YEARBOOK
2012-2013

International Court of Justice, Peace Palace,
2517 KJ The Hague, Netherlands
Tel. (+3170) 302 23 23
Website: www.icj-cij.org

ISSN 0074-445X
ISSN 978-92-1-170090-9

Sales number
Nº de vente: **1074**

INTERNATIONAL COURT OF JUSTICE

Yearbook
2012-2013

No. 67

I.C.J. - THE HAGUE - 2013

PRINTED IN FRANCE

In March 1947 the International Court of Justice instructed the Registrar to publish a *Yearbook* providing general information concerning its organization, jurisdiction, activities and administration.

The present volume – sixty-seventh of the series – covers the period from 1 August 2012 to 31 July 2013.

Seeking to strengthen complementarity between the *Yearbook* and the Court's other informational media, in particular its website and *Annual Report*, the Registrar ensures that the *Yearbook* is regularly updated and expanded, notably in order to enhance its instructional and explanatory role.

The *Yearbook* is produced by the Registry and in no way involves the responsibility of the Court; in particular, the summaries of judgments, advisory opinions and orders contained in Chapter V cannot be quoted against the actual texts of those judgments, advisory opinions and orders and do not constitute an interpretation of them.

Philippe COUVREUR,
Registrar of the Court.

––––––––––

TABLE OF CONTENTS

Page

INTRODUCTION

The International Court of Justice (ICJ), which has its seat in The Hague (Netherlands), is the principal judicial organ of the United Nations. It was established by the Charter of the United Nations in June 1945 and began its activities in April 1946. Of the six principal organs of the United Nations, it is the only one not located in New York.

It had as its predecessor the Permanent Court of International Justice (PCIJ), which was instituted by the League of Nations in 1920 and was dissolved in 1946.

The Court is composed of 15 judges elected for a nine-year term by the General Assembly and the Security Council of the United Nations. Independent of the United Nations Secretariat, it is assisted by a Registry, its own international secretariat, whose activities are both judicial and diplomatic, as well as administrative. The official languages of the Court are English and French.

Also known as the "World Court", it is the only court of a universal character with general jurisdiction. The Court has a two-fold role: first, to settle, in accordance with international law, legal disputes submitted to it by States (its judgments have binding force and are without appeal); and, second, to give advisory opinions on legal questions referred to it by duly authorized United Nations organs and agencies of the system.

I. BASIC TEXTS

The basic texts of the Court are the Charter of the United Nations and the Statute of the Court. Other texts are the Rules of Court and the Practice Directions supplementing them, as well as the resolution concerning the internal judicial practice of the Court.

These texts can be found on the Court's website, under the heading "Basic Documents". They are also published in the volume *I.C.J. Acts and Documents No. 6* (2007), which is also available on the Court's website under the heading "Publications".

1. Charter of the United Nations

The International Court of Justice was brought into being by the Charter of the United Nations, signed in San Francisco on 26 June 1945. The Charter deals with the Court in Article 7, paragraph 1, Article 36, paragraph 3, and Articles 92-96, which form Chapter XIV.

2. Statute of the Court

(a) Text of the Statute

The text of the Statute was based upon that of the Permanent Court of International Justice. The modifications, a list which can be found in the *I.C.J. Yearbook 1946-1947* (pp. 101-102), were few in number, most of them being formal adaptations designed to take account of the replacement of the League of Nations by the United Nations.

The text of the Statute, which was also signed in San Francisco on 26 June 1945, is annexed to the Charter, of which it forms an integral part. According to Article 69 of the Statute, amendments to that instrument can be made using the same procedure as is provided for amendments to the Charter (see Articles 108 to 109). It may also be amended in accordance with proposals made by the Court itself (see Article 70 of the Statute).

No amendments have so far been made to the Statute.

(b) States parties to the Statute

The question of the status as a party to the Statute of the Court is governed by Article 93 of the Charter. To date 193 States are parties to the Statute. The complete list of States parties to the Statute of the Court can be found on the ICJ website under "Jurisdiction/States Entitled to Appear before the Court".

3. Rules of Court and Practice Directions

(a) Rules of Court

Article 30 of the Statute provides that "the Court shall frame rules for carrying out its functions. In particular, it shall lay down rules of procedure".

The first Rules of Court were adopted on 6 May 1946. Revisions to these Rules were made in 1972, 1978, 2000 and 2005. A chronological summary of these revisions can be found in Annex 1 on page 134 of this *Yearbook*.

The text of the Rules of Court, as amended to date, can be found on the Court's website under the heading "Basic Documents". It is also published in the volume *I.C.J. Acts and Documents No. 6*, pp. 91-159 and on the website of the Court under the headings "Publications/Acts and Documents No. 6".

(b) Practice Directions

As part of the ongoing review of its procedures and working methods, in October 2001 the Court decided to adopt Practice Directions for use by the States appearing before it. In so doing, it wished to more effectively deal with the congested state of its List and the budgetary constraints facing it. These Practice Directions involve no alteration to the Rules of Court, but are additional thereto. The Court has since adopted new Practice Directions and amended others. This occurred in 2002, 2004, 2006 and 2009. A new Practice Direction was adopted during the period under review. On 21 March 2013, the Court adopted Practice Direction IX*quater*, which reads as follows:

"Practice Direction IX*quater*

1. Having regard to Article 56 of the Rules of Court, any party wishing to present audio-visual or photographic material at the hearings which was not previously included in the case file of the written proceedings shall submit a request to that effect sufficiently in advance of the date on which that party wishes to present that material to permit the Court to take its decision after having obtained the views of the other party.

2. The party in question shall explain in its request why it wishes to present the audio-visual or photographic material at the hearings.

3. A party's request to present audio-visual or photographic material must be accompanied by information as to the source of the material, the circumstances and date of its making and the extent to which it is available to the public. The party in question must also specify, wherever relevant, the geographic co-ordinates at which that material was taken.

4. The audio-visual or photographic material which the party in question is seeking to present shall be filed in the Registry in five copies. The Registrar shall communicate a copy to the other party and inform the Court accordingly.

5. It shall be for the Court to decide on the request, after considering any views expressed by the other party and taking account of any question relating to the sound administration of justice which might be raised by that request."

A chronological summary of the evolution of the Practice Directions can be found in Annex 2 on page 135 of this *Yearbook*.

4. *Resolution concerning the Internal Judicial Practice of the Court*

In accordance with Article 19 of the Rules of Court, "[t]he internal judicial practice of the Court shall . . . be governed by any resolutions on the subject adopted by the Court". The resolution currently in force was adopted on 12 April 1976. It can be found on the Court's website under the headings "Basic Documents/Other Texts". It can also be found in the volume *I.C.J Acts and Documents No. 6*, pp. 175-183.

It should nevertheless be noted that the Court remains entirely free to depart from the present resolution, or any part of it, in a given case, if it considers that the circumstances justify that course.

II. Summary of the Judicial Activities of the Court from 1 August 2012 to 31 July 2013

The first case entered in the General List of the Court *(Corfu Channel (United Kingdom* v. *Albania))* was submitted on 22 May 1947. Between then and 31 July 2013, the Court has had to deal with a total of 153 cases, i.e., 126 contentious cases and 27 advisory procedures (the full list of all the proceedings is annexed to this *Yearbook*, Annex 3, p. 136). In total, the Court has rendered 113 Judgments and 27 Advisory Opinions.

1. New Applications

During the period under review in this *Yearbook*, the Court received one new Application. On 24 April 2013, Bolivia instituted proceedings against Chile concerning a dispute in relation to "Chile's obligation to negotiate in good faith and effectively with Bolivia in order to reach an agreement granting Bolivia a fully sovereign access to the Pacific Ocean".

2. Public Hearings

Between 1 August 2012 and 31 July 2013, the Court held public hearings in four cases: from Monday 8 to Wednesday 17 October 2012, in the case concerning the *Frontier Dispute (Burkina Faso/Niger)*; from Monday 3 to Friday 14 December 2012, in the case concerning *Maritime Dispute (Peru* v. *Chile)*; from Monday 15 to Friday 19 April 2013, in the case concerning the *Request for Interpretation of the Judgment of 15 June 1962 in the Case concerning the* Temple of Preah Vihear (Cambodia *v.* Thailand) *(Cambodia* v. *Thailand)*; and from Wednesday 26 June to Tuesday 16 July 2013, in the case concerning *Whaling in the Antarctic (Australia* v. *Japan: New Zealand intervening)*.

3. Decisions

During the year under review, the Court delivered two Judgments on the merits, one on 19 November 2012, in the case concerning the *Territorial and Maritime Dispute (Nicaragua* v. *Colombia)*; and the other on 16 April 2013, in the case concerning the *Frontier Dispute (Burkina Faso/Niger)*.

It also handed down seven Orders: by its Order of 6 February 2013, the Court authorized New Zealand to intervene in the case concerning *Whaling in the Antarctic (Australia* v. *Japan)*; by two separate Orders dated 17 April 2013, the Court joined the proceedings in the case concerning *Certain Activities Carried Out by Nicaragua in the Border Area (Costa Rica* v. *Nicaragua)* and in the case concerning the *Construction of a Road in Costa Rica along the San Juan River (Nicaragua* v. *Costa Rica)*; by its Order dated 18 April 2013, the Court ruled on the four counter-claims submitted by Nicaragua in its Counter-Memorial filed in the case concerning *Certain Activities Carried Out by Nicaragua in the Border Area (Costa Rica v. Nicaragua)*; by its Order dated 12 July 2013, the Court nominated three experts who will assist the Parties in the operation of demarcation of their common frontier in the disputed area, pursuant to Article 7, paragraph 4, of the Special Agreement concluded between the Parties on 24 February 2009 and to paragraph 113 of the Judgment delivered by the Court on 16 April 2013 in the case concerning the *Frontier Dispute (Burkina Faso/ Niger)*; and by its Order dated 16 July 2013, the Court ruled on the requests submitted by Costa Rica and Nicaragua, respectively, for the modification of the provisional measures indicated by the Court on 8 March 2011 in the case concerning *Certain Activities Carried Out by Nicaragua in the Border Area (Costa Rica v. Nicaragua)*.

*

Proceedings pending before the Court during the period under review:

Title	Year
Gabčíkovo-Nagymaros Project (Hungary/Slovakia)	1993-
Armed Activities on the Territory of the Congo (Democratic Republic of the Congo v. Uganda)	1999-
Application of the Convention on the Prevention and Punishment of the Crime of Genocide (Croatia v. Serbia)	1999-
Territorial and Maritime Dispute (Nicaragua v. Colombia)	2001-2012
Maritime Dispute (Peru v. Chile)	2008-
Aerial Herbicide Spraying (Ecuador v. Colombia)	2008-
Whaling in the Antarctic (Australia v. Japan: New Zealand intervening)	2010-
Frontier Dispute (Burkina Faso/Niger)	2010-2013
Certain Activities Carried Out by Nicaragua in the Border Area (Costa Rica v. Nicaragua)	2010-
Request for Interpretation of the Judgment of 15 June 1962 in the Case concerning the Temple of Preah Vihear (Cambodia *v.* Thailand) *(Cambodia v. Thailand)*	2011-
Construction of a Road in Costa Rica along the San Juan River (Nicaragua v. Costa Rica)	2011-
Obligation to Negotiate Access to the Pacific Ocean (Bolivia v. Chile)	2013-

CHAPTER I

ORGANIZATION OF THE COURT

The organization of the International Court of Justice is governed by Articles 2-33 of the Statute of the Court and by Articles 1-18 and 32-37 of the Rules of Court.

I. MEMBERS OF THE COURT

1. Composition of the Court

The Court consists of 15 Members (Statute, Art. 3, para. 1). On 31 July 2013 the composition of the Court was as follows:

Order of precedence	Country	Date of expiry of term of office
President		
Peter Tomka	Slovakia	5 February 2021[1]
Vice-President		
Bernardo Sepúlveda-Amor	Mexico	5 February 2015[1]
Judges		
Hisashi Owada	Japan	5 February 2021
Ronny Abraham	France	5 February 2018
Kenneth Keith	New Zealand	5 February 2015
Mohamed Bennouna	Morocco	5 February 2015
Leonid Skotnikov	Russian Federation	5 February 2015
Antônio A. Cançado Trindade	Brazil	5 February 2018
Abdulqawi A. Yusuf	Somalia	5 February 2018
Christopher Greenwood	United Kingdom	5 February 2018
Xue Hanqin	China	5 February 2021
Joan E. Donoghue	United States	5 February 2015
Giorgio Gaja	Italy	5 February 2021
Julia Sebutinde	Uganda	5 February 2021
Dalveer Bhandari	India	5 February 2018

The Members of the Court are elected for nine years, one-third of the total number of judges being elected every three years; they may be re-elected (Statute, Art. 13). In the event of a vacancy, an election is held

---

[1] The terms of office of Judges Tomka and Sepúlveda-Amor as President and Vice-President respectively expire on 5 February 2015.

and the new judge holds office for the remainder of his/her predecessor's term (Statute, Arts. 14 and 15). Though replaced, Members of the Court finish any cases they have begun (Statute, Art. 13, para. 3).

As required by Article 7 of the Statute, the Secretary-General of the United Nations prepares for each election a list of the persons nominated in accordance with Articles 5 and 6. The Members of the Court are elected by the General Assembly and the Security Council of the United Nations, proceeding independently of each other and simultaneously (Statute, Arts. 8-12). The States parties to the Statute of the Court which are not Members of the United Nations take part in the election by the General Assembly in the same manner as Members of the United Nations (General Assembly resolution 264 (III) of 8 October 1948; see Chapter II, page 18, below).

Members of the Court elected during the same session of the General Assembly whose terms of office begin on the same date take precedence according to seniority of age; Members elected at a previous session take precedence; in the event of immediate re-election a Member retains his former precedence (Rules, Art. 3, paras. 2-4).

The Court elects its President and Vice-President; they are both elected for three years and take precedence over the other judges (Statute, Art. 21, para. 1; Rules, Art. 3, para. 5, Arts. 10-14, Art. 18, para. 2, and Art. 32).

2. Biographies of Members of the Court

No new judges took office between 1 August 2012 and 31 July 2013. Following the practice used by the Permanent Court of International Justice, only the biographies of judges whose terms of office commenced during the period under review will be included in the *Yearbook*. The biographical notes of current Members of the Court can be found on the ICJ website under "The Court/Members of the Court/Current Members". The biographical notes of former Members of the Court can be found in the *Yearbooks* covering the dates that their terms of office commenced.

3. Former Presidents and Vice-Presidents of the Court

A full list of all former Presidents and Vice-Presidents of the Court, including their terms in office, can be found in Annex 4, page 144 of this *Yearbook* and on the International Court of Justice website under the headings "The Court/Members of the Court/Presidency".

4. Former Members of the Court

A full list of all former Members of the Court, including their nationalities and terms in office, can be found in Annex 5, page 146 of this *Yearbook* and on the International Court of Justice website, under the headings: "The Court/Members of the Court/All Members".

II. Judges *Ad Hoc*

If in a case the Court, or a chamber of the Court, includes upon the Bench a judge of the nationality of one of the parties, any other party may choose a person to sit as judge; similarly, if the Court or the chamber includes upon the Bench no judge of the nationality of the parties, each of these parties may choose a judge (Statute, Art. 31; Rules, Arts. 7-8, Art. 17, para. 2, Arts. 35-37, Art. 91, para. 2, and Art. 102, para. 3, Practice Direction VII). Should there be several parties in the same interest they are reckoned for this purpose as one party only (Statute, Art. 31, para. 5; Rules, Art. 36 and Art. 37, para. 2).

A judge *ad hoc* does not necessarily have to have (and often does not have) the nationality of the designating State.

Only the biographies of judges *ad hoc* who were appointed during the period under review will be included in the present *Yearbook*. No new judges *ad hoc* were appointed during the period between 1 August 2012 and 31 July 2013.

The following list contains the names of cases currently pending before the Court to which judges *ad hoc* have been appointed (unless otherwise indicated, they held the nationality of the appointing party). The full list of all judges *ad hoc* can be found in Annex 6, page 149 of this *Yearbook* and on the International Court of Justice website, under the headings "The Court/Judges *Ad Hoc*/All Judges *Ad Hoc*".

Armed Activities on the Territory of the Congo (Democratic Republic of the Congo v. *Uganda).* Mr. Joe Verhoeven (Belgium) was chosen by the Democratic Republic of the Congo and Mr. James L. Kateka (Tanzania) was chosen by Uganda. Following the election of Ms Julia Sebutinde, of Ugandan nationality, as a Member of the Court with effect from 6 February 2012, the term of office of Mr. Kateka came to an end.

Application of the Convention on the Prevention and Punishment of the Crime of Genocide (Croatia v. *Serbia).* Mr. B. Vukas was chosen by Croatia and Mr. M. Kreća by Serbia.

Territorial and Maritime Dispute (Nicaragua v. *Colombia).* Nicaragua chose Mr. Mohammed Bedjaoui to sit as judge *ad hoc*; following the latter's resignation, it chose Mr. Giorgio Gaja. Following Mr. Gaja's election as a Member of the Court, it chose Mr. Thomas A. Mensah to sit as judge *ad hoc*. In view of that choice, Judge Gaja considered that it seemed appropriate for him, as the former judge *ad hoc* chosen by Nicaragua, not to take part in any further proceedings concerning the case. Colombia chose Mr. Yves L. Fortier to sit as judge *ad hoc*; following the latter's resignation, it chose Mr. Jean-Pierre Cot.

Maritime Dispute (Peru v. *Chile).* Mr. Gilbert Guillaume (France) was chosen by Peru. Mr. Francisco Orrego Vicuña was chosen by Chile.

Aerial Herbicide Spraying (Ecuador v. Colombia). Mr. Raúl Emilio Vinuesa (Argentina) was chosen by Ecuador. Mr. Jean-Pierre Cot (France) was chosen by Colombia.

Whaling in the Antarctic (Australia v. Japan: New Zealand intervening). Ms Hilary Charlesworth was chosen by Australia.

Frontier Dispute (Burkina Faso/Niger). Burkina Faso chose Mr. Jean-Pierre Cot to sit as judge *ad hoc.* Following the latter's resignation, Burkina Faso chose Mr. Yves Daudet. Niger chose Mr. Ahmed Mahiou.

Certain Activities Carried Out by Nicaragua in the Border Area (Costa Rica v. Nicaragua). Costa Rica chose Mr. John Dugard and Nicaragua chose Mr. Gilbert Guillaume.

Request for Interpretation of the Judgment of 15 June 1962 in the Case concerning the Temple of Preah Vihear (Cambodia *v.* Thailand) *(Cambodia v. Thailand).* Cambodia chose Mr. Gilbert Guillaume and Thailand chose Mr. Jean-Pierre Cot.

Construction of a Road in Costa Rica along the San Juan River (Nicaragua v. *Costa Rica).* Nicaragua chose Mr. Gilbert Guillaume and Costa Rica chose Mr. Bruno Simma to sit as judges *ad hoc.* Further to the Court's decision to join the proceedings in this case and in that concerning *Certain Activities Carried Out by Nicaragua in the Border Area (Costa Rica* v. *Nicaragua),* Mr. Simma resigned.

III. CHAMBERS

1. Provisions in the Rules relating to Chambers

Articles 15-18 and 90-93 of the Rules of Court contain the provisions relating to chambers.

2. Chamber of Summary Procedure

The Statute (Art. 29) provides that, with a view to the speedy despatch of business, the Court shall form annually a Chamber composed of five judges which, at the request of the parties, may hear and determine cases by summary procedure. The Court also selects two judges for the purpose of replacing judges who find it impossible to sit in the Chamber. Under Article 15 of the Rules of Court, the President and Vice-President are members of this Chamber ex officio, the other members and the substitutes being elected. The Chamber of Summary Procedure has never as yet been called upon to meet.

The Chamber of Summary Procedure is at present composed as follows: President Tomka; Vice-President Sepúlveda-Amor; Judges Yusuf, Xue and Donoghue, Members; Judges Skotnikov and Gaja, Substitute Members.

3. Chambers Provided for in Article 26, Paragraph 1, of the Statute

The Statute (Art. 26, para. 1) provides also that the Court may from time to time form one or more chambers, composed of three or more judges, as the Court may determine, for dealing with particular categories of cases: for example, labour cases and cases relating to transit and communications. Cases are heard and determined by these chambers if the parties so request.

In 1993, the Court established a Chamber for Environmental Matters, which was periodically reconstituted until 2006. In the Chamber's 13 years of existence, however, no State ever requested that a case be dealt with by it. The Court consequently decided in 2006 not to hold elections to re-elect a Bench for the said Chamber.

4. Chambers Provided for in Article 26, Paragraph 2, of the Statute

The Statute (Art. 26, para. 2) provides that the Court may form a chamber to deal with a particular case, the number of judges constituting such a chamber being determined by the Court with the approval of the parties.

Chambers of this kind have been formed at the joint request of the parties to deal with six cases. For the full list of these cases, including an indication of the date on which the respective chamber was constituted, the names of its members and the dates that the chambers were dissolved, please see Annex 7, page 157 of this *Yearbook*.

IV. ASSESSORS

Article 30, paragraph 2, of the Statute and Article 9 of the Rules of Court provide that the Court may, either *proprio motu* or upon a request made not later than the closure of the written proceedings, decide, for the purpose of a contentious case or request for advisory opinion, to appoint assessors to sit with it, without the right to vote. The chambers also have the power to appoint assessors.

These provisions have so far never been applied.

V. THE REGISTRAR

The Court appoints its Registrar (Statute, Art. 21, para. 2; Rules, Art. 22).

The present Registrar is Mr. Philippe Couvreur (see Chap. III, p. 24, below).

The biographical note of the Registrar can be found on the website of the Court under the headings "The Registry/The Registrar".

VI. Privileges and Immunities

Article 19 of the Statute provides: "The Members of the Court, when engaged on the business of the Court, shall enjoy diplomatic privileges and immunities."

In the Netherlands, pursuant to an exchange of correspondence between the President of the Court and the Minister for Foreign Affairs, dated 26 June 1946, they enjoy, in a general way, the same privileges, immunities, facilities and prerogatives as Heads of Diplomatic Missions accredited to Her Majesty the Queen of the Netherlands (*I.C.J. Acts and Documents No. 6*, pp. 205-211). In addition, in accordance with the terms of a letter dated 26 February 1971 from the Minister for Foreign Affairs of the Netherlands, the President of the Court takes precedence over the Heads of Mission, including the Dean of the Diplomatic Corps, who is immediately followed by the Vice-President of the Court and thereafter the precedence proceeds alternately between Heads of Mission and the Members of the Court (*ibid.*, pp. 215-217).

By resolution 90 (1) of 11 December 1946 (*ibid.*, pp. 211-215), the General Assembly of the United Nations approved the agreement concluded with the Government of the Netherlands in June 1946 and recommended that ". . . if a judge, for the purpose of holding himself permanently at the disposal of the Court, resides in some country other than his own, he should be accorded diplomatic privileges and immunities during the period of his residence there" and that

> "Judges should be accorded every facility for leaving the country where they may happen to be, for entering the country where the Court is sitting, and again for leaving it. On journeys in connection with the exercise of their functions, they should, in all countries through which they may have to pass, enjoy all the privileges, immunities and facilities granted by these countries to diplomatic envoys."

The same resolution contains also a recommendation calling upon Members of the United Nations to recognize and accept laissez-passer issued by the Court to the judges. Such laissez-passer have been issued since 1950. They are similar in form to those issued by the Secretary-General of the United Nations and are signed by the President of the Court and the Registrar.

Furthermore, Article 32, paragraph 8, of the Statute provides that the "salaries, allowances and compensation" received by judges "shall be free of all taxation".

CHAPTER II

JURISDICTION OF THE COURT

I. JURISDICTION IN CONTENTIOUS CASES

It is the function of the International Court of Justice to decide in accordance with international law such disputes as are submitted to it (Statute, Art. 38, para. 1). Its jurisdiction in this respect is defined in Article 93 of the Charter of the United Nations and in Articles 34-37 of the Statute of the Court.

1. Basis of the Court's Jurisdiction (Jurisdiction ratione materiae*)*

The jurisdiction of the Court in contentious proceedings is based on the consent of the States to which it is open. The form in which this consent is expressed determines the manner in which a case may be brought before the Court. The Court is competent to entertain a dispute only if the States concerned have accepted its jurisdiction in the following ways:

(a) *Special agreement*

Article 36, paragraph 1, of the Statute provides that the jurisdiction of the Court comprises all cases which the parties refer to it. Such cases normally come before the Court by notification to the Registry of an agreement known as a *special agreement* and concluded by the parties specially for this purpose. To date seventeen such cases have been submitted to the Court (for the list of these cases see Annex 8, page 159).

(b) *Cases provided for in treaties and conventions*

Article 36, paragraph 1, of the Statute provides also that the jurisdiction of the Court comprises all matters specially provided for in treaties and conventions in force. Over 300 treaties and conventions contain a clause to that effect. In such cases, a matter is normally brought before the Court by means of a written *application instituting proceedings*; this is a unilateral document which must indicate the subject of the dispute and the parties (Statute, Art. 40, para. 1) and, as far as possible, specify the provision on which the applicant founds the jurisdiction of the Court (Rules, Art. 38). With the exception of the cases which were brought by the notification of a special agreement, all contentious cases have been brought before the Court by means of an application instituting proceedings, irrespective of whether the Court's jurisdiction was founded on a provision in a treaty or convention, declarations recognizing the Court's jurisdiction as compulsory made by each of the parties to the dispute, or any other alleged form of consent.

The chronological list of treaties and other instruments *notified to the Registry* following registration, classification or recording at the Secretariat of the United Nations which (in addition to certain texts referred to in Section I of the present Chapter, the declarations mentioned in Section II and the special agreements whereby particular cases were submitted to the Court) contain clauses relating to the jurisdiction of the Court in contentious proceedings can be found on the website of the Court under the headings "Jurisdiction/Contentious Jurisdiction/Declarations Recognizing the Jurisdictions of the Court as Compulsory".

These instruments include treaties and conventions concluded earlier and conferring jurisdiction upon the Permanent Court of International Justice. For Article 37 of the Statute of the International Court of Justice stipulates that whenever a treaty or convention in force provides for reference of a matter to a tribunal to have been instituted by the League of Nations, or to the Permanent Court of International Justice, the matter shall, as between the parties to the Statute, be referred to the International Court of Justice. The Permanent Court of International Justice reproduced, in 1932, in its *Collection of Texts Governing the Jurisdiction of the Court (P.C.I.J., Series D, No. 6*, fourth edition) and subsequently in Chapter X of its *Annual Reports (P.C.I.J., Series E, Nos. 8-16)* the relevant provisions of the instruments governing its jurisdiction. By virtue of the Article referred to above, some of these provisions now govern the jurisdiction of the International Court of Justice.

(c) *Declarations recognizing the jurisdiction of the Court*

The Statute provides that a State may recognize as compulsory, in relation to any other State accepting the same obligation, the jurisdiction of the Court in legal disputes. These cases are brought before the Court by means of written applications. The conditions on which such compulsory jurisdiction may be recognized are stated in paragraphs 2-5 of Article 36 of the Statute, which reads as follows:

"2. The States parties to the present Statute may at any time declare that they recognize as compulsory *ipso facto* and without special agreement, in relation to any other State accepting the same obligation, the jurisdiction of the Court in all legal disputes concerning:

(a) the interpretation of a treaty;
(b) any question of international law;
(c) the existence of any fact which, if established, would constitute a breach of an international obligation;
(d) the nature or extent of the reparation to be made for the breach of an international obligation.

3. The declarations referred to above may be made unconditionally or on condition of reciprocity on the part of several or certain States, or for a certain time.

4. Such declarations shall be deposited with the Secretary-General

of the United Nations, who shall transmit copies thereof to the parties to the Statute and to the Registrar of the Court.

5. Declarations made under Article 36 of the Statute of the Permanent Court of International Justice and which are still in force shall be deemed, as between the parties to the present Statute, to be acceptances of the compulsory jurisdiction of the International Court of Justice for the period which they still have to run and in accordance with their terms."

The list of declarations recognizing as compulsory the jurisdiction of the Court (under Article 36, paragraph 2, of the Statute) can be found on the website of the Court under the headings "Jurisdiction/Contentious jurisdiction/Declarations recognizing the jurisdiction of the Court as compulsory".

As at 31 July 2013, a total of 70 such declarations have been deposited.

Only declarations filed during the period under review are reproduced in the *I.C.J. Yearbook*.

Three declarations were deposited during the current period: on 21 September 2012 by both Lithuania and Timor-Leste and on 24 April 2013, by the Marshall Islands. The texts of the three declarations are reproduced below:

LITHUANIA

21 IX 2012.

With reference to Article 36 of the Statute of the International Court of Justice, I have the honour to formulate on behalf of the Republic of Lithuania the following declaration:

1. The Republic of Lithuania declares that it recognizes as compulsory *ipso facto* and without special agreement, in relation to any other State accepting the same obligation, the jurisdiction of the International Court of Justice, in conformity with paragraph 2 of Article 36 of the Statute of the Court, until such time as notice may be given to the Secretary-General of the United Nations withdrawing the declaration and with effect as from the moment of such notification, over all disputes arising after the present declaration, with regard to situations or facts subsequent to this date, other than:

   (i)   any dispute which the parties thereto have agreed or shall agree to have recourse to some other method of peaceful settlement or which is subject to another method of peaceful settlement chosen by all the parties;

   (ii) any dispute relating to any matter excluded from compulsory adjudication or arbitration under any treaty, to which the Republic of Lithuania is a party, or other instrument imposing international obligations to the Republic of Lithuania;

   (iii) any dispute which arises from or is connected with a military operation carried out in accordance with a decision taken by consensus or unanimity by international security and defence organization or organization implementing common security and defence policy, to which the Republic of Lithuania is a member;

(iv) any dispute in respect of which any other party to the dispute has accepted the compulsory jurisdiction of the International Court of Justice only in relation to or for the purpose of the dispute; or where the acceptance of the Court's compulsory jurisdiction on behalf of any other party to the dispute was deposited or ratified less than twelve months prior to the filing of the application bringing the dispute before the Court.

2. The Republic of Lithuania also reserves the right at any time, by means of a notification addressed to the Secretary-General of the United Nations, and with effect as from the moment of such notification, either to add to, amend or withdraw any of the foregoing reservations, or any that may hereafter be added.

Done at Vilnius, 21 September 2012.

(Signed) Dalia GRYBAUSKAITĖ,
President of the Republic of Lithuania.

(Signed) Audronius AŽUBALIS,
Minister for Foreign Affairs
of the Republic of Lithuania.

TIMOR-LESTE

21 IX 2012.

On behalf of the Democratic Republic of Timor-Leste, I have the honour to declare that the Democratic Republic of Timor-Leste accepts as compulsory *ipso facto* and without special agreement, the jurisdiction of the International Court of Justice in conformity with Article 36, paragraph 2, of the Statute of the Court, until such time as notice may be given to terminate this acceptance. This declaration is effective immediately.

The Government of the Democratic Republic of Timor-Leste reserves the right at any time, by means of a notification addressed to the Secretary-General of the United Nations, either to amend the present declaration or to amend or withdraw an[y] reservation that may hereafter be added.

Dili, 21 September 2012.

(Signed) Kay Rala XANANA GUSMÃO,
Prime Minister of the Democratic Republic
of Timor-Leste.

THE MARSHALL ISLANDS

24 IV 2013.

I have the honour to declare on behalf of the Government of the Republic of the Marshall Islands that:

(1) The Government of the Republic of the Marshall Islands accepts as compulsory *ipso facto* and without special convention, on condition of reciprocity, the jurisdiction of the International Court of Justice, in conformity with paragraph 2 of Article 36 of the Statute of the Court, until such time as notice may be given to terminate the acceptance, over all disputes arising after 17 September 1991, with regard to situations or facts subsequent to the same date, other than:

   (i) any dispute which the Republic of Marshall Islands has agreed with the other party or parties there to settle by some other method of peaceful settlement;

   (ii) any dispute in respect of which any other party to the dispute has accepted the compulsory jurisdiction of the International Court of Justice only in relation to or for the purpose of the dispute.

(2) The Government of the Republic of the Marshall Islands also reserves the right at any time, by means of notification addressed to the Secretary-General of the United Nations, and with effect as from the moment of such notification, to add to, amend or withdraw either of the foregoing reservations or any that may hereafter be added.

Done at Majuro, Republic of the Marshall Islands this 15 March 2013.

(Signed) The Honourable Tony A. DEBRUM,

Minister in Assistance to the President
and Acting Minister of Foreign Affairs.

Since 1951, 15 other declarations relating to the jurisdiction of the International Court of Justice, either expressly or by virtue of Article 36, paragraph 5, of the Statute, have expired, been withdrawn or been terminated without being subsequently replaced. These were the declarations of the following States: Bolivia, Brazil, China, Colombia, El Salvador, France, Guatemala, Iran, Israel, Nauru (United Nations, *Treaty Series*, Vol. 1491, p. 199), Serbia and Montenegro (United Nations, *Treaty Series*, Vol. 2121, p. 422), South Africa, Thailand, Turkey and the United States.

In view of the provisions of Article 36, paragraph 5, of the Statute of the International Court of Justice, the ICJ website also contains the texts of declarations made under the Statute of the Permanent Court of International Justice, which have not lapsed or been withdrawn. There are now six such declarations.

(d) Forum prorogatum

In accordance with the present Rules of Court, which came into force on 1 July 1978, if a State has not recognized the jurisdiction of the Court at the time when an application instituting proceedings is filed against it, that State has the possibility of accepting such jurisdiction subsequently to enable the Court to entertain the case (Rules, Art. 38, para. 5).

Prior to 1 July 1978, the Court found in eight cases that it could take no further steps upon the applications because the opposing party did not accept its jurisdiction. For the list of these cases see Annex 9 (A), page 160.

Since 1 July 1978, Article 38, paragraph 5, was invoked 12 times. On ten of these occasions the jurisdiction of the Court was not accepted by the State against which the application was filed.

Notably, during the period under review, such an application was filed by Equatorial Guinea against France. For the list of all 10 applications see Annex 9 (B), page 161.

On only two occasions, in 2003 and in 2006, was the rule of *forum prorogatum* applied after the jurisdiction of the Court was accepted by the State against which the application was filed. For additional information, see Annex 10, page 163.

(e) *Determination of the Court's own jurisdiction*

Article 36, paragraph 6, of the Statute provides that in the event of a dispute as to whether the Court has jurisdiction, the matter shall be settled by the decision of the Court. Article 79 of the Rules lays down the conditions which govern the filing of preliminary objections. See Chap. III, Sec. III, Part *(c)*, page 43.

(f) *Interpretation of a judgment*

Article 60 of the Statute provides that in the event of dispute as to the meaning or scope of a judgment, the Court shall construe it upon the request of any party. The request for interpretation may be made either by means of a special agreement between the parties or of an application by one or more of the parties (Rules, Art. 98). Requests for interpretations of judgments of the Court were made on five occasions. For the list of these requests, see below, Annex 11, page 164.

(g) *Revision of a judgment*

An application for revision of a judgment may be made only when it is based upon the discovery of some fact of such a nature as to be a decisive factor, which fact was, when the judgment was given, unknown to the Court and also to the party claiming revision, always provided that such party's ignorance was not due to negligence (Statute, Art. 61, para. 1). A request for revision is made by means of an application (Rules, Art. 99). Applications for revision of judgments of the Court were filed on three occasions. For the list of these applications see Annex 12, page 165.

(h) *Applications from private persons*

Private persons frequently apply to the Court for the purpose of obtaining a decision on matters at issue between them and the authorities of their own or of another country. These individuals are subsequently informed that, according to Article 34 of the Statute, "only States may be parties in cases before the Court".

2. States Entitled to Appear before the Court
(*Jurisdiction* ratione personae)

Article 34, paragraph 1, of the Statute provides that: "Only States may be parties in cases before the Court." International organizations, other collectivities and private persons are therefore not entitled to institute proceedings before the International Court of Justice.

A State entitled to appear before the Court may fall into one of the three categories listed below:

(a) *States Members of the United Nations*

Article 35, paragraph 1, of the Statute provides that the Court shall be open to the States parties to the Statute.

Article 93, paragraph 1, of the Charter of the United Nations provides that all Members of the United Nations are *ipso facto* parties to the Statute.

On 31 July 2013, 193 States were Members of the United Nations and thus *ipso facto* parties to the Statute.

No additional States have joined the United Nations during the period currently under review.

The full list of the States Members of the United Nations can be found on the International Court of Justice website, under "Jurisdiction/ Contentious Jurisdiction/States Entitled to Appear before the Court".

(b) *States, not Members of the United Nations, parties to the Statute*[1]

Article 93, paragraph 2, of the Charter of the United Nations provides that States which are not Members of the United Nations may become parties to the Statute of the Court on conditions to be determined in each case by the General Assembly upon the recommendation of the Security Council. Japan (as from 2 April 1954), Liechtenstein (as from 29 March 1950), San Marino (as from 18 February 1954), Nauru (as from 29 January 1988) and Switzerland (as from 28 July 1948), fell into this category before joining the United Nations.

The conditions imposed have hitherto been the same in each case.

---

[1] The full text of the resolution referred to in this Section is given on pages 185-189 of *I.C.J. Acts and Documents No. 6.*

They were laid down for the first time as a result of a request by the Swiss Federal Council. On that occasion the General Assembly, on 11 December 1946, adopted resolution 91 (I), the full text of which can be found on the website of the United Nations at: http://www.un.org/documents/ga/res/1/ares1.htm.

The date on which the State concerned becomes a party to the Statute is that of the deposit with the Secretary-General of the United Nations of the instrument of acceptance of the above-mentioned conditions.

Pursuant to Article 4, paragraph 3, of the Statute, such States may participate in the election of Members of the Court under the conditions laid down in resolution 264 (III) adopted by the General Assembly, upon the recommendation of the Security Council, on 8 October 1948. The operative part of this resolution states that:

"1. Such a State shall be on an equal footing with the Members of the United Nations in respect to those provisions of the Statute which regulate the nominations of candidates for election by the General Assembly.

2. Such a State shall participate, in the General Assembly, in electing the Members of the Court in the same manner as the Members of the United Nations.

3. Such a State, when in arrears in the payment of its contribution to the expenses of the Court, shall not participate in electing the Members of the Court in the General Assembly if the amount of its arrears equals or exceeds the amount of the contribution due from it for the preceding two full years. The General Assembly may, nevertheless, permit such a State to participate in the elections if it is satisfied that the failure to pay is due to conditions beyond the control of that State (see Charter, Art.19)."

The participation of such States in the procedure for amending the Statute of the Court (Charter, Art. 108; Statute, Art. 69) is governed by the following provisions of resolution 2520 (XXIV) adopted by the General Assembly, upon the recommendation of the Security Council, on 4 December 1969:

"(a) A State which is a party to the Statute of the International Court of Justice, but is not a Member of the United Nations, may participate in the General Assembly in regard to amendments to the Statute in the same manner as the Members of the United Nations;

(b) Amendments to the Statute of the International Court of Justice shall come into force for all States which are parties to the Statute when they have been adopted by a vote of two-thirds of the States which are parties to the Statute and ratified in accordance with their respective constitutional processes by two-thirds of the States which are parties to the Statute and in accordance with the provisions of Article 69 of the Statute and Article 108 of the Charter of the United Nations."

(c) *States, not parties to the Statute, to which the Court may be open*

The Court, which is open to States parties to the Statute, as mentioned above, is also open to other States, in accordance with Article 35, paragraph 2, of the Statute. See also Rules, Article 26, paragraph 1 *(c)*, and Article 41. Article 35 provides that the conditions upon which the Court shall be open to such States shall, subject to the special provisions contained in treaties in force, be laid down by the Security Council, but in no case shall such conditions place the parties in a position of inequality before the Court.

On 15 October 1946, the Security Council adopted resolution 9 (1946) which reads as follows:

"The Security Council,

In virtue of the powers conferred upon it by Article 35, paragraph 2, of the Statute of the International Court of Justice and subject to the provisions of that Article,

Resolves that:

1. The International Court of Justice shall be open to a State which is not a party to the Statute of the International Court of Justice, upon the following condition, namely, that such State shall previously have deposited with the Registrar of the Court a declaration by which it accepts the jurisdiction of the Court, in accordance with the Charter of the United Nations and with the terms and subject to the conditions of the Statute and Rules of the Court, and undertakes to comply in good faith with the decision or decisions of the Court and to accept all the obligations of a Member of the United Nations under Article 94 of the Charter;

2. Such declaration may be either particular or general. A particular declaration is one accepting the jurisdiction of the Court in respect only of a particular dispute or disputes which have already arisen. A general declaration is one accepting the jurisdiction generally in respect of all disputes or of a particular class or classes of disputes which have already arisen or which may arise in the future. A State, in making such a general declaration, may, in accordance with Article 36, paragraph 2, of the Statute, recognize as compulsory, *ipso facto* and without special agreement, the jurisdiction of the Court, provided, however, that such acceptance may not, without explicit agreement, be relied upon vis-à-vis States parties to the Statute which have made the declaration in conformity with Article 36, paragraph 2, of the Statute of the International Court of Justice;

3. The original declarations made under the terms of this reso-lution shall be kept in the custody of the Registrar of the Court, in accordance with the practice of the Court. Certified true copies thereof shall be transmitted, in accordance with the practice of the

Court, to all States parties to the Statute of the International Court of Justice, and to such other States as shall have deposited a declaration under the terms of this resolution, and to the Secretary-General of the United Nations;

4. The Security Council reserves the right to rescind or amend this resolution by a resolution which shall be communicated to the Court, and on the receipt of such communication and to the extent determined by the new resolution, existing declarations shall cease to be effective except in regard to disputes which are already before the Court;

5. All questions as to the validity or the effect of a declaration made under the terms of this resolution shall be decided by the Court."

Such declarations have been filed by Albania (1947) and by Italy (1953), and general declarations by Cambodia (1952), Ceylon (1952), the Federal Republic of Germany (1955, 1956, 1961, 1965 and 1971), Finland (1953 and 1954), Italy (1955), Japan (1951), Laos (1952) and the Republic of Viet Nam (1952).

II. Advisory Jurisdiction

The advisory jurisdiction of the Court is governed by Article 65 of the Statute and Article 96 of the Charter of the United Nations.

By virtue of Article 65 of the Statute, the Court may give an advisory opinion on any legal question at the request of whatever body may be authorized by or in accordance with the Charter of the United Nations to make such a request. An exact statement of the questions upon which the advisory opinion is asked must be contained in a *request for an advisory opinion*. Article 96, paragraph 1, of the Charter provides that advisory opinions may be asked of the Court by the General Assembly or the Security Council on any legal question. Paragraph 2 of this Article adds:

"Other organs of the United Nations and specialized agencies, which may at any time be so authorized by the General Assembly, may also request advisory opinions of the Court on legal questions arising within the scope of their activities."

For the full list of organs and agencies at present authorized to request advisory opinions, see Annex 13 (A), page 166.

CHAPTER III

FUNCTIONING OF THE COURT AND ITS REGISTRY

In matters concerning its administration, the International Court of Justice applies Articles 2 to 33 of its Statute (dealing with the organization of the Court and the Registry) as well as Articles 19 to 29 of its Rules (dealing with the internal functioning of the Court).

I. Seat

The seat of the Court is in The Hague (Netherlands); this however, does not prevent the Court from sitting and exercising its functions elsewhere whenever the Court considers it desirable to do so, which to date, has not taken place (Statute, Art. 22, para. 1; Rules, Art. 55).

The Court occupies, in the Peace Palace, constructed between 1907 and 1913, at The Hague, the premises formerly occupied by the Permanent Court of International Justice (PCIJ) as well as a new wing built at the expense of the Netherlands Government and inaugurated in 1978. An extension of that new wing as well as a number of newly constructed offices on the third floor of the Peace Palace were inaugurated in 1978 and extended in 1997.

An agreement of 21 February 1946 between the United Nations and the Carnegie Foundation, which is responsible for the administration of the Peace Palace, determines the conditions under which the Court uses these premises. The agreement was approved by the General Assembly of the United Nations in resolution 84 (I) of 11 December 1946. It provides for the payment to the Carnegie Foundation of an annual contribution (see pp. 29-30).

II. Administration

1. The Presidency and the Committees of the Court

In accordance with Article 12 of the Rules of Court, "the President shall preside at all meetings of the Court; he shall direct the work and supervise the administration of the Court". Occasionally he can be requested by third persons to undertake tasks outside the judicial work of the Court. These activities are described in Annex 26, page 191.

Decisions which have to be taken by the Court on administrative matters are prepared by a Budgetary and Administrative Committee composed of the President (chair), the Vice-President and four to five judges who are elected tri-annually (at present composed of Judges Abraham, Bennouna, Yusuf and Xue).

In 1970 the Court established a Library Committee to review the programme of acquisitions for the library of the Court and supervise the continuous modernization of its services (at present composed of Judges Bennouna, Cançado Trindade and Gaja).

Finally, in 1979 the Court constituted the Rules Committee as a standing body. This committee advises the Court on procedural issues and working methods. Its Members are at present Judges Abraham, Keith, Skotnikov, Cançado Trindade, Donoghue and Gaja.

2. The Registry

Independent of the Secretariat of the United Nations, the Court is assisted by a Registry — its own international secretariat — whose activities are judicial, diplomatic and administrative in nature. The role of the Registry is defined by the Statute and the Rules (in particular Rules, Arts. 22-29). The organization of the Registry is prescribed by the Court on proposals submitted by the Registrar, and Instructions for the Registry are drawn up by the Registrar and approved by the Court (Rules, Art. 28, paras. 2 and 3, see Annex 14 on page 175). An organizational structure chart of the Registry appears on page 26.

The Registry is comprised of ten separate units: three departments and seven divisions (see organizational structure chart on page 26). For additional information concerning the substantive divisions and departments of the Registry, please consult pages 14-19 of the *I.C.J. Annual Report 2012-2013* on the Court's website under "The Court/Annual Reports".

(1) The Registrar

The Court appoints its Registrar from among candidates proposed by Members of the Court. The Registrar is elected for a term of seven years and may be re-elected (Statute, Art. 21, para. 2; Rules, Art. 22). The Court also appoints a Deputy-Registrar, under the same conditions and in the same way as the Registrar (Rules, Art. 23).

The general functions of the Registrar are defined by the Rules of Court (Art. 26) and the Instructions for the Registry (Art. 1). He or she is the regular channel of communications to and from the Court, and in particular, effects all communications, notifications and transmissions of documents required by the Statute or by the Rules; keeps a General List of all cases, entered and numbered in the order in which the documents instituting proceedings or requesting an advisory opinion are received in the Registry; is present, in person or by his/her deputy, at meetings of the Court, and of the Chambers, and is responsible for the preparation of minutes of such meetings; makes arrangements for such provision or verification of translations and interpretations into the Court's official languages (English and French) as the Court may require; together with the President, countersigns all judgments, advisory opinions and orders of the Court as well as the minutes; is responsible for the administration of the Registry and for the work of all its departments and divisions, including the accounts and financial administration in accordance with the financial procedures of the United Nations; assists in maintaining the Court's external relations, both with international organizations and States and in the fields of information and publications (official publications of the Court, press releases, etc.); finally, he/she has custody of the seals and stamps of the Court, of the archives of the Court, and of such other archives as may be entrusted to the Court (including the archives of the Nuremberg Tribunal).

The present Registrar is Mr. Philippe Couvreur, of Belgian nationality, who was elected on 10 February 2000 for a term of seven years. On 8 February 2007, he was re-elected for a second term of seven years starting on 10 February 2007. Mr. Couvreur, who joined the Court in 1982 as Special Assistant to the Registrar and the Deputy-Registrar, had risen to the rank of Secretary, then First Secretary, in the Legal Department and had served as Principal Legal Secretary since 1995. He has lectured in public international law at various universities, including the Université Catholique de Louvain, and he is the author of a number of publications on the Court. For the full list of previous Registrars of the Court, please see Annex 15, page 176 or consult the International Court of Justice website under "The Court/ The Registry/The Registrar".

(2) The Deputy-Registrar and the Staff of the Registry

(a) The Deputy-Registrar

The Deputy-Registrar assists the Registrar and acts as Registrar in the latter's absence; he/she has recently been entrusted with wider administrative responsibilities, including direct supervision of the Archives, Computerization and General Assistance Divisions.

On 11 February 2013, the Court elected Mr. Jean-Pelé Fomété, of Cameroonian nationality, to the post of Deputy-Registrar for a term of seven years as from 16 March 2013.

Prior to his election to this position, Mr. Fomété was Registrar of the United Nations Dispute Tribunal in Nairobi, a post which he has held from 2009 to date. Prior to that, he was for seven years Programmes Director in the Registry of the International Criminal Tribunal for Rwanda (ICTR), after having occupied for five years prior the post of Legal Adviser and Special Assistant to the Registrar.

Before joining the ICTR, he served *inter alia* as a Law Clerk at the International Criminal Tribunal for the former Yugoslavia (ICTY) and as Chief of the United Nations Political and Legal Affairs Service at the Ministry of External Relations of Cameroon.

For the full list of previous Deputy-Registrars of the Court, please see Annex 15, page 176 or consult the International Court of Justice website under the headings "The Court/The Registry/The Registrar".

(b) *The Staff of the Registry*

The officials of the Registry are appointed by the Court on proposals submitted by the Registrar (Statute, Art. 21, para. 2; Rules, Art. 25). General Service staff, however, are appointed by the Registrar with the approval of the President. Short-term staff are appointed by the Registrar. (Rules, Art. 25; Staff Regulations for the Registry, Art. 5; Instructions for the Registry, Art. 4). All officials of the Registry, whether permanent or temporary, must be proficient in English and French and those whose work involves linguistic responsibilities must have one of these languages as their first language.

According to Article 28, paragraph 4, of the Rules of Court, "the Staff of the Registry shall be subject to Staff Regulations drawn up by the Registrar, so far as possible in conformity with the United Nations Staff Regulations and Staff Rules, and approved by the Court", see Annex 14 on page 175.

3. *Privileges and Immunities*

In the Netherlands, in accordance with the terms of an exchange of letters, dated 26 June 1946, between the President of the Court and the Minister for Foreign Affairs of the Netherlands, the Registrar is, in a general way, accorded the same treatment as heads of diplomatic missions accredited to His Majesty the King of the Netherlands, and officials of the Registry are treated as officials of comparable rank attached to diplomatic missions at The Hague (*I.C.J. Acts and Documents No. 6*, pp. 205-211).

By resolution 90 (I) of 11 December 1946 (*ibid.*, pp. 211-215) the General Assembly of the United Nations recommended that, on journeys in connection with the exercise of his functions, the Registrar should enjoy all the privileges, immunities and facilities granted to diplomatic envoys and that the officials of the Registry should, in the same circumstances, enjoy such privileges, immunities and facilities for residence and travel as may be necessary for the independent exercise of their functions. This resolution also contains a recommendation calling upon Members of the United Nations to recognize and accept the United Nations laissez-passer issued by the Court to the Registrar and officials of the Registry. Such laissez-passer have been issued since 1950. They are similar in form to those issued by the Secretary-General of the United Nations. They are signed by the President of the Court and by the Registrar.

International Court of Justice: Organizational structure and post distribution as at 31 July 2013

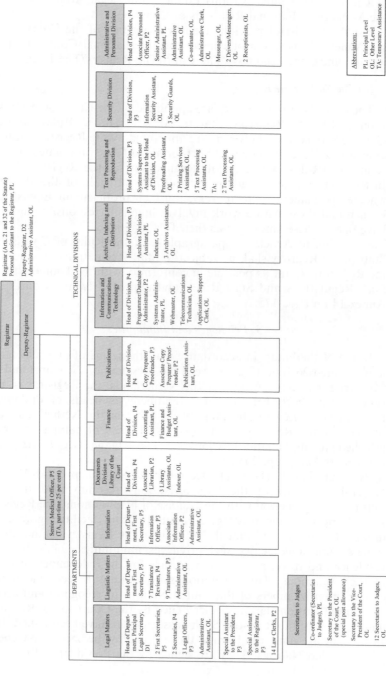

4. Finances of the Court

(a) Financial regulations

With regard to financial matters, the International Court of Justice applies Articles 32, 33, 35 and 64 of the Statute of the Court, Article 26, paragraph 1 (j), of the Rules of the Court, Articles 6, 24-36 and 55-63 of the Instructions for the Registry, the Staff Regulations for the Registry, the Financial Rules and Regulations of the United Nations and the relevant resolutions of the General Assembly of the United Nations.

(b) Method of covering expenditure

In accordance with Article 33 of the Statute of the Court, "The expenses of the Court shall be borne by the United Nations in such a manner as shall be decided by the General Assembly." As the budget of the Court has been incorporated in the budget of the United Nations, Member States participate in the expenses of both in the same proportion, in accordance with the scale of assessments determined by the General Assembly.

Under an established rule, sums derived from staff assessment, sales of publications (dealt with by the Sales Sections of the Secretariat), bank interest, and other revenues, are recorded as United Nations income.

(c) Drafting of the budget

In accordance with Articles 24 to 28 of the Instructions for the Registry, a preliminary draft budget is prepared by the Registrar. This preliminary draft is submitted for the consideration of the Budgetary and Administrative Committee of the Court and then for approval to the Court itself.

Once approved, the draft budget is forwarded to the Secretariat of the United Nations for incorporation in the draft budget of the United Nations (Volume I). It is then examined by the Advisory Committee on Administrative and Budgetary Questions (ACABQ) and is afterwards submitted to the Fifth Committee of the General Assembly. It is finally adopted by the General Assembly in plenary meeting, within the framework of decisions concerning the budget of the United Nations.

(d) Budget implementation

The Registrar is responsible for implementing the budget, with the assistance of the Head of the Finance Division. The Registrar ensures that proper use is made of the funds voted and sees that no expenses are incurred that are not provided for in the budget (Instructions for the Registry, Art. 29). He alone is entitled to incur liabilities in the name of the Court, subject to any possible delegations of authority (ibid., Art. 33). In accordance with a decision of the Court, the Registrar regularly communicates a statement of accounts to the Budgetary and Administrative Committee of the Court.

The accounts of the Court are regularly audited by the Board of Auditors appointed by the General Assembly and, periodically, by the internal auditors of the United Nations. At the beginning of each month, the closed accounts of the preceding month are forwarded to the Secretariat of the United Nations (Instructions for the Registry, Art. 25).

(e) *Budget of the Court for the biennium 2012-2013*

The Court was pleased to note that its requests for new posts and its other spending proposals were largely granted.

With the approval of the new posts and the conversion from temporary to established posts, the staffing strength of the Court has increased to a total of 117 posts, consisting of 59 established posts in the professional and higher categories, as well as 56 established and two temporary posts in the general services category.

For the revised budget for the biennium 2012-2013, after re-costing at the end of 2012, see Annex 16 of this *Yearbook* on page 177.

(f) *Budgetary requests for the biennium 2014-2015*

The budgetary requests for the 2014-2015 biennium were submitted to the United Nations Secretariat at the beginning of 2013. Therein, the Court requested the establishment of three posts: a post of Head of Procurement, Facilities Management and General Assistance (P-3), a post of Associate Legal Officer (P-2) for the Office of the President of the Court and a post of Administrative Assistant (General Service, Other Level) for the Office of the Registrar (for more details please see paragraphs 262-265 of the *I.C.J. Annual Report 2012-2013*, available on the website of the Court under "The Court".

In 2015, the Court is due to be included in the Umoja Project. Since the extent of this operation is as yet unknown, the Court has made provision in its budgetary requests for hardware, software and consultancy services in 2014-2015 to facilitate the migration to the Umoja/SAP (Systems, Applications, Products in Data Processing) software. The estimates — based on the hypothetical costs of the project — may prove insufficient to cover the actual costs.

As from 1 January 2014, the International Public Sector Accounting Standards (IPSAS) are due to be implemented across the United Nations. The Umoja Project will not be ready in time to provide the necessary support for this implementation. The Court has thus made provision in its budgetary requests for the biennium 2014-2015 to cover the costs of consultancy services, so as to ensure that its current accounting software (ACCPAC) meets IPSAS requirements. The Court will thus be in a position to produce IPSAS-compliant financial statements before Umoja becomes fully operational.

Finally, it should be noted that the Court will celebrate its seventieth anniversary on 18 April 2016. This event will be a unique opportunity to better inform the international community, through various means, about the activities and achievements of the principal judicial organ of the United Nations. Since most of the preparatory work for this celebration will take place in the course of the biennium 2014-2015, the Court has incorporated its funding requirements into the next budget.

(g) *Salaries and other emoluments of Members of the Court*

By virtue of Article 32, paragraph 5, of the Statute, the salaries, allowances and compensation paid to the judges are fixed by the General Assembly. With effect from 1 January 2012, the annual base salary of Members of the Court is fixed at $169,098. In this connection, the General Assembly adopted a series of resolutions and decisions, the latest one being resolution 65/258 of 16 March 2011. A full list of these resolutions and decisions can be found on pages 366-367 of the *I.C.J. Yearbook 2009-2010*.

More detailed information regarding the composition and emoluments of the Members of the Court (annual base salary, post adjustment, special allowances, pensions, education grants, travel and subsistence) can be found in Annex 17, page 179 of this *Yearbook*.

Under Article 32, paragraph 4, of the Statute, judges *ad hoc* chosen to sit in certain cases under Article 31 of the Statute shall receive compensation for each day in which they exercise their functions. Compensation to judges *ad hoc* has changed over time. With effect from 1 April 2008, the daily fee of judges *ad hoc* has been fixed at 1/365th of the annual salary of a Member of the Court plus post adjustment.

(h) *Salaries, allowances and expenses of the Registrar and officials of the Registry*

Salaries, pensions and other emoluments of the Registrar and other officials of the Registry are set out in the *I.C.J. Yearbook 2009-2010*, pp. 371-372.

The latest revision of the salary scale for staff in the professional and higher categories was approved by the General Assembly by resolution 66/235, effective 1 January 2012. The latest revision of the pensionable remuneration scale for this category of staff was promulgated by the International Civil Service Commission (ICSC), effective 1 February 2013. The ICSC promulgated the revised salary scale for The Hague for staff members in the general services category, effective 1 December 2012. For eligible temporary staff, the daily subsistence allowance for The Hague is fixed at 272 euros.

(i) *Common services*

The common services of the Court and of the Registry, as well as capital expenditures, come under special items in the budget. In particular, the Court pays to the Carnegie Foundation an annual contribution for the premises it occupies at the Peace Palace and in the new wing. The amount of the contribution has undergone successive alterations since it was first fixed by General Assembly resolution 84 (I) of 11 December 1946, and stands at 1,264,152 euros per annum as from 1 January 2012 and at 1,292,595 euros per annum as from 1 January 2013.

5. *Information, Publications and Documentation*

(a) *Relations with the Public*

Article 26, paragraph 1 *(a)*, of the Rules of Court states that the Registrar shall "be the regular channel for communications to and from the Court".

Consequently, correspondence of this nature should be addressed to:

> The Registrar
> International Court of Justice
> Peace Palace
> Carnegieplein 2
> 2517 KJ
> The Hague, Netherlands

The Court's switchboard number is (+31) 70 302 23 23.

All general queries (regarding employment/internship opportunities, visits to the seat of the Court, etc.) may be sent to the Registry, in either English or French, via the Court's website (www.icj-cij.org) under "Contact". Please note that it is not possible for the Registry to give legal advice or to enter into correspondence with private persons concerning any matter at issue between them and the authorities of their own or another country.

(b) *Information for Specialists and Members of the General Public*

Article 26, paragraph 1 *(k)* and *(m)*, of the Rules of Court provides that the Registrar shall "deal with enquiries concerning the Court and its work" and "ensure that information concerning the Court and its activities is made accessible to governments, the highest national courts of justice, professional and learned societies, legal faculties and law schools, and the media". For this purpose, the Registrar is assisted by the Information Department. The Registrar arranges as he considers necessary for the publication of information concerning the composition, jurisdiction and work of the Court, along with judgments, advisory opinions and orders relating to all cases and corresponding case documentation.

(i) Website of the Court

On 16 April 2007, to mark the end of its sixtieth anniversary year, the Court launched its new website. This website replaced the Court's original website launched in 1997. The website contains the entire jurisprudence of the Court, as well as that of its predecessor, the Permanent Court of International Justice. Information concerning the functioning of the

Court, its history, its elected Members, the judges *ad hoc* and the Registry are also featured.

The ICJ website offers detailed practical information for those wishing to attend proceedings of the Court, to see a presentation on the activities of the Court, or to visit the seat of the Court (it also includes a hearings schedule, online admission forms and a list of frequently asked questions (FAQ)).

The website features a "Press Room", which provides media representatives with all of the necessary information for covering the work of the Court and for accrediting themselves to Court proceedings. A multimedia gallery, from which digital photographs of recent public sessions of the Court, as well as video files (low resolution: flv. and high resolution mpeg2) and audio files (mp3) can be downloaded free of charge for non-commercial use, is also accessible.

Vacancy announcements and internship opportunities are also featured under "Registry", "Employment" or "Internships".

The website is available in the two official languages of the Court, English and French. A number of documents and files, including the ICJ video entitled "The Role and Activities of the ICJ", are also available in the other four official languages of the United Nations: Arabic, Chinese, Russian and Spanish. Among these documents are the United Nations Charter, the Statute and Rules of the Court, the Court's *Annual Reports* to the General Assembly since 1989-1990 and the summaries of decisions of the Court (from 1948 to 2002).

(ii) Information material published by the Registry

The Registry publishes a number of informative documents on the workings and activities of the Court. These include:

- a short description of the role and functioning of the Court called *The Court at a Glance* (available in English, French and Spanish);
- a booklet entitled *The International Court of Justice: Questions and Answers about the Principal Judicial Organ of the United Nations* (2000) (also known as the *Green Book*), published by the United Nations Department of Public Information in co-operation with the Court, available in English and French, as well as in Arabic, Chinese, Russian, Spanish and Dutch;
- a handbook entitled *The International Court of Justice* (2004) (also known as the *Blue Book*), available in English and French, along with a previous edition (1986) which was published in Arabic, Chinese, Russian, Spanish and German.

In addition, the updated illustrated edition of the *International Court of Justice Handbook* (in English and French) will be published in 2014. The updated PDF version will be posted on the website of the Court at the time of publication.

All of these documents are obtainable within the framework of the United Nations Programme of Assistance in Teaching, Study, Dissemination and Wider Appreciation of International Law, either from the Registry of the Court or from United Nations Information Centres.

This material is also available in English and French on the website of the Court under "Press Room/FAQ".

In 2006, on the occasion of the sixtieth anniversary of the Court, the Registry published a richly illustrated, bilingual coffee table book called *La Cour Internationale de Justice — The International Court of Justice.*

Over the course of 2013, in keeping with its wish to commemorate the ninetieth anniversary of the inauguration of the Permanent Court of International Justice, the Registry of the International Court of Justice will republish an explanatory book on the history and work of the first permanent international tribunal which was originally published in 1939 by the Registry of the Permanent Court of International Justice and which remained out of print for many years. The electronic version of the new trilingual edition (English, Spanish, French) is available on the website of the Court under the heading "Permanent Court of International Justice", free of charge. The clothbound version will be on sale in 2014. Purchasing information can be found on the Court's website at www.icj-cij.org.

For information regarding the sale of the Court's publications please see page 34 of this *Yearbook* or the website of the Court under the heading "Publications".

(iii) Presentation of the work and functioning of the Court and receiving groups

Groups often visit the Registry to receive presentations on the work of the Court. So far as the work of the Court permits, the Registrar accedes to requests of this kind. During the period under review the Court received a large number of groups, including diplomats, scholars and academics, judges and representatives of judicial authorities, lawyers and legal professionals, as well as journalists.

All requests for presentations on the history, workings and activities of the Court must be submitted via the Court's website at: www.icj-cij.org, under "Practical Information" at least six weeks in advance. Presentations are available in both English and French and are free of charge.

(c) Publications of the International Court of Justice and the Permanent Court of International Justice

The publications of the International Court of Justice are published by the Registry (Rules of Court, Art. 26, para. 1 *(i)*, and Art. 71, para. 6; Instructions for the Registry, Arts. 23, 43, 67-69 and 72). Information about the publications of the present Court and those of its forerunner, the Permanent Court of International Justice is given below.

(i) Series Published by the International Court of Justice

The publications of the Court are at present classified in series as shown hereunder.

Reports of Judgments, Advisory Opinions and Orders

This series contains the Reports of the decisions of the Court in both English and French. Each decision is published as soon as given, in an unbound fascicle which is sold separately.

An analytical index is published for each year's decisions. The collected decisions, with index, for each year may also be obtained ready bound together in one to three volumes.

Seventy-one bound volumes have so far been published, the first being the *I.C.J. Reports* for the years 1947 and 1948, which are collected in a single volume. The latest is the two bound volumes for 2011.

Official citation of the series: *I.C.J. Reports*, with an indication of the year. For a separate fascicle, the short title of the case, the countries (if a contentious case) and the nature of the decision should be given, e.g.: *Frontier Dispute (Burkino Faso/Niger), Judgment, I.C.J. Reports 2013*, p. 14; or *Whaling in the Antarctic (Australia v. Japan), Declaration of Intervention of New Zealand, Order of 6 February 2013, I.C.J. Reports 2013*, p. 3. For an exhaustive list of all case title citations for the *I.C.J. Reports*, please refer to the ICJ website under the heading "Publications/Judgments, Advisory Opinions and Orders".

Pleadings, Oral Arguments, Documents

Volumes in this series are published after the termination of each case and contain the documentation relating to the case in the original language, that is, in English or in French.

This comprises the document instituting proceedings, the written pleadings and their annexes, the verbatim record of the oral proceedings, and any documents submitted to the Court after the closure of the written proceedings.

Depending upon the length of the documents to be printed, one or more volumes are issued for each case.

Abbreviated reference: *I.C.J. Pleadings*, with the short title of the case and the countries involved in parenthesis, e.g.: *I.C.J. Pleadings, LaGrand (Germany v. United States of America)*, Vol. I. For an exhaustive list of all title citations for the *I.C.J. Pleadings*, please refer to the ICJ website under "Publications/Pleadings, Oral Arguments, Documents".

Acts and Documents concerning the Organization of the Court

This publication is a compilation of the basic documents of the Court. The latest edition, No. 6 was published in February 2007 and can be downloaded free of charge from the website of the Court under "Publications/Acts and Documents No. 6".

Abbreviated reference: *I.C.J. Acts and Documents No. 6.*

Yearbook

Each year a *Yearbook* is published in which an account is given of the work of the Court during the period from 1 August of the preceding year to 31 July of the current year. There is also a French edition of this publication, the *Annuaire*.

The present *Yearbook* is the sixty-seventh in the series, which started with *I.C.J. Yearbook 1946-1947*.

Abbreviated reference: *I.C.J. Yearbook*, with an indication of the year covered by the volume, e.g.: *I.C.J. Yearbook 2009-2010*. A PDF version of the most recent *I.C.J. Yearbook* can be found on the website of the Court under "Publications/I.C.J. Yearbook 2011-2012".

Bibliography of the International Court of Justice

Each year, the Registry issues a *Bibliography* listing such works and documents relating to the Court as have come to its attention during the previous year.

Bibliographies Nos. 1-18 formed Chapter IX in the appropriate *Yearbook* or *Annuaire* up to the 1963-1964 editions. Beginning with No. 19, later *Bibliographies* were issued as separate fascicles. The latest *I.C.J. Bibliography* published is No. 57 (year 2003).

Abbreviated reference: *I.C.J. Bibliography*, with the serial number of the volume, followed, if desired, by the entry number of the work cited. E.g.: *I.C.J. Bibliography No. 35:* 81: 150, as from 1981.

(ii) Dissemination of the Publications of the International Court of Justice

The publications of the Court are distributed free on request and as required to the governments or public services of all States entitled to appear before the Court. The *I.C.J. Reports*, the *I.C.J. Pleadings* and *Acts and Documents concerning the Organization of the Court* series are also published in electronic PDF format on the Court's website under the heading "Publications".

Printed publications are sold by the Sales and Marketing Sections of the United Nations Secretariat at:

> United Nations Publications,
> 300 East 42nd Street, Room IN-919 J,
> New York, NY 10017, United States of America.
> Tel.: +1-212-963-8302
> E-mail: publications@un.org

These publications may also be consulted in major law libraries, including many university libraries, certain depository libraries for United

Nations publications, and libraries aided by the United Nations Programme of Assistance in the Teaching, Study, Dissemination and Wider Appreciation of International Law. They may also be obtained from any bookseller selling United Nations publications. *Orders and requests for information should be sent to these addresses and not to the Registry.*

A Catalogue is issued in English and French. It lists the sales number of each publication and its price in US dollars. It is updated each year, by means either of an addendum or of a new edition. A free copy of the Catalogue may be obtained by applying to the Sales Sections of the United Nations. A PDF version is also available on the Court's website at: http://www.icj-cij.org.publications/en/catalogue.pdf.

(iii) Publications of the Permanent Court of International Justice

Between 1922 and 1946 the Permanent Court of International Justice published the following series:

Series A (Nos. 1-24): *Collection of Judgments* (up to and including 1930)

Series B (Nos. 1-18): *Collection of Advisory Opinions* (up to and including 1930)

Series A/B (Nos. 40-80): *Judgments, Orders and Advisory Opinions* (beginning in 1931)

Series C (Nos. 1-19): *Acts and Documents relating to Judgments and Advisory Opinions given by the Court* (up to and including 1930)

Series C (Nos. 52-88): *Pleadings, Oral Statements and Documents* (beginning in 1931)

Series D (Nos. 1-6): *Acts and Documents concerning the Organization of the Court*

Series E (Nos. 1-16): *Annual Reports*

Series F (Nos. 1-4): *General Indexes*

They may be consulted in certain universities and other libraries with a substantial legal section.

It is recalled that in 2012, to celebrate the ninetieth anniversary of the creation of the Permanent Court of International Justice, the Court published a deluxe special edition of the original 1939 booklet supplemented with additional photographs, information, a foreword and afterword. This new edition is entitled *The Permanent Court of International Justice (PCIJ), 1922-2012,* and is a trilingual (French, English, Spanish) edition.

(d) *Library and Archives of the Court*

(i) *Library*

The principal role of the Court's library is to assist Members of the Court and the different departments and divisions of the Registry, notably the Department of Legal Matters and the Linguistics Department, with their research. The library also compiles annual bibliographies of the Court, which inventory those books and periodical articles that make reference to the International Court of Justice or the Permanent Court of International Justice.

The library of the International Court of Justice, which succeeded the library of the Permanent Court of International Justice created in 1931, is distinct from the Peace Palace Library. The two libraries, however, maintain a privileged relationship based on rules established in 1931 and confirmed by a *modus vivendi* dating from 1946.

The library's collection also includes the Archives of the International Military Tribunal at Nuremberg (see point *(ii)* below).

Information regarding the library of the Court is available on the website of the Court, under "The Registry". The Court's library is not open to members of the public.

(ii) Archives of the Court, the PCIJ and the International Military Tribunal at Nuremberg

The archives of the International Military Tribunal at Nuremberg were entrusted to the International Court of Justice by a decision of the Tribunal on 1 October 1946. These archives were transported to the Peace Palace, where representatives of the Tribunal and the staff of the Court took delivery of them on 14 March 1950. They have remained in the library's collection ever since.

All questions regarding consultation of these archives should be addressed in writing to the Registrar of the Court at the address mentioned on page 30 above. Neither the archives of the International Court of Justice nor the Permanent Court of International Justice are open to the public (Rules, Art. 26, para. 1 *(n)*).

CHAPTER IV

PRACTICE OF THE COURT WITH REGARD TO PROCEDURE

In matters concerning its procedure, the International Court of Justice applies Articles 39-64 and 65-68 of its Statute (related respectively to procedure and to advisory opinions), as well as Articles 30-101 and 102-109 of its Rules (related respectively to proceedings in contentious cases and in advisory proceedings).

1. General

(a) Official languages

The official languages of the Court are English and French (Statute, Art. 39; Rules, Arts. 51, 70 and 71).

(b) Official communications

In all cases submitted to the Court, communications and documents for the Court are delivered to the Registrar and he is the regular channel for communications or notifications from the Court (Rules, Art. 26, para. 1, and Art. 30; Instructions for the Registry, Arts. 3, 11 and 13).

Communications in a case which are intended for a State party thereto are sent to its agent at the Hague address it designates for the purpose (Rules, Art. 40, para. 1).

For communications with other States, the Registrar requests the foreign ministers of States entitled to appear before the Court to indicate the channel through which their Governments would wish to receive such communications. The channel of communication indicated is usually the Embassy in The Hague or the Ministry of Foreign Affairs of the State in question.

For public international organizations, the Registrar addresses the communications of the Court to the Director General or Secretary-General of the organization, as the case may be.

(c) Minutes

The Registrar is present at all sittings and meetings of the Court and is responsible for drawing up the minutes. After being signed by the President and the Registrar, these minutes are filed in the archives (Statute, Art. 47; Rules, Art. 21, Art. 26, para. 1 *(f)-(i)*, and Art. 71; Instructions for the Registry, Art. 19).

(d) *General List*

The Registrar prepares and keeps up to date a General List of cases submitted to the Court (Rules, Art. 26, para. 1 *(b)*, and Art. 38, para. 5; Instructions for the Registry, Art. 6, para. 1, and Art. 46, para. 3).

(For the General List of the Permanent Court of International Justice, see *P.C.I.J., Series E, No. 16*, pp. 92-147.) This publication is available on the website of the Court under "PCIJ/Series E".

2. Procedure in Contentious Cases

(a) *Institution of proceedings and appointment of agents*

As soon as proceedings are instituted, the special agreement or the application, filed in one of the two official languages of the Court, is translated and printed in a bilingual edition by the Registry, then communicated to all concerned and to the States entitled to appear before the Court (Statute, Art. 40; Rules, Art. 38, paras. 4 and 5; Art. 39, para. 1, and Art. 42).

The Registrar instructs the Information Department to publish a press release informing the general public and the media that proceedings have been instituted. Copies of the special agreement or application and the press release are published on the website of the Court.

The party which files a document instituting proceedings informs the Court at the same time of the name of the agent who will be its representative in the proceedings and take steps on its behalf; the other party then appoints its agent as soon as possible (Statute, Art. 42; Rules, Art. 40; Practice Direction VIII). A party may also appoint a co-agent, a deputy-agent or an additional agent. Agents, and counsel and advocates also, enjoy such privileges and immunities as may be required for the independent exercise of their duties (Statute, Art. 42, para. 3; *I.C.J. Acts and Documents No. 6*, pp. 211-215).

The President, who is required to ascertain the views of the parties on questions of procedure, summons the agents to meet him as soon as possible after their appointment and whenever necessary thereafter (Rules, Art. 31).

(b) *Written proceedings*

The written proceedings comprise the filing of pleadings within time-limits fixed in orders made by the Court or, if it is not sitting, the President; the pleadings are in principle confined to a Memorial and a Counter-Memorial, though the Court may if it thinks fit authorize or direct that there be a Reply and a Rejoinder (Statute, Art. 43; Rules, Arts. 44-46 and 48; Instructions for the Registry, Art. 14; Practice Direction I).

The party's submissions are set out in each pleading (Rules, Art. 49; Practice Direction II).

The agent of the party filing the pleading supplies the Registry (Statute, Art. 43, paras. 3 and 4; Rules, Arts. 50-52; Practice Directions III[1] and IV) with the following:

- an original copy of the pleading, signed by the agent, to which is annexed a certified copy of any relevant document adduced in support of the contentions put forward;
- an English or French translation, certified by the agent to be accurate, of any part of a pleading or annexed document submitted in another language;
- a copy, certified by the agent, of the pleading and annexed documents, for communication to the other party;
- 125 further copies of the pleading and annexed documents (75 of which should be on paper, while 50 may be on USB stick);
- an electronic copy of any pleading;
- in the case of any document of which only parts are relevant and only necessary extracts have been annexed to the pleading, a copy of the whole document.

The format for the pleadings and annexes is 19 × 26 cm. If they are submitted in printed form, which is not compulsory, it is recommended that the Court's Typographical Rules (supplied by the Registry on request) be complied with.

The Registry usually translates, for the judges, pleadings and annexed documents, filed in one of the official languages of the Court, into the other official language (Rules, Art. 26, para. 1 *(g)*).

The Registrar arranges for the publication of press releases giving information concerning the course of the written proceedings. Moreover, the Court may, after ascertaining the views of the parties, communicate the pleadings on request to any State entitled to appear before the Court.

It may also, after ascertaining the parties' views, make the pleadings available to the general public and the media on or after the opening of the oral proceedings (Rules, Art. 53); this is generally done by posting them on the Court's website and by depositing copies in a number of libraries, including the Peace Palace Library. The pagination of the pleadings and annexed documents, which may thus be made accessible, is provisional in character. They are not given their final pagination until they are published in the *I.C.J. Pleadings* series (see *(e)* below).

(c) *Oral proceedings*

Upon the closure of the written proceedings, a case is ready for hearing. The opening date of the oral proceedings is fixed by the Court or, if it is not sitting, the President (Rules, Art. 54). Public sittings are held at the seat of the Court, on weekdays. They are devoted to hearing the arguments of counsel and such evidence of witnesses or experts[2] as the parties may call;

---

[1] The text of Practice Direction III was modified in January 2009, see Annex 2 of this *Yearbook* on page 135.

[2] The Court heard witnesses and/or expert witnesses in 11 cases. For a list of these cases, see Annex 18, p. 181.

the Court itself may also arrange for a witness to be heard, entrust any individual, body or organization with the task of giving an expert opinion or decide on an inspection *in loco*[1] (Statute, Arts. 43-46 and 48-51; Rules, Arts. 57-68; Instructions for the Registry, Art. 20; Practice Direction VI).

The Court settles the order in which the parties are heard, the number of counsel who will address the Court, and the method of handling the evidence (Rules, Art. 58, para. 2). It is customary for the parties to present their arguments in the order in which their pleadings have been deposited or, in the case of proceedings instituted by special agreement, in the order laid down by the Court after consultations with the agents of the parties. Speeches and statements are normally made in one of the Court's two official languages and are (simultaneously) interpreted into the other; arrangements may be made for some other language to be used (Statute, Art. 39; Rules, Art. 70; Instructions for the Registry, Art. 17).

When the Court or a judge puts a question to the agents, counsel and advocates, the answer may be given either immediately or within a time-limit fixed by the President; if given in writing it is communicated to the other party (Rules, Art. 61, paras. 2-4, and Art. 72), but is not made public.

A provisional verbatim record of each public sitting is drawn up by the Registry in the official language used, and translated into the other; copies in the original official language are then communicated to the parties and to the witnesses and experts in order that mistakes may be corrected under the supervision of the Court (Statute, Art. 47; Rules, Art. 71). A period of 24 hours is usually allowed for the submission of corrections by the parties, a non-corrected version is published online within a few hours of the conclusion of the hearings.

In the course of the hearings each party reads out its final submissions and hands the Registrar copies of the text (Rules, Art. 60, para. 2). The filing of new documents after closure of the written proceedings is permissible only with the other party's consent or the authorization of the Court (Practice Direction IX); such documents must be filed in the same number of copies as the pleadings; the Registrar transmits them to the other party with a request for observations. No reference may be made to the contents of any document which has not been duly produced, unless the document is part of a publication readily available (Statute, Art. 52; Rules, Art. 56)[2].

The Registrar issues press releases giving all necessary information as to the dates of the hearings (Instructions for the Registry, Arts. 10 and 51). Members of the diplomatic corps, representatives of the media and any person who comes to the Peace Palace on the occasion of a hearing are

---

[1] The Court conducted an inspection *in loco* at the site of the hydroelectric dam project in the case concerning *Gabčíkovo-Nagymaros Project (Hungary/Slovakia)*, but did not accede to requests concerning an inspection *in loco* in either the case concerning *South West Africa (Ethiopia* v. *South Africa; Liberia* v. *South Africa)* or the case concerning the *Land, Island and Maritime Frontier Dispute (El Salvador/Honduras: Nicaragua intervening)*.

[2] The full text of the Practice Directions can be found on the website of the Court, under "Basic Documents".

welcome to attend, subject to accreditation or admission procedures. Photographs may be taken by the press for a few minutes at the opening of hearings, under strict conditions (see the ICJ website under the heading "Press Room"). Filming by the press is permitted under the same rules.

(d) *Deliberations*

After the close of the oral proceedings, the Court withdraws to deliberate in private and to prepare a judgment. The deliberations of the Court are conducted *in camera* and remain confidential. This applies to all aspects of the deliberations, including the schedule of meetings (Statute, Arts. 54-55; Rules, Arts. 19-21; Instructions for the Registry, Art. 16).

The manner in which the Court conducts its deliberations is governed by a resolution concerning the internal judicial practice of the Court, the most recent version of which was adopted on 12 April 1976 (see *I.C.J. Acts and Documents No. 6*, pp. 175-183).

(e) *Judgment*

The judgment is read out at a public sitting for which similar arrangements are made as for a hearing in open court, in particular with regard to the admission of the public and the assistance provided to representatives of the press (see *(c)* above).

The judgment is prepared in both official languages, of which one is indicated as authoritative (Statute, Art. 39; Rules, Art. 96). If it does not represent in whole or in part the unanimous opinion of the judges, any judge is entitled to attach a dissenting or separate opinion, or a declaration which records his position without stating his reasons; the judgment indicates the names of the judges constituting the majority (Statute, Arts. 56-58; Rules, Arts. 94 and 95).

Three original copies of the judgment are signed by the President and the Registrar and are then sealed; one is placed in the archives of the Court and the others are handed to the parties (Rules, Art. 95, para. 3; Instructions for the Registry, Art. 21).

Immediately after the public reading, copies of the judgment are placed at the disposal of the judges and the representatives of the parties. At the same time an unofficial summary of the decision and the press release are issued, on the authority of the Registrar, to all those attending. They are also published on the Court's website and sent by email to all those registered to the press release mailing list.

As soon as possible after the judgment is issued, the printed text of the judgment becomes available as a separate fascicle in the *I.C.J. Reports* series, which is sent to States entitled to appear before the Court and is placed on sale. Subsequently, the documentation of the case is published in one or more printed volumes of the series entitled *I.C.J. Pleadings, Oral Arguments, Documents*. It is these printed texts (see the Court's website under the heading "Publications/Pleadings, Oral Arguments, Documents") which should be used for all purposes of quotation or citation.

(f) *Expenses and costs*

The expenses of the Court, including amounts payable to witnesses or experts appearing at the instance of the Court (Rules, Art. 68; Instructions for the Registry, Art. 18), are borne out of the United Nations budget; if a party to a case does not contribute to the United Nations budget, the Court itself fixes the amount payable by that party as a contribution towards the expenses of the Court for the case.

Each party bears its own costs, unless the Court makes an order in favour of a party for the payment of the costs (Statute, Art. 64; Rules, Art. 95, para. 1, and Art. 97).

(g) *Trust Fund*

In addition, there exists a Secretary-General's Trust Fund to Assist States in the Settlement of Disputes through the International Court of Justice, established on 1 November 1989 (see United Nations doc. A/ 44/ PV.43 (1989)). The Fund is designed to encourage States to settle their disputes peaceably by submitting them to the Court. The Fund is open to States in all circumstances where the jurisdiction of the Court (or the admissibility of the application) is not or is no longer the subject of dispute on their part. A further purpose of the Fund is to help States parties to a dispute to comply with the judgment rendered by the Court.

A Report (UN doc. A/67/494) regarding the Secretary-General's Trust Fund was published on 4 October 2012, indicating that as at 30 June 2012, the Fund balance, net of awards already paid, was $2,959,966.39.

3. Incidental Proceedings in Contentious Cases

(a) *Provisional measures*

The Court has the power to indicate provisional measures (Statute, Art. 41). A request for such measures is treated as a matter of urgency, and the Court's decision is given in an order (Rules, Arts. 73-78). Such provisional measures have been requested in 41 cases. For the complete list of these cases see Annex 18 below, page 181.

The following requests were made during the period under review:

On 23 May 2013, Costa Rica presented the Court with a request for the modification of the Order of 8 March 2011 in the case concerning *Certain Activities Carried Out by Nicaragua in the Border Area (Costa Rica v. Nicaragua)*. That request made reference to Article 41 of the Statute of the Court and Article 76 of the Rules of Court.

. In its written observations, Nicaragua asked the Court to reject Costa Rica's request, while in its turn requesting the Court to modify or adapt the Order of 8 March 2011 on the basis of Article 76 of the Rules of Court. By an Order dated 16 July 2013, the Court ruled on the requests submitted by Costa Rica and Nicaragua (for more information, see page 116 of this *Yearbook*, or the *I.C.J. Annual Report 2012-2013*, which can be found on the ICJ website).

On 25 September 2012, Equatorial Guinea filed in the Registry of the Court a document, with annexes, entitled "Application instituting proceedings including request for provisional measures". In accordance with Article 38, paragraph 5, of the Rules of Court, a copy of the above-mentioned document received from Equatorial Guinea has been transmitted to the Government of France. No action shall be taken in the proceedings and the case shall not be entered in the General List unless and until France consents to the Court's jurisdiction in this case. (for more information, see press release 2012/26 available on the website of the Court under "Press Room").

More detailed information regarding provisional measures can be found in the *Handbook* of the International Court of Justice, available on the website of the Court.

(b) *Joinder of proceedings*

The Court may direct that the proceedings in two or more cases be joined (Rules, Art. 47). It does this by means of an order.

On 17 April 2013, the Court, by two separate orders joined the cases concerning *Certain Activities Carried Out by Nicaragua in the Border Area (Costa Rica* v. *Nicaragua)* and *Construction of a Road in Costa Rica along the San Juan River (Nicaragua* v. *Costa Rica)*. In both orders, the Court, "in conformity with the principle of the sound administration of justice and with the need for judicial economy", considered it appropriate to join the proceedings.

It is recalled that on 21 May 1961 and on 26 April 1968, respectively, proceedings were joined in the cases concerning *South West Africa (Ethiopia* v. *South Africa; Liberia* v. *South Africa)* and *North Sea Continental Shelf (Federal Republic of Germany/Denmark; Federal Republic of Germany/Netherlands)*.

(c) *Preliminary objections*

Preliminary objections must be filed as soon as possible, and not later than three months after the delivery of the Memorial (Rules, Art. 79). Notwithstanding that provision, the Court, following the submission of the application in a case and after the President has met and consulted with the parties, may decide that any questions of jurisdiction and admissibility shall be determined separately. Where the Court so decides, the parties shall submit any pleadings as to jurisdiction and admissibility within the time-limits fixed by the Court and in the order determined by it. Preliminary objections suspend the proceedings on the merits and may be answered by the observations and submissions of the opposing party, to be filed within a time-limit fixed by an order. In accordance with Practice Direction V, this time-limit should generally not exceed four months from the date of the filing of the preliminary objections. Oral proceedings on the objections ensue; the party which raised them being called upon to speak first. The Court gives its decision on the objections in a judgment; if it dismisses them, the proceedings on the merits are resumed from the point of interruption; they are likewise resumed if it declares that the objections do not possess an exclusively preliminary character. The Court gave its decision on the preliminary objections raised in 34 cases, see Annex 20 below, page 184. The latest being on 18 February 2011, in the case concerning *Application of the International Convention on the Elimination of All Forms of Racial Discrimination (Georgia v. Russian Federation)*. In seven other cases the Court was not called upon to give a decision on such objections, either because they were withdrawn or as a result of a discontinuance. For the list of all these cases see also Annex 20 below, page 184.

The Court gave effect to an agreement between the parties that objections should be heard and determined within the framework of the merits in the cases concerning *Elettronica Sicula S.p.A. (ELSA) (United States of America v. Italy)* and *East Timor (Portugal v. Australia)*. Preliminary objections were joined to the merits under the pre-1972 Rules of Court by agreement between the parties in the following case: *Certain Norwegian Loans (France v. Norway)* and by a decision of the Court in the following two cases: *Right of Passage over Indian Territory (Portugal v. India)* and *Barcelona Traction, Light and Power Company, Limited (New Application: 1962) (Belgium v. Spain)*.

It can occur that a Respondent contests jurisdiction or admissibility, but not by means of a preliminary objection; and sometimes the Court decides *proprio motu* to examine a preliminary point about which no formal objection has been raised. The Court has thus had to pronounce on questions of jurisdiction and/or admissibility in a number of cases, a list of which can be found in Annex 21 on page 186.

(d) *Counter-claims*

Counter-claims may be presented if they are directly connected with the subject-matter of the claim of the other party and come within the jurisdiction of the Court. They are to be made by a party in its Counter-Memorial, as part of the submissions. In case of doubt, it is for the Court to decide whether a counter-claim is admissible and shall form part of the proceedings (Rules, Art. 80). Counter-claims were made by the respondent States and admitted by the Court in four cases. For a list of these cases see Annex 22 below, page 187.

(e) *Intervention*

A third State may request to be permitted to intervene if it considers that it has an interest of a legal nature which may be affected by the decision in the case; it is for the Court to decide upon such a request (Statute, Art. 62; Rules, Arts. 81 and 83-85). Applications for permission to intervene under Article 62 and declarations under Article 63 were submitted in 13 cases, the latest in the case concerning *Whaling in the*

Antarctic (Australia v. *Japan)*. By an Order dated 6 February 2013, the Court authorized New Zealand to intervene in the case. A list of cases in which declarations of intervention have been filed can be found in Annex 23 on page 188.

Additionally, if the dispute relates to the construction of a convention to which States other than those concerned in the case are parties, these States are notified forthwith and have the right to intervene in the proceedings (Statute, Art. 63; Rules, Arts. 43, 82-84 and 86).

Similarly, public international organizations may, at the request of the Court or a party or on their own initiative, furnish the Court with information relevant to cases before it; whenever the construction of their constituent instruments or of a convention adopted thereunder is in question, they are notified (Statute, Art. 34, paras. 2 and 3; Rules, Art. 69).

(f) *Default*

If one of the parties does not appear before the Court or fails to defend its case, the other party may call upon the Court to decide in favour of its claim (Statute, Art. 53). Twelve judgments and orders were delivered in the absence of one of the parties. For the list of these cases see Annex 24 below, page 189.

(g) *Settlement, discontinuance*

The Court, or the President if the Court is not sitting, may, by way of an order, officially record the conclusion of a settlement or a discontinuance (Rules, Arts. 88 and 89). Twenty-three cases ended in discontinuance. Two of these ended in discontinuance as regarded the question of reparation which the judgment had left to be settled. For the list of these cases see Annex 25 below, page 190. The latest case to end in discontinuance is that concerning *Certain Criminal Proceedings in France (Republic of the Congo* v. *France)*, which was removed from the Court's General List, by an Order dated 16 November 2010, at the request of the Republic of the Congo.

(h) *Interpretation or revision of judgments*

The judgments of the Court are binding, final and without appeal (Charter, Art. 94, para. 1; Statute, Arts. 59-60; Rules, Art. 94, para. 2). The parties may, however, make a request for interpretation or, in certain circumstances, for revision of a judgment.

The decision of the Court on such requests is given in the form of a judgment (Statute, Arts. 60-61; Rules, Arts. 98-100). The Court gave five decisions on requests for interpretation. See Annex 11 below, page 164. The Court gave decisions on applications for revision in three cases. See Annex 12 below, page 165. A Chamber of the Court gave one decision on an application for revision. So far, the International Court of Justice has never accepted to revise any of its decisions.

Article 94, paragraph 2, of the Charter of the United Nations states that, if any party to a case fails to perform the obligations incumbent upon it under a judgment, the other party may have recourse to the Security Council.

(i) *Special reference to the Court*

When a matter which has been the subject of proceedings before some other international body is brought before the Court, the provisions of the Statute and of the Rules apply (Rules, Art. 87). The Court was on one occasion in 1971, seised in the case *Appeal Relating to the Jurisdiction of the ICAO Council (India* v. *Pakistan)*.

4. Procedure in Advisory Proceedings

In addition to the Rules of Court which are expressly applicable to proceedings in regard to advisory opinions, the Court is guided by the provisions which apply in contentious proceedings (Statute, Art. 68; Rules, Art. 102). It may thus be led to apply the articles of the Statute concerning judges *ad hoc* (Chap. I, p. 8, above).

The practical information given concerning the course of the procedure in contentious cases (see Section 2, pp. 38-42, above) applies *mutatis mutandis* to the procedure in regard to advisory opinions, in particular as regards arrangements for the public and the press.

(a) *Request*

Notice of a request for an advisory opinion (see Chap. II, p. 21, above) is addressed to the Court by the Secretary-General of the United Nations or the chief administrative officer of the organization authorized to make the request; all documents likely to throw light upon the question are to be transmitted at the same time as the request or as soon as possible thereafter (Statute, Art. 65, para. 2; Rules, Art. 104).

Notice of the request for an advisory opinion is given to all States entitled to appear before the Court (Statute, Art. 66, para. 1).

In addition, the Court gives the States and international organizations considered likely to be able to furnish information on the question an opportunity to submit their views in writing, orally, or both (Statute, Art. 66, paras. 2-4).

(b) *Written and oral proceedings*

A request for an opinion usually gives rise to written proceedings followed by oral proceedings (Statute, Art. 66; Rules, Arts. 105 and 106). In the case of urgency, the Court takes all necessary steps to accelerate the procedure (Rules, Art. 103). The Court decided to accelerate the procedure in accordance with Article 103 of the Rules in the following advisory proceedings: *Interpretation of the Agreement of 25 March 1951 between the*

WHO and Egypt; *Applicability of the Obligation to Arbitrate under Section 21 of the United Nations Headquarters Agreement of 26 June 1947*; *Legality of the Threat or Use of Nuclear Weapons* and *Legal Consequences of the Construction of a Wall in the Occupied Palestinian Territory*.

(c) *Deliberations*

The deliberations are conducted in the same manner as in contentious cases (Rules, Arts. 19-21 and 107; resolution concerning the Internal Judicial Practice of the Court, Art. 10).

(d) *Advisory opinion*

The advisory opinion is read in open Court; if it does not represent in whole or in part the unanimous opinion of the judges, any judge is entitled to attach a dissenting or separate opinion, or a declaration which records his position without stating his reasons; the advisory opinion indicates the names of the judges constituting the majority (Statute, Art. 67; Rules, Arts. 107 and 108).

One of the original copies of the advisory opinion is transmitted to the body which made the request (Rules, Art. 109), after which copies are distributed to those attending. The text of the advisory opinion, a summary and a press release are then posted on the website of the Court.

The opinions given by the Court are purely advisory in character. In certain cases, the instrument by which the Court is seised provides that the advisory opinion has binding force.

5. Practice Directions

Practice Directions are the result of the Court's ongoing review of its working methods. Any amendments to the Practice Directions, following their adoption by the Court, are posted on the Court's website and published in the Court's *Yearbook*, with a note of any temporal reservations relating to their applicability.

The full text of the Practice Directions can be found on the website of the International Court of Justice under the headings "Basic Documents/Practice Directions".

6. Occasional Functions Entrusted to the President of the International Court of Justice

These functions are not described individually; however, a general presentation of them is given in Annex 26 on page 191 of this *Yearbook*.

CHAPTER V

JUDICIAL WORK AND OTHER ACTIVITIES OF THE COURT IN 2012-2013

I. Proceedings before the Court

A detailed overview of developments in all the proceedings pending before the Court during the period from 1 August 2012 to 31 July 2013 is provided below. For a brief summary of the judicial work of the Court during the period under review, see page 4 of this *Yearbook*.

1. *Gabčíkovo-Nagymaros Project (Hungary/Slovakia)*

On 2 July 1993, Hungary and Slovakia jointly notified to the Court a Special Agreement, signed between them on 7 April 1993, for the submission of certain issues arising out of differences regarding the implementation and the termination of the Budapest Treaty of 16 September 1977 on the construction and operation of the Gabčíkovo-Nagymaros barrage system.

In Article 2 of the Special Agreement:

"(1) The Court is requested to decide on the basis of the Treaty and rules and principles of general international law, as well as such other treaties as the Court may find applicable,

(*a*) whether the Republic of Hungary was entitled to suspend and subsequently abandon, in 1989, the works on the Nagymaros Project and on the part of the Gabčíkovo Project for which the Treaty attributed responsibility to the Republic of Hungary;

(*b*) whether the Czech and Slovak Federal Republic was entitled to proceed, in November 1991, to the 'provisional solution' and to put into operation from October 1992 this system, described in the Report of the Working Group of Independent Experts of the Commission of the European Communities, the Republic of Hungary and the Czech and Slovak Federal Republic dated 23 November 1992 (damming up of the Danube at river kilometre 1851.7 on Czechoslovak territory and resulting consequences on water and navigation course);

(*c*) what are the legal effects of the notification, on 19 May 1992, of the termination of the Treaty by the Republic of Hungary.

(2) The Court is also requested to determine the legal consequences, including the rights and obligations for the Parties, arising from its Judgment on the questions in paragraph (1) of this Article."

Each of the Parties filed a Memorial, a Counter-Memorial and a Reply within the time-limits fixed by the Court or its President.

Public hearings in the case were held between 3 March and 15 April 1997. From 1 to 4 April 1997, the Court paid a site visit (the first ever in its history) to the Gabčíkovo-Nagymaros Project, by virtue of Article 66 of the Rules of Court.

In its Judgment of 25 September 1997 (*I.C.J. Reports 1997*, p. 7) the Court found that both Hungary and Slovakia had breached their legal obligations. It called on both States to negotiate in good faith in order to ensure the achievement of the objectives of the 1977 Budapest Treaty, which it declared was still in force, while taking account of the factual situation that had developed since 1989.

On 3 September 1998 Slovakia filed in the Registry of the Court a request for an additional judgment in the case. Such an additional judgment was necessary, according to Slovakia, because of the unwillingness of Hungary to implement the judgment delivered by the Court in that case on 25 September 1997.

Hungary filed a written statement of its position on the request for an additional judgment made by Slovakia within the time-limit of 7 December 1998 fixed by the President of the Court.

The Parties have subsequently resumed negotiations and have informed the Court on a regular basis of the progress made. The President of the Court holds meetings with their agents when he deems it necessary. The case remains pending.

2. Armed Activities on the Territory of the Congo (Democratic Republic of the Congo v. Uganda)

On 23 June 1999, the Democratic Republic of the Congo filed an Application instituting proceedings against Uganda for "acts of armed aggression perpetrated . . . in flagrant violation of the Charter of the United Nations and of the Charter of the Organization of African Unity" (see *I.C.J. Annual Report 1998-1999, et seq.*).

In its Application, the Democratic Republic of the Congo requested the Court to adjudge and declare that Uganda was guilty of an act of aggression contrary to Article 2, paragraph 4, of the United Nations Charter and that it was committing repeated violations of the Geneva Conventions of 1949 and the Additional Protocols of 1977. The Democratic Republic of the Congo further asked the Court to adjudge and declare that all Ugandan armed forces and Ugandan nationals, both natural and legal persons, should be withdrawn from Congolese territory; and that the Democratic Republic of the Congo was entitled to compensation (see *I.C.J. Annual Report 1998-1999*).

In its Counter-Memorial, filed on 20 April 2001, Uganda presented three counter-claims. The first concerned alleged acts of aggression against it by the Democratic Republic of the Congo; the second related to attacks on Ugandan diplomatic premises and personnel in Kinshasa and on Ugandan nationals for which the Democratic Republic of the Congo was alleged to be responsible; and the third dealt with alleged violations by the Democratic Republic of the Congo of the Lusaka Agreement (see *I.C.J. Annual Report 2000-2001*).

By an Order of 29 November 2001, the Court found that the first two of the counter-claims submitted by Uganda against the Democratic Republic of the Congo were "admissible as such and [formed] part of the current proceedings", but that the third was not (see *I.C.J. Annual Report 2001-2002*).

Public hearings on the merits of the case were held from 11 to 29 April 2005 (see *I.C.J. Annual Report 2004-2005*).

In the Judgment which it rendered on 19 December 2005 (see *I.C.J. Annual Report 2005-2006*), the Court found in particular that Uganda, by engaging in military activities against the Democratic Republic of the Congo on the latter's territory, by occupying Ituri and by actively extending support to irregular forces having operated on the territory of the DRC, had violated the principle of non-use of force in international relations and the principle of non-intervention; that it had violated, in the course of hostilities between Ugandan and Rwandan military forces in Kisangani, its obligations under international human rights law and international humanitarian law; that it had violated, by the conduct of its armed forces towards the Congolese civilian population and in particular as an occupying Power in Ituri district, other obligations incumbent on it under international human rights law and international humanitarian law; and that it had violated its obligations under international law by acts of looting, plundering and exploitation of Congolese natural resources committed by members of its armed forces in the territory of the DRC and by its failure to prevent such acts as an occupying Power in Ituri district.

Regarding the second counter-claim submitted by Uganda, having rejected the first, the Court found that the Democratic Republic of the Congo had for its part violated obligations owed to the Republic of Uganda under the Vienna Convention on Diplomatic Relations of 1961, through maltreatment of or failure to protect the persons and property protected by the said Convention.

The Court therefore found that the Parties were under obligation to one another to make reparation for the injury caused; it decided that, failing agreement between the Parties, the question of reparation would be settled by the Court. It reserved for this purpose the subsequent procedure in the case. Since then, the Parties have transmitted to the Court certain information concerning the negotiations they are holding to settle the question of reparation, as referred to in points (6) and (14) of the operative clause of the Judgment and paragraphs 260, 261 and 344 of the reasoning in the Judgment. The case therefore remains pending.

3. Application of the Convention on the Prevention and Punishment of the Crime of Genocide (Croatia v. Serbia)

On 2 July 1999 Croatia instituted proceedings against Serbia (then known as the Federal Republic of Yugoslavia (FRY)) with respect to a dispute concerning alleged violations of the 1948 Convention on the Prevention and Punishment of the Crime of Genocide alleged to have been committed between 1991 and 1995.

In its Application, Croatia contended *inter alia* that, "[b]y directly controlling the activity of its armed forces, intelligence agents, and various paramilitary detachments, on the territory of . . . Croatia, in the Knin region, eastern and western Slavonia, and Dalmatia", Serbia was liable for "ethnic cleansing" committed against Croatian citizens, "a form of genocide which resulted in large numbers of Croatian citizens being displaced, killed, tortured, or illegally detained, as well as [causing] extensive property destruction".

Accordingly, Croatia requested the Court to adjudge and declare that Serbia had "breached its legal obligations" to Croatia under the Genocide Convention and that it had

> "an obligation to pay to . . . Croatia, in its own right and as *parens patriae* for its citizens, reparations for damages to persons and property, as well as to the Croatian economy and environment caused by the foregoing violations of international law in a sum to be determined by the Court".

As basis for the jurisdiction of the Court, Croatia invoked Article IX of the Genocide Convention, to which, it claims, both States are parties.

By an Order of 14 September 1999, the Court fixed 14 March 2000 and 14 September 2000 as the respective time-limits for the filing of a Memorial by Croatia and a Counter-Memorial by Serbia. These time-limits were twice extended, by Orders of 10 March 2000 and 27 June 2000. Croatia filed its Memorial within the time-limit as extended by the latter Order.

On 11 September 2002, within the time-limit for the filing of its Counter-Memorial as extended by the Order of 27 June 2000, Serbia raised certain preliminary objections on jurisdiction and admissibility. It maintained in particular that the Court lacked jurisdiction over the dispute because the FRY was not party to the Genocide Convention on 2 July 1999, the date proceedings were instituted before the Court. Serbia contended that it did not become party to the Convention until 10 June 2001, after its admission to the United Nations on 1 November 2000, and, in addition, that it never became bound by Article IX of the Genocide Convention because it entered a reservation to that Article when it acceded to the Convention. Serbia further argued that Croatia's Application was inadmissible in so far as the most serious incidents and omissions described therein occurred prior to 27 April 1992, the date on which the FRY came into being, and could not therefore be attributed to it. Lastly, it asserted that certain specific claims made by Croatia were inadmissible or moot. Pursuant to Article 79 of the Rules of Court, the proceedings on the merits were suspended. Croatia filed a written statement of its observations and submissions on Serbia's preliminary objections on 25 April 2003, within the time-limit fixed by the Court.

Public hearings on the preliminary objections on jurisdiction and admissibility were held from 26 to 30 May 2008. (See *I.C.J. Annual Report 2007-2008*.)

On 18 November 2008, the Court rendered its judgment on the preliminary objections (*I.C.J. Reports 2008*, p. 412; *I.C.J. Yearbook 2008-2009*, p. 230).

In its Judgment, the Court found *inter alia* that, subject to its statement concerning the second preliminary objection raised by the Respondent, it had jurisdiction, on the basis of Article IX of the Genocide Convention, to entertain Croatia's Application. The Court added that Serbia's second preliminary objection did not, in the circumstances of the case, possess an exclusively preliminary character. It then rejected the third preliminary objection raised by Serbia.

By an Order of 20 January 2009, the President of the Court fixed 22 March 2010 as the time-limit for the filing of the Counter-Memorial of Serbia. That pleading, containing counter-claims, was filed within the time-limit thus prescribed. By an Order of 4 February 2010, the Court directed the submission of a Reply by the Republic of Croatia and a Rejoinder by the Republic of Serbia concerning the claims presented by the Parties. It fixed 20 December 2010 and 4 November 2011, respectively, as the time-limits for the filing of those written pleadings. Those pleadings were filed within the time-limits thus fixed.

By an Order of 23 January 2012, the Court authorized the submission by Croatia of an additional written pleading relating solely to the counter-claims submitted by Serbia. It fixed 30 August 2012 as the time-limit for the filing of that written pleading which was filed by Croatia within the time-limit thus fixed. Public hearings on the merits of the case are scheduled for early 2014.

4. Territorial and Maritime Dispute (Nicaragua v. Colombia)

On 6 December 2001, Nicaragua filed an Application instituting proceedings against Colombia in respect of a dispute concerning "a group of related legal issues subsisting" between the two States "concerning title to territory and maritime delimitation" in the western Caribbean.

In its Application, Nicaragua requested the Court to adjudge and declare:

"*First*, that . . . Nicaragua has sovereignty over the islands of Providencia, San Andres and Santa Catalina and all the appurtenant islands and keys, and also over the Roncador, Serrana, Serranilla and Quitasueño keys (in so far as they are capable of appropriation);

Second, in the light of the determinations concerning title requested above, the Court is asked further to determine the course of the single maritime boundary between the areas of continental shelf and exclusive economic zone appertaining respectively to Nicaragua and Colombia, in accordance with equitable principles and relevant circumstances recognized by general international law as applicable to such a delimitation of a single maritime boundary."

Nicaragua further indicated that it

"reserves the right to claim compensation for elements of unjust enrichment consequent upon Colombian possession of the islands of San Andres and Providencia as well as the keys and maritime spaces up to the 82 meridian, in the absence of lawful title".

It also "reserves the right to claim compensation for interference with fishing vessels of Nicaraguan nationality or vessels licensed by Nicaragua" (see *I.C.J. Annual Report 2001-2002, et seq.*).

As basis for the Court's jurisdiction, Nicaragua invokes Article XXXI of the Pact of Bogotá, to which both Nicaragua and Colombia are parties, as well as the declarations of the two States recognizing the compulsory jurisdiction of the Court.

By an Order of 26 February 2002 (*I.C.J. Reports 2002*, p. 189), the Court fixed 28 April 2003 and 28 June 2004 as the time-limits for the filing of a Memorial by Nicaragua and of a Counter-Memorial by Colombia. The Memorial of Nicaragua was filed within the time-limit thus fixed.

Copies of the pleadings and documents annexed were requested by the Governments of Honduras, Jamaica, Chile, Peru, Ecuador and Venezuela by virtue of Article 53, paragraph 1, of the Rules of Court. Pursuant to that same provision, the Court, after ascertaining the views of the Parties, acceded to those requests.

On 21 July 2003, within the time-limit for the submission of its Counter-Memorial, Colombia filed preliminary objections to the jurisdiction of the Court. Public hearings on the preliminary objections were held from 4 to 8 June 2007.

On 13 December 2007, the Court rendered its judgment (*I.C.J. Reports 2007 (II)*, p. 832 and *I.C.J Yearbook 2007-2008*, p. 261), in which it found that Nicaragua's Application was admissible in so far as it concerned sovereignty over the maritime features claimed by the Parties other than the islands of San Andrés, Providencia and Santa Catalina, and in respect of the maritime delimitation between the Parties (see *I.C.J. Annual Report 2007-2008*).

By an Order of 11 February 2008 (*I.C.J. Reports 2008*, p. 3) the President of the Court fixed 11 November 2008 as the time-limit for the filing of the Counter-Memorial of Colombia. The Counter-Memorial was filed within the time-limit thus fixed.

By an Order of 18 December 2008 (*ibid.*, p. 645), the Court directed Nicaragua to submit a Reply and Colombia a Rejoinder, and fixed

18 September 2009 and 18 June 2010 as the respective time-limits for the filing of those written pleadings, which were filed within the time-limits thus fixed.

On 25 February 2010, Costa Rica filed an Application for permission to intervene in the case. In its Application, Costa Rica states among other things that "[b]oth Nicaragua and Colombia, in their boundary claims against each other, claim maritime area to which Costa Rica is entitled". Costa Rica has indicated in its Application that it is not seeking to intervene in the proceedings as a party. The Application was immediately communicated to Nicaragua and Colombia, and the Court fixed 26 May 2010 as the time-limit for the filing of written observations by those States. The written observations were filed within the time-limit thus fixed.

On 10 June 2010, the Republic of Honduras also filed an Application for permission to intervene in the case. It is asserted in the Application that Nicaragua, in its dispute with Colombia, is putting forward maritime claims that lie in an area of the Caribbean Sea in which Honduras has rights and interests. Honduras states in its Application that it is seeking primarily to intervene in the proceedings as a party. Honduras's Application was immediately communicated to Nicaragua and Colombia. The President of the Court fixed 2 September 2010 as the time-limit for these two States to furnish written observations. The written observations were filed within the time-limit thus fixed.

Public hearings on the admission of Costa Rica's Application for permission to intervene were held from 11 to 15 October 2010.

In its Judgment of 4 May 2011, the Court, by nine votes to seven, found that the Application for permission to intervene in the proceedings filed by Costa Rica could not be granted.

Public hearings on the admission of Honduras's Application for permission to intervene took place from 18 to 22 October 2010.

In its Judgment of 4 May 2011, the Court, by thirteen votes to two, found that the Application for permission to intervene in the proceedings filed by Honduras could not be granted.

Public hearings on the merits of the case were held from 23 April to 4 May 2012. At the conclusion of their oral arguments, the Parties presented the following final submissions to the Court:

For the Republic of Nicaragua,

"In accordance with Article 60 of the Rules of Court and having regard to the pleadings, written and oral, the Republic of Nicaragua,

I. May it please the Court to adjudge and declare that:

(1) The Republic of Nicaragua has sovereignty over all maritime features off her Caribbean coast not proven to be part of the

'San Andrés Archipelago' and in particular the following cays: the Cayos de Albuquerque; the Cayos del Este Sudeste; the Cay of Roncador; North Cay, Southwest Cay and any other cays on the bank of Serrana; East Cay, Beacon Cay and any other cays on the bank of Serranilla; and Low Cay and any other cays on the bank of Bajo Nuevo.

(2) If the Court were to find that there are features on the bank of Quitasueño that qualify as islands under international law, the Court is requested to find that sovereignty over such features rests with Nicaragua.

(3) The appropriate form of delimitation, within the geographical and legal framework constituted by the mainland coasts of Nicaragua and Colombia, is a continental shelf boundary dividing by equal parts the overlapping entitlements to a continental shelf of both Parties.

(4) The islands of San Andrés and Providencia and Santa Catalina be enclaved and accorded a maritime entitlement of 12 nautical miles, this being the appropriate equitable solution justified by the geographical and legal framework.

(5) The equitable solution for any cay, that might be found to be Colombian, is to delimit a maritime boundary by drawing a 3-nautical-mile enclave around them.

II. Further, the Court is requested to adjudge and declare that:

Colombia is not acting in accordance with her obligations under international law by stopping and otherwise hindering Nicaragua from accessing and disposing of her natural resources to the east of the 82nd meridian."

For the Republic of Colombia,

"In accordance with Article 60 of the Rules of Court, for the reasons set out in Colombia's written and oral pleadings, taking into account the Judgment on preliminary objections and rejecting any contrary submissions of Nicaragua, Colombia requests the Court to adjudge and declare:

(a) That Nicaragua's new continental shelf claim is inadmissible and that, consequently, Nicaragua's Submission I (3) is rejected.

(b) That Colombia has sovereignty over all the maritime features in dispute between the Parties: Alburquerque, East-Southeast, Roncador, Serrana, Quitasueño, Serranilla and Bajo Nuevo, and all their appurtenant features, which form part of the Archipelago of San Andrés.

(c) That the delimitation of the exclusive economic zone and the continental shelf between Nicaragua and Colombia is to be

effected by a single maritime boundary, being the median line every point of which is equidistant from the nearest points on the baselines from which the breadth of the territorial seas of the Parties is measured . . .

(d) That Nicaragua's written Submission II is rejected."

At a public sitting which was held on 19 November 2012, the Court delivered its Judgment (see *I.C.J. Reports 2012 (II)*, p. 624), a summary of which is given below:

Chronology of the procedure (paras. 1-17)

The Court recalls that, on 6 December 2001, the Republic of Nicaragua (hereinafter "Nicaragua") filed in the Registry of the Court an Application instituting proceedings against the Republic of Colombia (hereinafter "Colombia") in respect of a dispute "concerning title to territory and maritime delimitation" in the western Caribbean. The Court further recalls that on 13 December 2007 it rendered a Judgment on preliminary objections to the jurisdiction of the Court raised by Colombia, in which it concluded that it had jurisdiction, under Article XXXI of the Pact of Bogotá, to adjudicate upon the dispute concerning sovereignty over the maritime features claimed by the Parties, other than the islands of San Andrés, Providencia and Santa Catalina[1], and upon the dispute concerning the maritime delimitation between the Parties.

I. Geography (paras. 18-24)

The area where the maritime features in dispute (Alburquerque Cays, East-Southeast Cays, Roncador, Serrana, Quitasueño, Serranilla and Bajo Nuevo) are located and within which the delimitation sought is to be carried out lies in the Caribbean Sea (see sketch-map No. 1: Geographical context on page 57 of this *Yearbook*).

II. Sovereignty (paras. 25-103)

1. Whether the maritime features in dispute are capable of appropriation

Before addressing the question of sovereignty, the Court must determine whether the maritime features in dispute are capable of appropriation. It is well established in international law that islands, however small, are capable of appropriation. By contrast, low-tide elevations (features which are above water at low tide but submerged at high tide) cannot be appropriated, although a coastal State has sovereignty over low-tide

---

[1] In its 2007 Judgment on preliminary objections, the Court held that it had no jurisdiction with regard to Nicaragua's claim to sovereignty over the islands of San Andrés, Providencia and Santa Catalina, because the question of sovereignty over these three islands had been determined by the Treaty concerning Territorial Questions at Issue between Colombia and Nicaragua, signed at Managua on 24 March 1928, by which Nicaragua recognized Colombian sovereignty over these islands.

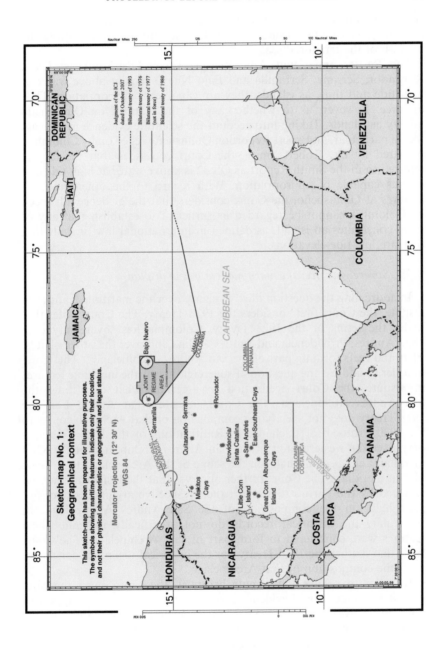

Sketch-map No. 1:
Geographical context

This sketch-map has been prepared for illustrative purposes.
The symbols showing maritime features indicate only their location,
and not their physical characteristics or geographical and legal status.

Mercator Projection (12° 30' N)
WGS 84

elevations which are situated within its territorial sea, and these low-tide elevations may be taken into account for the purpose of measuring the breadth of the territorial sea.

The Parties agree that Alburquerque Cays, East-Southeast Cays, Roncador, Serrana, Serranilla and Bajo Nuevo remain above water at high tide and thus, as islands, they are capable of appropriation. They disagree, however, as to whether any of the features on Quitasueño qualify as islands. Taking into account the scientific evidence in the case file, in particular, an Expert Report on Quitasueño relied on by Colombia, prepared by Dr. Robert Smith, the Court concludes that the feature referred to in the Smith Report as QS 32 is above water at high tide and is thus capable of appropriation. With regard to the other maritime features at Quitasueño, the Court considers that the evidence advanced by Colombia cannot be regarded as sufficient to establish that any of them constitutes an island, as defined in international law; it finds that they are low-tide elevations.

2. Sovereignty over the maritime features in dispute

In addressing the question of sovereignty over the maritime features in dispute, the Court first considers the 1928 Treaty. The Court notes that under the terms of the 1928 Treaty, Colombia has sovereignty over "San Andrés, Providencia and Santa Catalina and over the other islands, islets and reefs forming part of the San Andrés Archipelago". Therefore, in order to address the question of sovereignty over the maritime features in dispute, the Court needs first to ascertain what constitutes the San Andrés Archipelago. The Court observes that Article I of the 1928 Treaty does not specify the composition of that Archipelago. As to the 1930 Protocol of Exchange of Ratifications of the 1928 Treaty, it only fixes the western limit of the San Andrés Archipelago at the 82nd meridian and sheds no light on the scope of the Archipelago to the east of that meridian. The Court further observes that the historical material adduced by the Parties to support their respective arguments does not shed light on the composition of the San Andrés Archipelago. In particular, the historical records do not specifically indicate which features were considered to form part of that Archipelago. The Court finds that neither the 1928 Treaty nor the historical records is conclusive as to the composition of that Archipelago.

In order to resolve the dispute before it, the Court must therefore examine arguments and evidence submitted by the Parties in support of their respective claims to sovereignty, which are not based on the composition of the Archipelago under the 1928 Treaty.

The Court thus turns to the claims of sovereignty asserted by both Parties on the basis of *uti possidetis juris* (a principle according to which, upon independence, new States inherit territories and boundaries of former colonial provinces). The Court concludes that, in the present case, the principle of *uti possidetis juris* affords inadequate assistance in determining sovereignty over the maritime features in dispute between Nicaragua and Colombia because nothing in the historical record clearly indicates whether these features were attributed to the colonial provinces of Nicaragua or of Colombia prior to or upon independence from Spain.

The Court next considers whether sovereignty can be established on the basis of *effectivités* (State acts manifesting a display of authority on a given territory). The Court notes that it is Colombia's submission that *effectivités* confirm its prior title to the maritime features in dispute. The Court considers the different categories of *effectivités* presented by Colombia, namely: public administration and legislation, regulation of economic activities, public works, law enforcement measures, naval visits and search and rescue operations and consular representation. On the basis of the evidence on the case file, the Court finds that, for many decades, Colombia continuously and consistently acted *à titre de souverain* in respect of the maritime features in dispute. This exercise of sovereign authority was public and there is no evidence that it met with any protest from Nicaragua prior to 1969, when the dispute crystallized. Moreover, the evidence of Colombia's acts of administration with respect to the islands is in contrast to the absence of any evidence of acts *à titre de souverain* on the part of Nicaragua. The Court concludes that the facts provide very strong support for Colombia's claim of sovereignty over the maritime features in dispute.

The Court also notes that, while not being evidence of sovereignty, Nicaragua's conduct with regard to the maritime features in dispute, the practice of third States and maps afford some support to Colombia's claim.

The Court concludes that Colombia, and not Nicaragua, has sovereignty over the islands at Alburquerque, Bajo Nuevo, East-Southeast Cays, Quitasueño, Roncador, Serrana and Serranilla.

III. Admissibility of Nicaragua's claim for delimitation of a continental shelf extending beyond 200 nautical miles (paras. 104-112)

The Court observes that, from a formal point of view, the claim made in Nicaragua's final submission I (3) — requesting the Court to effect a continental shelf boundary dividing by equal parts the overlapping entitlements to a continental shelf of both Parties (see sketch-map No. 2: Delimitation claimed by Nicaragua, on page 60 of this *Yearbook*) — is a new claim in relation to the claims presented in the Application and the Memorial, in which the Court was requested to determine the "single maritime boundary" between the continental shelf areas and exclusive economic zones appertaining respectively to Nicaragua and Colombia in the form of a median line between the mainland coasts of the two States. The Court is not, however, convinced by Colombia's contentions that this revised claim transforms

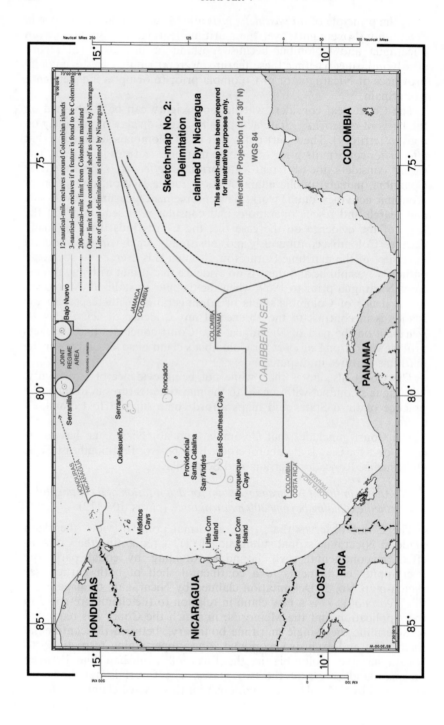

Sketch-map No. 2:
Delimitation
claimed by Nicaragua

This sketch-map has been prepared
for illustrative purposes only.

Mercator Projection (12° 30' N)

WGS 84

12-nautical-mile enclaves around Colombian islands
3-nautical-mile enclaves if a feature is found to be Colombian
200-nautical-mile limit from Colombian mainland
Outer limit of the continental shelf as claimed by Nicaragua
Line of equal delimitation as claimed by Nicaragua

CARIBBEAN SEA

HONDURAS

NICARAGUA

COSTA
RICA

PANAMA

COLOMBIA

JAMAICA
COLOMBIA

COLOMBIA
PANAMA

COLOMBIA
COSTA RICA

COSTA RICA
PANAMA

HONDURAS
NICARAGUA

Colombia / Jamaica

JOINT
REGIME
AREA

Bajo Nuevo

Serranilla

Serrana

Quitasueño

Roncador

Providencia/
Santa Catalina
San Andrés

East-Southeast Cays

Alburquerque
Cays

Miskitos
Cays

Little Corn
Island

Great Corn
Island

the subject-matter of the dispute brought before the Court. The fact that Nicaragua's claim to an extended continental shelf is a new claim does not, in itself, render the claim inadmissible. In the Court's view, the claim to an extended continental shelf falls within the dispute between the Parties relating to maritime delimitation and cannot be said to transform the subject-matter of that dispute. Moreover, it arises directly out of that dispute. The Court concludes that the claim contained in final submission I (3) by Nicaragua is admissible.

IV. Consideration of Nicaragua's claim for delimitation of a continental shelf extending beyond 200 nautical miles (paras. 113-131)

The Court turns to the question whether it is in a position to delimit a maritime boundary between an extended continental shelf of Nicaragua and Colombia's continental shelf as requested by Nicaragua in its final submission I (3). The Court notes that Colombia is not a State party to the United Nations Convention on the Law of the Sea (UNCLOS) and that, therefore, the law applicable in the case is customary international law. The Court considers that the definition of the continental shelf set out in Article 76, paragraph 1, of UNCLOS forms part of customary international law. At this stage, in view of the fact that the Court's task is limited to the examination of whether it is in a position to carry out a continental shelf delimitation as requested by Nicaragua, it does not need to decide whether other provisions of Article 76 of UNCLOS form part of customary international law.

The Court further observes that in the case concerning *Territorial and Maritime Dispute between Nicaragua and Honduras in the Caribbean Sea (Nicaragua v. Honduras)*, it stated that "any claim of continental shelf rights beyond 200 miles [by a State party to UNCLOS] must be in accordance with Article 76 of UNCLOS and reviewed by the Commission on the Limits of the Continental Shelf established thereunder". Given the object and purpose of UNCLOS, as stipulated in its Preamble, the fact that Colombia is not a party thereto does not relieve Nicaragua of its obligations under Article 76. The Court notes that Nicaragua submitted to the Commission only "Preliminary Information" which, by its own admission, falls short of meeting the requirements for the Commission to be able to make a recommendation relating to the establishment of the outer limits of the continental shelf.

As the Court was not presented with any further information, it finds that, in the present proceedings, Nicaragua has not established that it has a continental margin that extends far enough to overlap with Colombia's 200-nautical-mile entitlement to the continental shelf, measured from Colombia's mainland coast. The Court is therefore not in a position to delimit the maritime boundary as requested by Nicaragua. The Court concludes that Nicaragua's claim contained in its final submission I (3) cannot be upheld.

V. Maritime boundary (paras. 132-247)

1. The task now before the Court

In light of the decision it has taken regarding Nicaragua's proposed maritime delimitation as set out in its final submission I (3), the Court must consider what maritime delimitation should be effected. The Court observes that Colombia, for its part, has requested that the delimitation of the exclusive economic zone and the continental shelf between Nicaragua and Colombia be effected by a single maritime boundary, constructed as a median line between Nicaraguan fringing islands and the islands of the San Andrés Archipelago (see sketch-map No. 3: Delimitation claimed by Colombia, on page 63 of this *Yearbook*).

The Court notes that there is an overlap between Nicaragua's entitlement to a continental shelf and exclusive economic zone extending to 200 nautical miles from its mainland coast and adjacent islands and Colombia's entitlement to a continental shelf and exclusive economic zone derived from the islands over which the Court has held that Colombia has sovereignty. Thus, notwithstanding its decision regarding Nicaragua's final submission I (3), the Court is still called upon to effect a delimitation between the overlapping maritime entitlements of Colombia and Nicaragua within 200 nautical miles of the Nicaraguan coast.

2. Applicable law

As the Court has already noted, the law applicable to this delimitation is customary international law. The Court considers that the principles of maritime delimitation enshrined in Articles 74 and 83 and the legal régime of islands set out in UNCLOS Article 121 reflect customary international law.

3. Relevant coasts

The Court begins by determining what the relevant coasts of the Parties are, namely, those coasts the projections of which overlap. After briefly setting out the positions of the Parties regarding their respective coasts (see sketch-map No. 4: The relevant coasts and the relevant area according to Nicaragua, and sketch-map No. 5: The relevant coasts and the relevant area according to Colombia, on pages 64 and 65 respectively of this *Yearbook*).

For Nicaragua, the Court finds that the relevant coast is its whole coast with the exception of the short stretch of coast near Punta de Perlas, which faces due south and thus does not project into the area of overlapping potential entitlements. The Court also considers that Nicaragua's entitlement to a 200-nautical-mile continental shelf and exclusive economic zone has to be measured from the islands fringing the Nicaraguan coast. The east-facing coasts of the Nicaraguan islands are

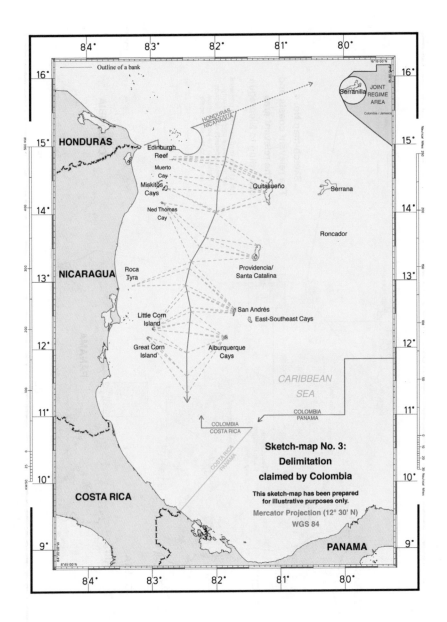

Sketch-map No. 3:
Delimitation
claimed by Colombia

This sketch-map has been prepared
for illustrative purposes only.
Mercator Projection (12° 30' N)
WGS 84

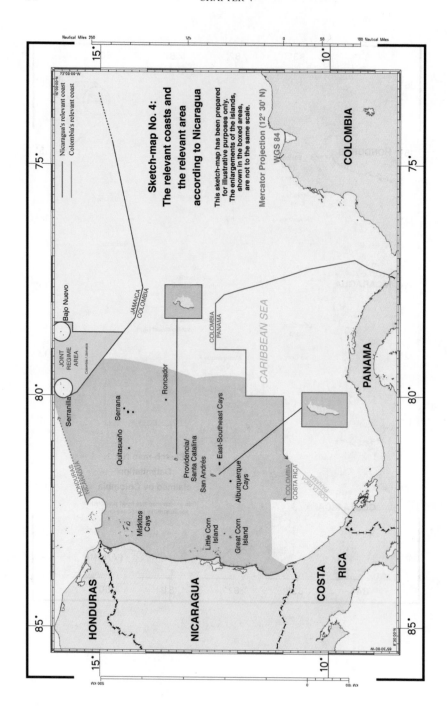

Sketch-map No. 4:
The relevant coasts and
the relevant area
according to Nicaragua

This sketch-map has been prepared
for illustrative purposes only.
The enlargements of the islands,
shown in the boxed areas,
are not to the same scale.

Mercator Projection (12° 30' N)
WGS 84

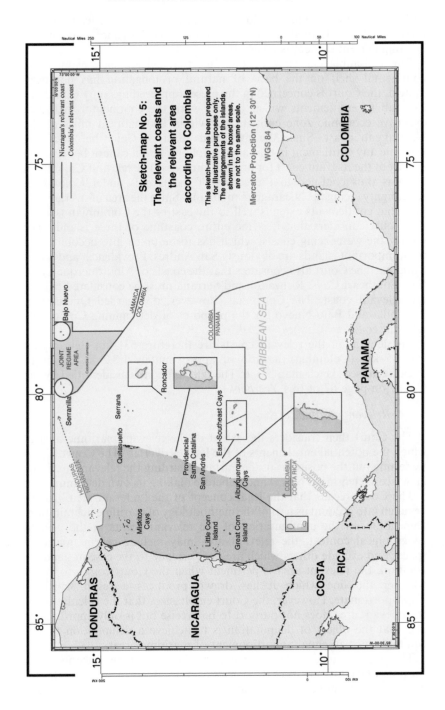

parallel to the mainland and do not, therefore, add to the length of the relevant coast, although they contribute to the baselines from which Nicaragua's entitlement is measured.

For Colombia, in view of the fact that Nicaragua's claim to a continental shelf on the basis of natural prolongation has not been upheld, the Court is concerned in the present proceedings only with those Colombian entitlements which overlap with the continental shelf and exclusive economic zone entitlements within 200 nautical miles of the Nicaraguan coast. Since the mainland coast of Colombia does not generate any entitlement in that area, it follows that it cannot be regarded as part of the relevant coast for present purposes. The relevant Colombian coast is thus confined to the coasts of the islands under Colombian sovereignty facing the Nicaraguan mainland. Since the area of overlapping potential entitlements extends well to the east of the Colombian islands, the Court considers that it is the entire coastline of these islands, not merely the west-facing coasts, which has to be taken into account. The most important islands are obviously San Andrés, Providencia and Santa Catalina. The Court also considers that the coasts of Alburquerque Cays, East-Southeast Cays, Roncador and Serrana must be considered part of the relevant coast. The Court has, however, disregarded Quitasueño, Serranilla and Bajo Nuevo for the purposes of determining Colombia's relevant coast.

The lengths of the relevant coasts are therefore 531 km (Nicaragua) and 65 km (Colombia), a ratio of approximately 1:8.2 in favour of Nicaragua (see sketch-map No. 6: The relevant coasts as identified by the Court, on page 67 of this *Yearbook*).

4. Relevant maritime area

The Court then considers the extent of the relevant maritime area in which the potential entitlements of the Parties overlap. The Court begins by setting out the positions of the Parties regarding the relevant maritime area (see sketch-maps Nos. 4 and 5) before making its own determination.

The Court recalls that the legal concept of the "relevant area" has to be taken into account as part of the methodology of maritime delimitation. Depending on the configuration of the relevant coasts in the general geographical context, the relevant area may include certain maritime spaces and exclude others which are not germane to the case in hand. In addition, the relevant area is pertinent when the Court comes to verify whether the line which it has drawn produces a result which is disproportionate. However, the Court emphasizes that the calculation of the relevant area does not purport to be precise but is only approximate and that the object of delimitation is to achieve a delimitation that is equitable, not an equal apportionment of maritime areas.

The relevant area comprises that part of the maritime space in which the potential entitlements of the parties overlap. Accordingly, the relevant area extends from the Nicaraguan coast to a line in the east 200 nautical

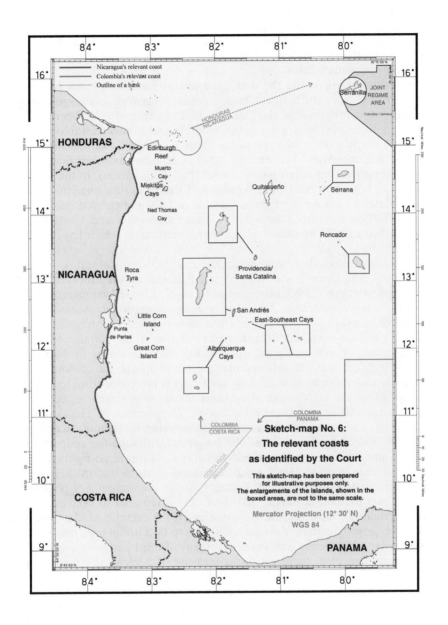

Sketch-map No. 6:
The relevant coasts
as identified by the Court

This sketch-map has been prepared
for illustrative purposes only.
The enlargements of the islands, shown in the
boxed areas, are not to the same scale.

Mercator Projection (12° 30' N)
WGS 84

miles from the baselines from which the breadth of Nicaragua's territorial sea is measured. Since Nicaragua has not yet notified the Secretary-General of the location of those baselines under Article 16, paragraph 2, of UNCLOS, the eastern limit of the relevant area can be determined only on an approximate basis.

In both the north and the south, the interests of third States become involved. In the north, there is a boundary between Nicaragua and Honduras, established by the Court in its Judgment of 8 October 2007, and a maritime boundary between Colombia and Jamaica established in 1993 through a bilateral agreement. There is also a Colombia-Jamaica "Joint Regime Area" (an area in which Colombia and Jamaica have agreed upon shared development, rather than delimitation). In the south, there is a boundary between Colombia and Panama established pursuant to a bilateral agreement which was signed in 1976 and entered into force in 1977. There is also a boundary between Colombia and Costa Rica established in 1977 by means of a bilateral agreement, which has not yet been ratified.

The Court notes that, while the agreements between Colombia, on the one hand, and Costa Rica, Jamaica and Panama, on the other, concern the legal relations between the parties to each of those agreements, they are *res inter alios acta* so far as Nicaragua is concerned. Accordingly, none of those agreements can affect the rights and obligations of Nicaragua vis-à-vis Costa Rica, Jamaica or Panama; nor can they impose obligations, or confer rights, upon Costa Rica, Jamaica or Panama vis-à-vis Nicaragua. It follows that, when it effects the delimitation between Colombia and Nicaragua, the Court is not purporting to define or to affect the rights and obligations which might exist as between Nicaragua and any of these three States. The position of Honduras is somewhat different. The boundary between Honduras and Nicaragua was established by the Court's 2007 Judgment, although the endpoint of that boundary was not determined. Nicaragua can have no rights to the north of that line and Honduras can have no rights to the south. It is in the final phase of delimitation, however, not in the preliminary phase of identifying the relevant area, that the Court is required to take account of the rights of third parties. Nevertheless, if the exercise of identifying, however approximately, the relevant area is to be a useful one, then some awareness of the actual and potential claims of third parties is necessary. In the present case, there is a large measure of agreement between the Parties as to what this task must entail. Both Nicaragua and Colombia have accepted that the area of their overlapping entitlements does not extend beyond the boundaries already established between either of them and any third State.

The Court recalls that the relevant area cannot extend beyond the area in which the entitlements of both Parties overlap. Accordingly, if either Party has no entitlement in a particular area, whether because of an agreement it has concluded with a third State or because that area lies beyond a judicially determined boundary between that Party and a third State, that area cannot be treated as part of the relevant area for present purposes. Since Colombia has no potential entitlements to the south and east of the boundaries which it has agreed with Costa Rica and Panama, the relevant area cannot extend beyond those boundaries. In addition, although the Colombia-Jamaica "Joint Regime Area" is an area in which Colombia and Jamaica have agreed upon shared development, rather than delimitation, the Court considers that it has to be treated as falling outside the relevant area. The Court notes that more than half of the "Joint Regime Area" (as well as the island of Bajo Nuevo and the waters within a 12-nautical-mile radius thereof) is located more than 200 nautical miles from Nicaragua and thus could not constitute part of the relevant area in any event. It also recalls that neither Colombia, nor (at least in most of its pleadings) Nicaragua, contended that it should be included in the relevant area. Although the island of Serranilla and the waters within a 12-nautical-mile radius of the island are excluded from the "Joint Regime Area", the Court considers that they also fall outside the relevant area for the purposes of the present case, in view of potential Jamaican entitlements and the fact that neither Party contended otherwise.

The Court therefore concludes that the boundary of the relevant area in the north follows the maritime boundary between Nicaragua and Honduras, laid down in the Court's Judgment of 8 October 2007, until it reaches latitude 16 degrees north. It then continues due east until it reaches the boundary of the Colombia-Jamaica "Joint Regime Area". From that point, it follows the boundary of that area, skirting a line 12 nautical miles from Serranilla, until it intersects with the line 200 nautical miles from Nicaragua. In the south, the boundary of the relevant area begins in the east at the point where the line 200 nautical miles from Nicaragua intersects with the boundary line agreed between Colombia and Panama. It then follows the Colombia-Panama line to the west until it reaches the line agreed between Colombia and Costa Rica. It follows that line westwards and then northwards, until it intersects with a hypothetical equidistance line between the Costa Rican and Nicaraguan coasts. (See sketch-map No. 7: The relevant maritime area as identified by the Court. This sketch-map is reproduced on page 70 of the present *Yearbook*.)

The relevant area thus drawn has a size of approximately 209,280 sq km.

5. Entitlements generated by maritime features

The Parties agree that San Andrés, Providencia and Santa Catalina are entitled to a territorial sea, exclusive economic zone and continental shelf. In principle, that entitlement is capable of extending up to 200 nautical miles in each direction. The Parties differ regarding the entitlements which may be generated by Alburquerque Cays, East-Southeast Cays, Roncador, Serrana, Serranilla and Bajo Nuevo.

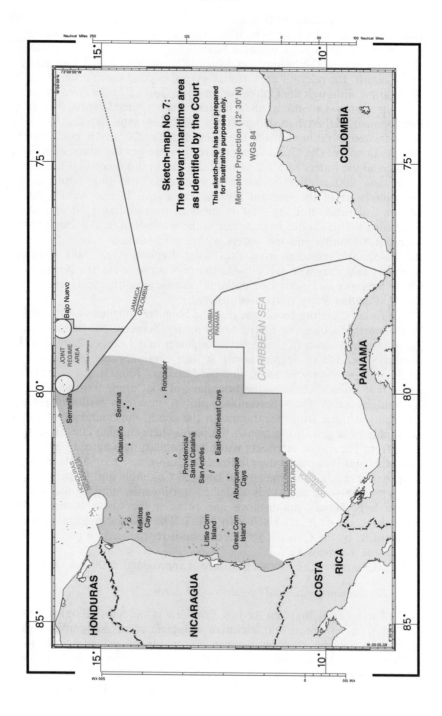

Sketch-map No. 7:
The relevant maritime area
as identified by the Court

This sketch-map has been prepared
for illustrative purposes only.

Mercator Projection (12° 30' N)
WGS 84

The Court begins by recalling that Serranilla and Bajo Nuevo fall outside the relevant area as defined in the preceding section of the Judgment and that it is accordingly not called upon in the present proceedings to determine the scope of their maritime entitlements. With regard to Alburquerque Cays, East-Southeast Cays, Roncador and Serrana, the Court observes that international law today sets the breadth of the territorial sea which the coastal State has the right to establish at 12 nautical miles. These features are therefore each entitled to a territorial sea of 12 nautical miles, irrespective of whether they fall within the exception stated in Article 121, paragraph 3, of UNCLOS. The Court does not deem it necessary to determine the precise status of the smaller islands, since any entitlement to maritime spaces which they might generate within the relevant area (outside the territorial sea) would entirely overlap with the entitlement to a continental shelf and exclusive economic zone generated by the islands of San Andrés, Providencia and Santa Catalina.

The Court finds that Colombia is entitled to a territorial sea of 12 nautical miles around QS 32 at Quitasueño. Moreover, in measuring that territorial sea, Colombia is entitled to use those low-tide elevations within 12 nautical miles of QS 32 for the purpose of measuring the breadth of its territorial sea. The Court observes that it has not been suggested by either Party that QS 32 is anything other than a rock which is incapable of sustaining human habitation or economic life of its own under Article 121, paragraph 3, of UNCLOS, so this feature generates no entitlement to a continental shelf or exclusive economic zone.

6. Method of delimitation

To effect the delimitation, the Court follows the three-stage methodology employed in its case law. In the first stage, the Court establishes a provisional delimitation line between territories (including the island territories) of the Parties. The line is constructed using the most appropriate base points on the coasts of the Parties. In the second stage, the Court considers whether there are any relevant circumstances which may call for an adjustment or shifting of the provisional equidistance/median line so as to achieve an equitable result. In the third and final stage, the Court conducts a disproportionality test in which it assesses whether the effect of the line, as adjusted or shifted, is that the Parties' respective shares of the relevant area are markedly disproportionate to their respective relevant coasts.

7. Determination of base points and construction of the provisional median line

For the Nicaraguan coast, the Court uses base points located on Edinburgh Reef, Muerto Cay, Miskitos Cays, Ned Thomas Cay, Roca Tyra, Little Corn Island and Great Corn Island.

So far as the Colombian coast is concerned, the Court considers that

Quitasueño should not contribute to the construction of the provisional median line. The part of Quitasueño which is undoubtedly above water at high tide is a minuscule feature, barely 1 sq m in dimension. When placing base points on very small maritime features would distort the relevant geography, it is appropriate to disregard them in the construction of a provisional median line. In the Court's view, neither should a base point be placed on Serrana or on Low Cay. The base points on the Colombian side will, therefore, be located on Santa Catalina, Providencia and San Andrés islands and on Alburquerque Cays.

The provisional median line constructed from these two sets of base points is, therefore, controlled in the north by the Nicaraguan base points on Edinburgh Reef, Muerto Cay and Miskitos Cays and Colombian base points on Santa Catalina and Providencia, in the centre by base points on the Nicaraguan islands of Ned Thomas Cay and Roca Tyra and the Colombian islands of Providencia and San Andrés, and in the south by Nicaraguan base points on Little Corn Island and Great Corn Island and Colombian base points on San Andrés and Alburquerque Cays. (See sketch-map No. 8: Construction of the provisional median line, on page 73 of this *Yearbook*.)

8. Relevant circumstances

The Court notes that the Parties invoked several different circumstances which they found relevant to the achievement of an equitable solution, which the Court now considers in turn.

A. Disparity in the lengths of the relevant coasts

The Court begins by observing that a substantial difference in the lengths of the Parties' respective coastlines may be a factor to be taken into consideration in order to adjust or shift the provisional delimitation line. In the present case, the disparity between the relevant Colombian coast and that of Nicaragua is approximately 1:8.2. This is undoubtedly a substantial disparity and the Court considers that it requires an adjustment or shifting of the provisional line, especially given the overlapping maritime areas to the east of the Colombian islands.

B. Overall geographical context

The Court does not believe that any weight should be given to Nicaragua's contention that the Colombian islands are located on "Nicaragua's continental shelf". It has repeatedly made clear that geological and geomorphological considerations are not relevant to the delimitation of overlapping entitlements within 200 nautical miles of the coasts of States.

The Court agrees, however, that the achievement of an equitable solution requires that, so far as possible, the line of delimitation should allow the coasts of the Parties to produce their effects in terms of maritime entitlements in a reasonable and mutually balanced way. The effect of

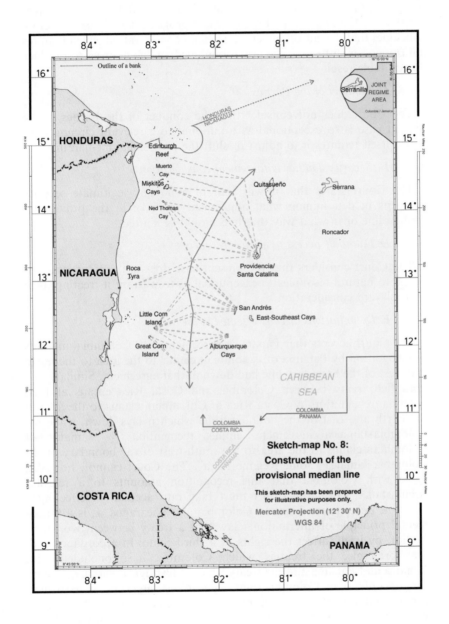

Sketch-map No. 8:
Construction of the
provisional median line

This sketch-map has been prepared
for illustrative purposes only.

Mercator Projection (12° 30' N)
WGS 84

the provisional median line is to cut Nicaragua off from some three-quarters of the area into which its coast projects. The Court therefore concludes that the cut-off effect is a relevant consideration which requires adjustment or shifting of the provisional median line in order to produce an equitable result.

C. Conduct of the Parties

The Court does not consider that the conduct of the Parties in the present case is so exceptional as to amount to a relevant circumstance which itself requires it to adjust or shift the provisional median line.

D. Security and law enforcement considerations

The Court states that it will bear in mind any legitimate security concerns in determining what adjustment to make to the provisional median line or in what way that line should be shifted.

E. Equitable access to natural resources

The Court considers that the present case does not present issues of access to natural resources so exceptional as to warrant it treating them as a relevant consideration.

F. Delimitations already effected in the area

The Court accepts that Panama's agreement with Colombia amounts to recognition by Panama of Colombian claims to the area to the north and west of the boundary line laid down in that agreement. Similarly the unratified treaty between Colombia and Costa Rica entails at least potential recognition by Costa Rica of Colombian claims to the area to the north and east of the boundary line which it lays down, while the Colombia-Jamaica agreement entails recognition by Jamaica of Colombian claims to the area to the south-west of the boundary of the Colombia-Jamaica "Joint Regime Area". The Court cannot, however, agree with Colombia that this recognition amounts to a relevant circumstance which the Court must take into account in effecting a maritime delimitation between Colombia and Nicaragua. It is a fundamental principle of international law that a treaty between two States cannot, by itself, affect the rights of a third State. In accordance with that principle, the treaties which Colombia has concluded with Jamaica and Panama and the treaty which it has signed with Costa Rica cannot confer upon Colombia rights against Nicaragua and, in particular, cannot entitle it, vis-à-vis Nicaragua, to a greater share of the area in which its maritime entitlements overlap with those of Nicaragua than it would otherwise receive.

The Court further observes that, as Article 59 of the Statute of the Court makes clear, it is axiomatic that a judgment of the Court is not binding on any State other than the parties to the case. Moreover, the

Court has always taken care not to draw a boundary line which extends into areas where the rights of third States may be affected. The Judgment, by which the Court delimits the boundary, addresses only Nicaragua's rights as against Colombia and vice versa and is, therefore, without prejudice to any claim of a third State or any claim which either party may have against a third State.

9. Course of the maritime boundary

Having thus identified relevant circumstances which mean that a maritime boundary following the course of the provisional median line would not produce an equitable result, the Court proceeds by way of shifting the provisional median line. In this context, the Court draws a distinction between that part of the relevant area which lies between the Nicaraguan mainland and the western coasts of Alburquerque Cays, San Andrés, Providencia and Santa Catalina, where the relationship is one of opposite coasts, and the part which lies to the east of those islands, where the relationship is more complex. In the first, western, part of the relevant area, the relevant circumstances call for the provisional median line to be shifted eastwards. The disparity in coastal lengths is so marked as to justify a significant shift. The line cannot, however, be shifted so far that it cuts across the 12-nautical-mile territorial sea around any of the Colombian islands.

The Court notes that there are various techniques which allow for relevant circumstances to be taken into consideration in order to reach an equitable solution. In the present case, the Court proceeds by giving a weighting of one to each of the Colombian base points and a weighting of three to each of the Nicaraguan base points. The Court notes that, while all of the Colombian base points contribute to the construction of this line, only the Nicaraguan base points on Miskitos Cays, Ned Thomas Cay and Little Corn Island control the weighted line. As a result of the fact that the line is constructed using a 3:1 ratio between Nicaraguan and Colombian base points, the effect of the other Nicaraguan base points is superseded by those base points. The line ends at the last point that can be constructed using three base points. The weighted line, constructed on this basis, has a curved shape with a large number of turning points (see sketch-map No. 9: Construction of the weighted line, on page 76 of this Yearbook).

Mindful that such a configuration of the line may create difficulties in its practical application, the Court proceeds to a further adjustment by reducing the number of turning points and connecting them by geodetic lines. This produces a simplified weighted line (see sketch-map No. 10: The simplified weighted line, on page 77 of this Yearbook). The line thus constructed forms the boundary between the maritime entitlements of the two States between points 1 and 5.

The Court considers, however, that to extend that line into the parts

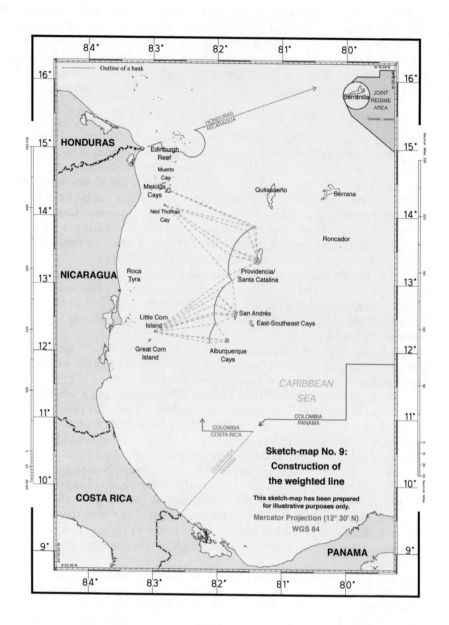

Sketch-map No. 9:
Construction of
the weighted line

This sketch-map has been prepared
for illustrative purposes only.
Mercator Projection (12° 30' N)
WGS 84

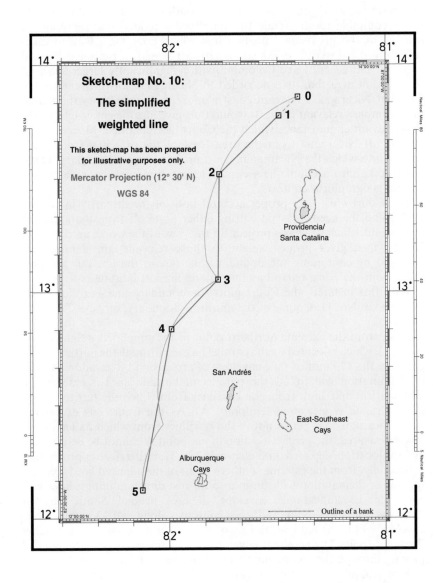

of the relevant area north of point 1 or south of point 5 would not lead to an equitable result. While the simplified weighted line represents a shifting of the provisional median line which goes some way towards reflecting the disparity in coastal lengths, it would, if extended beyond points 1 and 5, still leave Colombia with a significantly larger share of the relevant area than that accorded to Nicaragua, notwithstanding the fact that Nicaragua's relevant coast is more than eight times the length of Colombia's relevant coast. It would thus give insufficient weight to the first relevant circumstance which the Court has identified. Moreover, by cutting off Nicaragua from the areas east of the principal Colombian islands into which the Nicaraguan coast projects, such a boundary would fail to take into account the second relevant circumstance, namely, the overall geographical context.

The Court must take proper account both of the disparity in coastal length and the need to avoid cutting either State off from the maritime spaces into which its coasts project. In the view of the Court an equitable result which gives proper weight to those relevant considerations is achieved by continuing the boundary line out to the line 200 nautical miles from the Nicaraguan baselines along lines of latitude.

With this in mind, the Court plots the boundary line as follows (see sketch-map No. 11: Course of the maritime boundary, on page 79 of this *Yearbook*).

First, from the extreme northern point of the simplified weighted line (point 1), which is located on the parallel passing through the northernmost point on the 12-nautical-mile envelope of arcs around Roncador, the line of delimitation will follow the parallel of latitude until it reaches the 200-nautical-mile limit from the baselines from which the territorial sea of Nicaragua is measured (endpoint A). As the Court has explained, since Nicaragua has yet to notify the baselines from which its territorial sea is measured, the precise location of endpoint A cannot be determined and the location, depicted on sketch-map No. 11, is therefore approximate.

Secondly, from the extreme southern point of the adjusted line (point 5), the line of delimitation will run in a south-east direction until it intersects with the 12-nautical-mile envelope of arcs around South Cay of Alburquerque Cays (point 6). It then continues along that 12-nautical-mile envelope of arcs around South Cay of Alburquerque Cays until it reaches the point (point 7) where that envelope of arcs intersects with the parallel passing through the southernmost point on the 12-nautical-mile envelope of arcs around East-Southeast Cays. The boundary line then follows that parallel until it reaches the southernmost point of the 12-nautical-mile envelope of arcs around East-Southeast Cays (point 8) and continues along that envelope of arcs until its most eastward point (point 9). From that point the boundary line follows the parallel of latitude until it reaches the 200-nautical-mile limit from the baselines from which the territorial sea of Nicaragua is measured (endpoint B, the approximate location of which is shown on sketch-map No. 11).

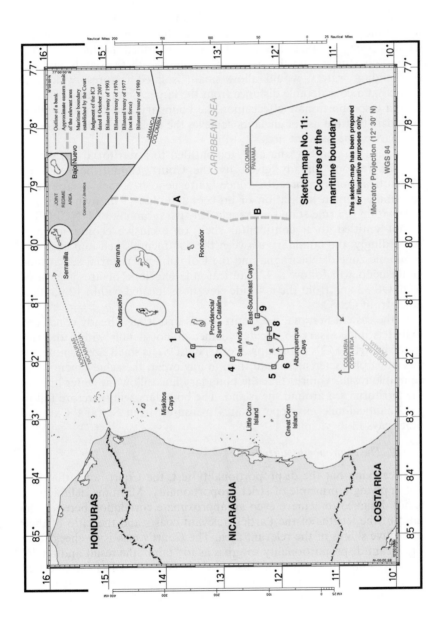

Sketch-map No. 11:
Course of the
maritime boundary

This sketch-map has been prepared
for illustrative purposes only.

Mercator Projection (12° 30′ N)
WGS 84

That leaves Quitasueño and Serrana, both of which the Court has held fall on the Nicaraguan side of the boundary line described above. In the Court's view, to take the adjusted line described in the preceding paragraphs further north, so as to encompass these islands and the surrounding waters, would allow small, isolated features, which are located at a considerable distance from the larger Colombian islands, to have a disproportionate effect upon the boundary. The Court therefore considers that the use of enclaves achieves the most equitable solution in this part of the relevant area.

Quitasueño and Serrana are each entitled to a territorial sea which, for the reasons already given by the Court, cannot be less than 12 nautical miles in breadth. Since Quitasueño is a rock incapable of sustaining human habitation or an economic life of its own and thus falls within the rule stated in Article 121, paragraph 3, of UNCLOS, it is not entitled to a continental shelf or exclusive economic zone. Accordingly, the boundary between the continental shelf and exclusive economic zone of Nicaragua and the Colombian territorial sea around Quitasueño will follow a 12-nautical-mile envelope of arcs measured from QS 32 and from the low-tide elevations located within 12 nautical miles from QS 32.

In the case of Serrana, the Court recalls that it has already concluded that it is unnecessary to decide whether or not it falls within the rule stated in Article 121, paragraph 3, of UNCLOS. Its small size, remoteness and other characteristics mean that, in any event, the achievement of an equitable result requires that the boundary line follow the outer limit of the territorial sea around the island. The boundary will therefore follow a 12-nautical-mile envelope of arcs measured from Serrana Cay and other cays in its vicinity.

10. The disproportionality test

In carrying out the disproportionality test, the Court notes that it is not applying a principle of strict proportionality. Maritime delimitation is not designed to achieve even an approximate correlation between the ratio of the lengths of the Parties' relevant coasts and the ratio of their respective shares of the relevant area. The Court's task is to check for a significant disproportionality so gross as to "taint" the result and render it inequitable. In the present case, the boundary line has the effect of dividing the relevant area between the Parties in a ratio of approximately 1:3.44 in Nicaragua's favour, while the ratio of relevant coasts is approximately 1:8.2. The question, therefore, is whether, in the circumstances of the present case, this disproportion is so great as to render the result inequitable. The Court concludes that, taking account of all the circumstances of the present case, the result achieved by the maritime delimitation does not entail such a disproportionality as to create an inequitable result.

VI. Nicaragua's request for a declaration (paras. 248-250)

In addition to its claims regarding a maritime boundary, in its final submissions, Nicaragua requested that the Court adjudge and declare that "Colombia is not acting in accordance with her obligations under international law by stopping and otherwise hindering Nicaragua from accessing and disposing of her natural resources to the east of the 82nd meridian".

The Court observes that Nicaragua's request for this declaration is made in the context of proceedings regarding a maritime boundary which had not been settled prior to the decision of the Court. The consequence of the Court's Judgment is that the maritime boundary between Nicaragua and Colombia throughout the relevant area has now been delimited as between the Parties. In this regard, the Court observes that the Judgment attributes to Colombia part of the maritime spaces in respect of which Nicaragua seeks a declaration regarding access to natural resources. In this context, the Court considers that Nicaragua's claim is unfounded.

VII. Operative clause (para. 251)

"THE COURT,

(1) Unanimously,

Finds that the Republic of Colombia has sovereignty over the islands at Alburquerque, Bajo Nuevo, East-Southeast Cays, Quitasueño, Roncador, Serrana and Serranilla;

(2) By fourteen votes to one,

Finds admissible the Republic of Nicaragua's claim contained in its final submission I (3) requesting the Court to adjudge and declare that '[t]he appropriate form of delimitation, within the geographical and legal framework constituted by the mainland coasts of Nicaragua and Colombia, is a continental shelf boundary dividing by equal parts the overlapping entitlements to a continental shelf of both Parties';

IN FAVOUR: *President* Tomka; *Vice-President* Sepúlveda-Amor; *Judges* Abraham, Keith, Bennouna, Skotnikov, Cançado Trindade, Yusuf, Greenwood, Xue, Donoghue, Sebutinde; *Judges* ad hoc Mensah, Cot;

AGAINST: *Judge* Owada;

(3) Unanimously,

Finds that it cannot uphold the Republic of Nicaragua's claim contained in its final submission I (3);

(4) Unanimously,

Decides that the line of the single maritime boundary delimiting the continental shelf and the exclusive economic zones of the Republic of

Nicaragua and the Republic of Colombia shall follow geodetic lines connecting the points with co-ordinates:

Latitude north	Longitude west
1. 13° 46′ 35.7″	81° 29′ 34.7″
2. 13° 31′ 08.0″	81° 45′ 59.4″
3. 13° 03′ 15.8″	81° 46′ 22.7″
4. 12° 50′ 12.8″	81° 59′ 22.6″
5. 12° 07′ 28.8″	82° 07′ 27.7″
6. 12° 00′ 04.5″	81° 57′ 57.8″

From point 1, the maritime boundary line shall continue due east along the parallel of latitude (co-ordinates 13° 46′ 35.7″ N) until it reaches the 200-nautical-mile limit from the baselines from which the breadth of the territorial sea of Nicaragua is measured. From point 6 (with co-ordinates 12° 00′ 04.5″ N and 81° 57′ 57.8″ W), located on a 12-nautical-mile envelope of arcs around Alburquerque, the maritime boundary line shall continue along that envelope of arcs until it reaches point 7 (with co-ordinates 12° 11′ 53.5″ N and 81° 38′ 16.6″ W) which is located on the parallel passing through the southernmost point on the 12-nautical-mile envelope of arcs around East-Southeast Cays. The boundary line then follows that parallel until it reaches the southernmost point of the 12-nautical-mile envelope of arcs around East-Southeast Cays at point 8 (with co-ordinates 12° 11′ 53.5″ N and 81° 28′ 29.5″ W) and continues along that envelope of arcs until its most eastward point (point 9 with co-ordinates 12° 24′ 09.3″ N and 81° 14′ 43.9″ W). From that point the boundary line follows the parallel of latitude (co-ordinates 12° 24′ 09.3″ N) until it reaches the 200-nautical-mile limit from the baselines from which the territorial sea of Nicaragua is measured;

(5) Unanimously,

Decides that the single maritime boundary around Quitasueño and Serrana shall follow, respectively, a 12-nautical-mile envelope of arcs measured from QS 32 and from low-tide elevations located within 12 nautical miles from QS 32, and a 12-nautical-mile envelope of arcs measured from Serrana Cay and the other cays in its vicinity;

(6) Unanimously,

Rejects the Republic of Nicaragua's claim contained in its final submissions requesting the Court to declare that the Republic of Colombia is not acting in accordance with its obligations under international law by preventing the Republic of Nicaragua from having access to natural resources to the east of the 82nd meridian."

Judge Owada appended a dissenting opinion to the Judgment of the Court; Judge Abraham appended a separate opinion; Judges Keith and

Xue appended declarations; Judge Donoghue appended a separate opinion to the Judgment of the Court; Judges *ad hoc* Mensah and Cot append declarations to the Judgment of the Court.

Eleven sketch-maps are attached to the Judgment of the Court. These sketch-maps are reproduced in this *Yearbook* and are titled respectively:

— Sketch-map No. 1: Geographical context;
— Sketch-map No. 2: Delimitation claimed by Nicaragua;
— Sketch-map No. 3: Delimitation claimed by Colombia;
— Sketch-map No. 4: The relevant coasts and the relevant area according to Nicaragua;
— Sketch-map No. 5: The relevant coasts and the relevant area according to Colombia;
— Sketch-map No. 6: The relevant coasts as identified by the Court;
— Sketch-map No. 7: The relevant maritime area as identified by the Court;
— Sketch-map No. 8: Construction of the provisional median line;
— Sketch-map No. 9: Construction of the weighted line;
— Sketch-map No. 10: The simplified weighted line;
— Sketch-map No. 11: Course of the maritime boundary.

The above summary, along with summaries of opinions and declarations, as well as the full text of this Judgment (and sketch-maps) are available on the website of the Court under the headings "Cases/Contentious Cases".

5. Maritime Dispute (Peru v. Chile)

On 16 January 2008 Peru filed an Application instituting proceedings against Chile before the Court concerning a dispute in relation to

"the delimitation of the boundary between the maritime zones of the two States in the Pacific Ocean, beginning at a point on the coast called Concordia, . . . the terminal point of the land boundary established pursuant to the Treaty . . . of 3 June 1929"[1]

and also to the recognition in favour of Peru of a "maritime zone lying within 200 nautical miles of Peru's coast, and thus appertaining to Peru, but which Chile considers to be part of the high seas".

In its Application, Peru claims that "the maritime zones between Chile and Peru have never been delimited by agreement or otherwise" and that, accordingly, "the delimitation is to be determined by the Court in accordance with customary international law". Peru states that, "since the 1980s, [it] has consistently endeavoured to negotiate the various issues in dispute, but . . . has constantly met a refusal from Chile to enter into negotiations". It asserts that a Note of 10 September 2004 from the

---

[1] Treaty between Chile and Peru for the settlement of the dispute regarding Tacna and Arica, signed at Lima on 3 June 1929.

Minister for Foreign Affairs of Chile to the Minister for Foreign Affairs of Peru made further attempts at negotiation impossible.

Peru,

"requests the Court to determine the course of the boundary between the maritime zones of the two States in accordance with international law . . . and to adjudge and declare that Peru possesses exclusive sovereign rights in the maritime area situated within the limit of 200 nautical miles from its coast but outside Chile's exclusive economic zone or continental shelf".

As basis for the Court's jurisdiction, Peru invokes Article XXXI of the American Treaty on Pacific Settlement (the Pact of Bogotá) of 30 April 1948, to which both States are parties without reservation.

By an Order of 31 March 2008, the Court fixed 20 March 2009 and 9 March 2010 as the respective time-limits for the filing of a Memorial by Peru and a Counter-Memorial by Chile. Those pleadings were filed within the time-limits thus prescribed.

Colombia and Ecuador, relying on Article 53, paragraph 1, of the Rules of Court, requested copies of the pleadings and annexed documents produced in the case. In accordance with that provision, the Court, after ascertaining the views of the Parties, acceded to those requests.

By an Order of 27 April 2010, the Court authorized the submission of a Reply by Peru and a Rejoinder by Chile. It fixed 9 November 2010 and 11 July 2011 as the respective time-limits for the filing of those pleadings. The Reply and Rejoinder were filed within the time-limits thus fixed.

Public hearings were held from 3 to 14 December 2012. At the conclusion of those hearings, the Parties presented the following final submissions to the Court:

For the Republic of Peru:

"For the reasons set out in Peru's Memorial and Reply and during the oral proceedings, the Republic of Peru requests the Court to adjudge and declare that:

(1) The delimitation between the respective maritime zones between the Republic of Peru and the Republic of Chile, is a line starting at 'Point Concordia' (defined as the intersection with the low-water mark of a 10-kilometre radius arc, having as its centre the first bridge over the River Lluta of the Arica-La Paz railway) and equidistant from the baselines of both Parties, up to a point situated at a distance of 200 nautical miles from those baselines, and

(2) Beyond the point where the common maritime border ends, Peru is entitled to exercise exclusive sovereign rights over a maritime area lying out to a distance of 200 nautical miles from its baselines."

For the Republic of Chile:

"Chile respectfully requests the Court to:

(a) dismiss Peru's claims in their entirety;
(b) adjudge and declare that:

(i) the respective maritime zone entitlements of Chile and Peru have been fully delimited by agreement;
(ii) those maritime zone entitlements are delimited by a boundary following the parallel of latitude passing through the most seaward boundary marker of the land boundary between Chile and Peru, known as Hito No. 1, having a latitude of 18° 21′ 00″ S under WGS84 Datum; and
(iii) Peru has no entitlement to any maritime zone extending to the south of that parallel."

The Judgment of the Court will be delivered at a public sitting on a date to be announced in due course.

6. Aerial Herbicide Spraying (Ecuador v. Colombia)

On 31 March 2008, Ecuador filed an Application instituting proceedings against Colombia with respect to a dispute concerning the alleged "aerial spraying [by Colombia] of toxic herbicides at locations near, at and across its border with Ecuador".

Ecuador maintains that "the spraying has already caused serious damage to people, to crops, to animals, and to the natural environment on the Ecuadorian side of the frontier, and poses a grave risk of further damage over time". It further contends that it has made "repeated and sustained efforts to negotiate an end to the fumigations" but that "these negotiations have proved unsuccessful". (See *I.C.J. Annual Report 2007-2008, et seq.*)

Ecuador accordingly requests the Court "to adjudge and declare" that:

"*(a)* Colombia has violated its obligations under international law by causing or allowing the deposit on the territory of Ecuador of toxic herbicides that have caused damage to human health, property and the environment;
(b) Colombia shall indemnify Ecuador for any loss or damage caused by its internationally unlawful acts, namely the use of herbicides, including by aerial dispersion, and in particular:

(i) death or injury to the health of any person or persons arising from the use of such herbicides; and
(ii) any loss of or damage to the property or livelihood or human rights of such persons; and
(iii) environmental damage or the depletion of natural resources; and
(iv) the costs of monitoring to identify and assess future risks to

public health, human rights and the environment resulting from Colombia's use of herbicides; and

(v) any other loss or damage; and

(c) Colombia shall:

(i)   respect the sovereignty and territorial integrity of Ecuador; and

(ii)   forthwith, take all steps necessary to prevent, on any part of its territory, the use of any toxic herbicides in such a way that they could be deposited onto the territory of Ecuador; and

(iii) prohibit the use, by means of aerial dispersion, of such herbicides in Ecuador, or on or near any part of its border with Ecuador."

As basis for the Court's jurisdiction, Ecuador invokes Article XXXI of the American Treaty on Pacific Settlement (the "Pact of Bogotá") of 30 April 1948, to which both States are parties. Ecuador also relies on Article 32 of the 1988 United Nations Convention against Illicit Traffic in Narcotic Drugs and Psychotropic Substances.

In its Application, Ecuador reaffirms its opposition "to the export and consumption of illegal narcotics", but stresses that the issues it presents to the Court "relate exclusively to the methods and locations of Colombia's operations to eradicate illicit coca and poppy plantations — and the harmful effects in Ecuador of such operations".

By an Order of 30 May 2008, the Court fixed 29 April 2009 and 29 March 2010 as the respective time-limits for the filing of a Memorial by Ecuador and a Counter-Memorial by Colombia. Those pleadings were filed within the time-limits thus prescribed.

By an Order of 25 June 2010, the Court directed the submission of a Reply by Ecuador and a Rejoinder by Colombia. It fixed 31 January and 1 December 2011, respectively, as the time-limits for the filing of those pleadings. The Reply of Ecuador was filed within the time-limit thus fixed.

By an Order of 19 October 2011, the President of the Court extended from 1 December 2011 to 1 February 2012 the time-limit for the filing of a Rejoinder by Colombia. That pleading was filed within the time-limit thus extended.

Pursuant to Article 54, paragraph 1, of the Rules of Court, the Court fixed Monday, 30 September 2013, as the date for the opening of the oral proceedings in the case.

7. Whaling in the Antarctic (Australia v. *Japan: New Zealand intervening)*

On 31 May 2010, Australia instituted proceedings against Japan, alleging that

"Japan's continued pursuit of a large-scale program of whaling under the Second Phase of its Japanese Whale Research Program under Special Permit in the Antarctic ('JARPA II') [is] in breach of obligations assumed by Japan under the International Convention for the Regulation of Whaling ('ICRW'), as well as its other international obligations for the preservation of marine mammals and marine environment."

The Applicant contends in particular that Japan

"has breached and is continuing to breach the following obligations under the ICRW:

(a) the obligation under paragraph 10 (e) of the Schedule to the ICRW to observe in good faith the zero catch limit in relation to the killing of whales for commercial purposes; and

(b) the obligation under paragraph 7 (d) of the Schedule to the ICRW to act in good faith to refrain from undertaking commercial whaling of humpback and fin whales in the Southern Ocean Sanctuary."

Australia points out that "having regard to the scale of the JARPA II program, to the lack of any demonstrated relevance for the conservation and management of whale stocks, and to the risks presented to targeted species and stocks, the JARPA II program cannot be justified under Article VIII of the ICRW" (this Article regulates the granting of special permits to kill, take and treat whales for purposes of scientific research). Australia alleges further that Japan has also breached and is continuing to breach, *inter alia*, its obligations under the Convention on International Trade in Endangered Species of Wild Fauna and Flora and under the Convention on Biological Diversity.

At the end of its Application, Australia requests the Court to adjudge and declare that "Japan is in breach of its international obligations in implementing the JARPA II program in the Southern Ocean", and to order that Japan:

"(a) cease implementation of JARPA II;

(b) revoke any authorizations, permits or licences allowing the activities which are the subject of this Application to be undertaken; and

(c) provide assurances and guarantees that it will not take any further action under the JARPA II or any similar program until such program has been brought into conformity with its obligations under international law."

Australia explains in its Application that it has consistently opposed the JARPA II program, both through individual protests and demarches to Japan and through relevant international forums, including the International Whaling Commission ("IWC").

As the basis for the jurisdiction of the Court, the Applicant invokes the provisions of Article 36, paragraph 2, of the Court's Statute, referring to the declarations recognizing the Court's jurisdiction as compulsory made by Australia on 22 March 2002 and by Japan on 9 July 2007.

By an Order of 13 July 2010, the Court fixed 9 May 2011 as the time-limit for the filing of a Memorial by Australia and 9 March 2012 as the time-limit for the filing of a Counter-Memorial by Japan. Those pleadings were filed within the time-limits thus prescribed.

The Court subsequently decided that the filing of a Reply by Australia and a Rejoinder by Japan was not necessary and that the written phase of the proceedings was therefore closed. The subsequent procedure was reserved for further decision.

On 20 November 2012, New Zealand filed in the Registry a Declaration of Intervention in the case. In order to avail itself of the right of intervention conferred by Article 63 of the Statute of the Court, New Zealand relied on its "status as a party to the International Convention for the Regulation of Whaling". It contended that "[a]s a party to the Convention, [it] has a direct interest in the construction that might be placed upon the Convention by the Court in its decision in these proceedings".

In its Declaration, New Zealand further explained that its intervention was directed to the questions of construction arising in the case, in particular with respect to Article VIII of the Convention, which provides, *inter alia*, that

> "any Contracting Government may grant to any of its nationals a special permit authorizing that national to kill, take and treat whales for purposes of scientific research subject to such restrictions as to number and subject to such other conditions as the Contracting Government thinks fit".

Given its long-standing participation in the work of the International Whaling Commission (the "IWC"), and its views with respect to the interpretation and application of the Convention, in particular with regard to whaling under special permit, New Zealand declared that it was necessary for it to intervene in the case "in order to be able to place its interpretation of the relevant provisions of the Convention before the Court".

At the end of its Declaration, New Zealand provided the following summary of its interpretation of Article VIII:

> "*(a)* Article VIII forms an integral part of the system of collective regulation established by the Convention.
> *(b)* Parties to the Convention may engage in whaling by special permit only in accordance with Article VIII.
> *(c)* Article VIII permits the killing of whales under special permit only if:
>
>> (i) an objective assessment of the methodology, design and characteristics of the programme demonstrates that the killing is only 'for purposes of scientific research'; and

(ii) the killing is necessary for, and proportionate to, the objectives of that research and will have no adverse effect on the conservation of stocks; and

(iii) the Contracting Government issuing the special permit has discharged its duty of meaningful co-operation with the Scientific Committee and the IWC.

(d) Whaling under special permit that does not meet these requirements of Article VIII, and not otherwise permitted under the Convention, is prohibited."

New Zealand underlined in its Declaration "that it d[id] not seek to be a party to the proceedings" and "confirm[ed] that, by availing itself of its right to intervene, it accept[ed] that the construction given by the judgment in the case w[ould] be equally binding upon it".

In accordance with Article 83 of the Rules of Court, Australia and Japan were invited to furnish written observations on New Zealand's Declaration of Intervention by Friday, 21 December 2012 at the latest. Those written observations were filed within the time-limit thus fixed.

In its Order dated 6 February 2013 (see *I.C.J. Reports 2013*, p. 3), the Court, taking note of the concerns expressed by Japan relating to certain procedural issues regarding the equality of the Parties, recalled that intervention under Article 63 of the Statute was limited to submitting observations on the construction of the Convention in question and did not allow the intervener, which did not become a party to the proceedings, to deal with any other aspect of the case before the Court. It considered that such an intervention could not affect the equality of the Parties. Having noted that New Zealand met the requirements set out in Article 82 of the Rules of Court, that its Declaration of Intervention fell within the provisions of Article 63 of the Statute and, moreover, that the Parties had raised no objection to the admissibility of the Declaration, the Court concluded that New Zealand's Declaration of Intervention was admissible. By the same Order, the Court fixed 4 April 2013 as the time-limit for the filing by New Zealand of the written observations referred to in Article 86, paragraph 1, of the Rules of Court; it also authorized the filing by Australia and Japan of written observations on those written observations of New Zealand and fixed 31 May 2013 as the time-limit for such filings. Those pleadings were filed within the time-limits thus fixed.

Public hearings were held from 26 June to 16 July 2013. At the conclusion of those hearings, the Parties presented the following final submissions to the Court:

On behalf of Australia:

"1. Australia requests the Court to adjudge and declare that the Court has jurisdiction to hear the claims presented by Australia.

2. Australia requests the Court to adjudge and declare that Japan is in breach of its international obligations in authorizing and

implementing the Japanese Whale Research Program under Special Permit in the Antarctic Phase II (JARPA II) in the Southern Ocean.

3. In particular, the Court is requested to adjudge and declare that, by its conduct, Japan has violated its international obligations pursuant to the International Convention for the Regulation of Whaling to:

    (a) observe the zero catch limit in relation to the killing of whales for commercial purposes in paragraph 10 *(e)* of the Schedule;

    (b) refrain from undertaking commercial whaling of fin whales in the Southern Ocean Sanctuary in paragraph 7 *(b)* of the Schedule;

    (c) observe the moratorium on taking, killing or treating of whales, except minke whales, by factory ships or whale catchers attached to factory ships in paragraph 10 *(d)* of the Schedule; and

    (d) comply with the requirements of paragraph 30 of the Schedule.

4. Further, the Court is requested to adjudge and declare that JARPA II is not a program for purposes of scientific research within the meaning of Article VIII of the International Convention for the Regulation of Whaling.

5. Further, the Court is requested to adjudge and declare that Japan shall:

    (a) refrain from authorizing or implementing any special permit whaling which is not for purposes of scientific research within the meaning of Article VIII;

    (b) cease with immediate effect the implementation of JARPA II; and

    (c) revoke any authorization, permit or licence that allows the implementation of JARPA II."

On behalf of Japan:

    "Japan requests that the Court adjudge and declare:

1. —   that it lacks jurisdiction over the claims brought against Japan by Australia, referred to it by the Application of Australia of 31 May 2010; and

    — that, consequently, the Application of New Zealand for permission to intervene in the proceedings instituted by Australia against Japan lapses;

2. in the alternative, that the claims of Australia are rejected."

New Zealand presented its oral observations to the Court on Monday, 8 July 2013.

The Court will deliver its Judgment at a public sitting, the date of which will be announced in due course.

8. Frontier Dispute (Burkina Faso/Republic of Niger)

On 20 July 2010, Burkina Faso and Niger jointly submitted a frontier dispute between them to the Court. By a joint letter dated 12 May 2010 and filed in the Registry on 20 July 2010, the two States notified to the Court a Special Agreement signed in Niamey on 24 February 2009, which entered into force on 20 November 2009. Under the terms of Article 1 of this Special Agreement, the Parties have agreed to submit their frontier dispute to the Court, and that each of them will choose a judge *ad hoc*.

Article 2 of the Special Agreement indicates the subject of the dispute as follows:

"The Court is requested to:

1. determine the course of the boundary between the two countries in the sector from the astronomic marker of Tong-Tong (latitude 14° 25′ 04″ N; longitude 00° 12′ 47″ E) to the beginning of the Botou bend (latitude 12° 36′ 18″ N; longitude 01° 52′ 07″ E);
2. place on record the Parties' agreement on the results of the work of the Joint Technical Commission on demarcation of the Burkina Faso-Niger boundary with regard to the following sectors:

   (a) the sector from the heights of N'Gouma to the astronomic marker of Tong-Tong;
   (b) the sector from the beginning of the Botou bend to the River Mekrou."

In Article 3, paragraph 1, the Parties request the Court to authorize the following written proceedings:

"*(a)* a Memorial filed by each Party not later than nine (9) months after the seising of the Court;
(b) a Counter-Memorial filed by each Party not later than nine (9) months after exchange of the Memorials;
(c) any other pleading whose filing, at the request of either of the Parties, shall have been authorized or directed by the Court."

Article 7 of the Special Agreement, entitled "Judgment of the Court", reads as follows:

"1. The Parties accept the Judgment of the Court given pursuant to this Special Agreement as final and binding upon them.
2. From the day on which the Judgment is rendered, the Parties

shall have eighteen (18) months in which to commence the work of demarcating the boundary.

3. In case of difficulty in the implementation of the Judgment, either Party may seise the Court pursuant to Article 60 of its Statute.

4. The Parties request the Court to nominate, in its Judgment, three (3) experts to assist them in the demarcation."

Lastly, Article 10 contains the following "Special Undertaking":

"Pending the Judgment of the Court, the Parties undertake to maintain peace, security and tranquility among the populations of the two States in the frontier region, refraining from any act of incursion into the disputed areas and organizing regular meetings of administrative officials and the security services.

With regard to the creation of socio-economic infrastructure, the Parties undertake to hold preliminary consultations prior to implementation."

The Special Agreement was accompanied by an exchange of Notes dated 29 October and 2 November 2009, embodying the agreement between the two States on the delimited sectors of the frontier.

By Order of 14 September 2010, the Court fixed 20 April 2011 and 20 January 2012 as the respective time-limits for the filing of a Memorial and Counter-Memorial by each of the Parties. Both were filed within the time-limits thus prescribed.

Pursuant to Article 54, paragraph 1, of the Rules of Court, the Court fixed Monday 8 October 2012 as the date of the opening of the oral proceedings in the case.

Public hearings were held from 8 to 17 October 2012.

At the end of the oral proceedings, the Parties presented the following final submissions to the Court:

For Burkina Faso:

"In view of all the considerations set out in its Memorial, its Counter-Memorial and its oral argument, Burkina Faso has the honour to request that it may please the International Court of Justice to adjudge and declare that the frontier between Burkina Faso and the Republic of Niger follows the course described hereafter:

1. from the heights of N'Gouma to the Tong-Tong astronomic marker, the frontier takes the following course: a series of straight lines connecting the following points in turn[1]: Mount N'Gouma

---

[1] The co-ordinates which follow are those adopted in the record of the work of the Joint Survey Mission of the erected markers, 3 July 2009, Memorial of Burkina Faso (MBF), Ann. 101. The co-ordinates are measured by GPS.

(Lat. 14° 54′ 46.0″ N; Long. 0° 14′ 36.4″ E), Kabia Ford (Lat. 14° 53′ 09.8″ N; Long. 0° 13′ 06.3″ E), Mount Arwaskoye (Lat. 14° 50′ 44.7″ N; Long. 0° 10′ 35.8″ E), Mount Bellé Banguia (Lat. 14° 45′ 05.2″ N; Long. 0° 14′ 09.6″ E), Takabougou (Lat. 14° 37′ 54.5″ N; Long. 0° 10′ 16.1″ E), Mount Douma Fendé (Lat. 14° 32′ 00.6″ N; Long. 0° 09′ 42.1″ E) and the Tong-Tong astronomic marker (Lat. 14° 24′ 53.2″ N; Long. 0° 12′ 51.7″ E);

2. from the Tong-Tong astronomic marker to the beginning of the Botou bend, the frontier takes the following course:

— a straight line as far as the Tao astronomic marker (Lat. 14° 03′ 04.7″ N; Long. 0° 22′ 51.8″ E)[1];
— from that point, a straight line up to the point where the frontier reaches the River Sirba at Bossébangou (Lat. 13° 21′ 06.5″ N; Long. 1° 17′ 11.0″ E[2];
— from that point, the frontier follows the right bank of the River Sirba, from east to west, up to the point on the right bank with the co-ordinates: Lat. 13° 19′ 53.5″ N; Long. 1° 07′ 20.4″ E;
— from that point, the frontier follows the line on the 1:200,000-scale map of the Institut géographique national de France, 1960 edition, as far as the point with the co-ordinates: Lat. 13° 22′ 30.0″ N; Long. 0° 59′ 40.0″ E;
— from that point, the frontier runs south in a straight line, ending at the intersection of the right bank of the River Sirba with the Say parallel (Lat. 13° 06′ 10.7″ N; Long. 0° 59′ 40.0″);
— from that point, the frontier runs in a straight line up to the beginning of the Botou bend (Tyenkilibi) (Lat. 12° 36′ 19.2″ N; Long. 1° 52′ 06.9″ E)[3];

3. from the beginning of the Botou bend as far as the River Mekrou, the frontier takes the following course:

— a series of straight lines connecting the following points in turn: Jackal Mountain (Lat. 12° 41′ 33.1″ N; Long. 1° 55′ 43.9″ E), Laguil (Lat. 12° 41′ 31.9″ N; Long. 1° 57′ 1.3″ E) and Nonbokoli (Lat. 12° 44′ 12.9″ N; Long. 1° 58′ 47.0″ E);
— from the latter point, the frontier follows the median line of the Dantiabonga *marigot*, passes to the south of Dantiandou

[1] The co-ordinates of this point were measured by GPS by Burkina. The co-ordinates of this marker on the Clarke 1880 ellipsoid are: Lat. 14° 03′ 13″ N; Long. 00° 22′ 53″ E.

[2] The co-ordinates of this point, and the following ones, are given on the Clarke 1880 ellipsoid.

[3] The co-ordinates of this point, and the following ones, are those adopted in the record of the work of Joint Survey Mission of the markers erected, 3 July 2009, MBF, Ann. 101. The co-ordinates were measured by GPS (WGS84 ellipsoid).

and then follows the line of the Yoga Djoaga hills as far as the confluence of the Dyamongou and Dantiabonga Rivers (Lat. 12° 43′ 15.1″ N; Long. 2° 05′ 14.9″ E);

— from that point, the frontier follows the median line of the River Dyamongou as far as the confluence of the Dyamongou marigot and the Boulel Fouanou (Lat. 12° 43′ 44.0″ N; Long. 2° 06′ 23.9″ E;

— from that point, the frontier runs in a series of straight lines connecting the following points in turn: Boulel (Lat. 12° 42′ 15.1″ N; Long. 2° 06′ 53.3″ E), Boulel East (Teylinga) (Lat. 12° 41′ 09.5″ N; Long. 2° 09′ 43.2″ E), Dyapionga North (Lat. 12° 39′ 42.3″ N; Long. 2° 09′ 37.3″ E), Dyapionga South (Lat. 12° 38′ 55.4″ N; Long. 2° 09′ 08.1″ E), Kanleyenou (Lat. 12° 37′ 21.7″ N; Long. 2° 11′ 57.1″ E), Niobo Farou (Caiman Pool) (Lat. 12° 35′ 19.6″ N; Long. 2° 13′ 23.9″ E), the eastern crests of Mount Tambouadyoaga (Lat. 12° 31′ 19.7″ N; Long. 2° 13′ 48.0″ E), Banindyididouana (Lat. 12° 27′ 52.7″ N; Long. 2° 16′ 27.2″ E) and the confluence of the Banindyidi Fouanou and Tapoa Rivers (Lat. 12° 25′ 30.5″ N; Long. 2° 16′ 40.6″ E);

— from the latter of those points, the frontier follows the median line of the River Tapoa as far as the point where it intersects with the former boundary of the Fada and Say *cercles*[1] (Lat. 12° 21′ 04.88″ N; Long. 2° 04′ 12.77″ E);

— from the latter point, the frontier runs in a straight line, corresponding to the former boundary of the Fada and Say *cercles*, up to the point where it intersects with the River Mekrou (Lat. 11° 54′ 07.83″ N; Long. 2° 24′ 15.25″ E).

Pursuant to Article 7, paragraph 4, of the Special Agreement, Burkina Faso further requests the Court to nominate, in its Judgment, three experts to assist the Parties as necessary in the demarcation."

For the Republic of Niger:

"The Republic of Niger requests the Court to adjudge and declare that the frontier between the Republic of Niger and Burkina Faso takes the following course:

In the Téra sector:

— Starting from the Tong-Tong astronomic marker (co-ordinates: 14° 25′ 04″ N, 00° 12′ 47″ E);

— from that point: a straight line as far as the Vibourié marker (co-ordinates: 14° 21′ 44″ N, 0° 16′ 25″ E);

— from that point: a straight line as far as the Tao astronomic

---

[1] The co-ordinates of the following points are those adopted in the record of the meeting to ascertain the co-ordinates of the unmarked points in Sector B, 15 October 2009, MBF, Ann. 105. They were derived from the IGN France 1:200,000-scale map (Clarke 1880).

marker (co-ordinates: 14° 03′ 02.2″ N, 00° 22′ 52.1″ E);
— from that point the frontier follows the 1960 IGN line (Téra sheet) as far as the point having co-ordinates 14° 01′ 55″ N, 00° 24′ 11″ E;
— from that point, it runs in a straight line to the frontier point on the new Téra-Dori road (co-ordinates: 14° 00′ 04.2″ N, 00° 24′ 16.3″ E) (to the west of Petelkolé);
— from that point, it runs in a straight line to the point with co-ordinates 13° 59′ 03″ N, 00° 25′ 12″ E, and reaches the IGN line (at the point with co-ordinates 13° 58′ 38.9″ N, 00° 26′ 03.5″ E), which it follows as far as the break in the line of crosses north of Ihouchaltane (Oulsalta on the 1960 IGN map, Sebba sheet), at the point with co-ordinates 13° 55′ 54″ N, 00° 28′ 21″ E;
— from this point the frontier skirts Ihouchaltane (Oulsalta), passing through the points with co-ordinates 13° 54′ 42″ N, 00° 26′ 53.3″ E, then 13° 53′ 30″ N, 00° 28′ 07″ E;
— from that point, it rejoins the IGN line (at the point having co-ordinates 13° 53′ 24″ N, 00° 29′ 58″ E), which it follows as far as the tripoint of the former boundaries of the *cercles* of Say, Tillabéry and Dori (co-ordinates 13° 29′ 08″ N, 01° 01′ 00″ E).

Where there are gaps in the course of the IGN line, these will be filled by straight lines or, where there is a watercourse, by following its bed.

In the Say sector:
— Starting from the tripoint of the former boundaries of the *cercles* of Say, Tillabéry and Dori (co-ordinates 13° 29′ 08″ N, 01° 01′ 00″ E), the frontier runs in a straight line as far as the point having co-ordinates 13° 04′ 52″ N, 00° 55′ 47″ E (where it cuts the River Sirba at the level of the Say parallel), then from that point a straight line passing through a point situated 4 km to the south-west of Dogona with co-ordinates 13° 01′ 44″ N, 01° 00′ 25″ E, as far as the frontier marker with co-ordinates 12° 37′ 55.7″ N, 01° 34′ 40.7″ E, and finally from there to the point fixed by agreement between the Parties, the co-ordinates of which are the following: 12° 36′ 18″ N, 01° 52′ 07″ E.″

At a public sitting which was held on 16 April 2013, the Court delivered its Judgment (see *I.C.J. Reports 2013*, p. 43) a summary of which is given below:

I. Procedural and factual background of the case (paras. 1-34)

The Court recalls that, by a joint letter of notification dated 12 May 2010, Burkina Faso and the Republic of Niger transmitted to the Registrar a Special Agreement which was signed at Niamey on

24 February 2009 and entered into force on 20 November 2009, whereby they agreed to submit to the Court the frontier dispute between them over a section of their common boundary. Attached to this letter were the Protocol of Exchange of the Instruments of Ratification of the said Special Agreement and an exchange of Notes, dated 29 October and 2 November 2009, placing on record the agreement *("entente")* between the two States on the results of the work of the Joint Technical Commission on Demarcation concerning the demarcated sectors of the frontier running, in the north, from the heights of N'Gouma to the astronomic marker of Tong-Tong and, in the south, from the beginning of the Botou bend to the River Mekrou. The Court further recalls that it was requested, in Article 2 of the said Special Agreement, to determine the course of the boundary between Burkina Faso and Niger in the sector from the astronomic marker of Tong-Tong to the beginning of the Botou bend and to place on record the Parties' agreement *("leur entente")* on the results of the work of the Joint Technical Commission on Demarcation of the boundary. It then sets out the historical and factual background of the dispute between these two former colonies, which were part of French West Africa until they gained independence in 1960.

Before examining the dispute between the Parties regarding the course of their common frontier between the astronomic marker of Tong-Tong and the beginning of the Botou bend, the Court deals with the request submitted by Burkina Faso concerning the two demarcated sectors of the frontier.

II. The request concerning the two sectors running, in the north, from the heights of N'Gouma to the Tong-Tong astronomic marker and, in the south, from the beginning of the Botou bend to the River Mekrou (paras. 35-39)

The Court notes that in points 1 and 3 of its final submissions, Burkina Faso requests it to adjudge and declare that its frontier with Niger follows, in the two demarcated sectors, a course which consists of lines linking points whose co-ordinates it provides, which correspond to those recorded in 2009 by the joint mission tasked with conducting surveys based on the work of the Joint Technical Commission. It further notes that Burkina Faso asks the Court to include that course in the operative part of its Judgment, so that the Parties will be bound by it, in the same way that they will be bound with regard to the frontier line in the sector that remains in dispute. The Court observes that, in its final submissions, Niger only requests the Court to draw the frontier between the two States in the section in dispute, which runs from the Tong-Tong astronomic marker to the beginning of the Botou bend. Taking the view that there already exists an agreement between the Parties regarding the two demarcated sectors, Niger is of the opinion that there is no need to include a reference to those sectors in the operative part of the Judgment.

However, it does consider that the said agreement should be noted by the Court in the reasoning of its Judgment.

The Court indicates that, when it is seised on the basis of a special agreement, any request made by a party in its final submissions can fall within the jurisdiction of the Court only if it remains within the limits defined by the provisions of that special agreement. However, it considers that the request made by Burkina Faso in its final submissions does not exactly correspond to the terms of the Special Agreement, since that State does not request the Court to "place on record the Parties' agreement" *("leur entente")* regarding the delimitation of the frontier in the two demarcated sectors, but rather to delimit the frontier according to a line that corresponds to the conclusions of the Joint Technical Commission. According to the Court, however, it is one thing to note the existence of an agreement between the Parties and to place it on record for them; it is quite a different matter to appropriate the content of that agreement in order to make it the substance of a decision of the Court itself. The Court considers that, taken literally, Burkina Faso's request could therefore be rejected as exceeding the limits of the Court's jurisdiction as defined by the Special Agreement. It recognizes, however, that it has the power to interpret the final submissions of the Parties in such a way as to maintain them, so far as possible, within the limits of its jurisdiction under the Special Agreement and, consequently, to interpret the final submissions of Burkina Faso as seeking that the Court place on record the agreement of the Parties.

Nevertheless, the Court takes the view that that would not be sufficient to entertain such a request, since it would still have to be verified that the object of that request falls within the Court's judicial function as defined by its Statute, which is "to decide in accordance with international law such disputes as are submitted to it". The Court notes that, in the present case, neither of the Parties has ever claimed that a dispute continued to exist between them concerning the delimitation of the frontier in the two sectors in question on the date when the proceedings were instituted — nor that such a dispute has subsequently arisen. It observes that, if the Parties have appeared to argue differently, it is on the question of whether the *"entente"* referred to in the Special Agreement has already resulted in an agreement which is legally binding for the two Parties under international law. In its opinion, however, the decisive question is whether a dispute existed between the Parties concerning these two sectors on the date when the proceedings were instituted; it matters little, from the point of view of the judicial function of the Court, whether or not the *"entente"* reached by the Parties has already been incorporated into a legally binding instrument. Accordingly, the Court considers that Burkina Faso's request exceeds the limits of its judicial function.

III. The course of the section of the frontier remaining in dispute
(paras. 60-112)

A. Applicable law (paras. 60-69)

The Court notes that Article 6 of the Special Agreement, entitled "Applicable law", stipulates that:

> "[t]he rules and principles of international law applicable to the dispute are those referred to in Article 38, paragraph 1, of the Statute of the International Court of Justice, including the principle of the intangibility of boundaries inherited from colonization and the Agreement of 28 March 1987."

It observes that, amongst the rules of international law applicable to the dispute, the above-mentioned provision highlights "the principle of the intangibility of boundaries inherited from colonization and the Agreement of 28 March 1987". It states that the Special Agreement provides specific indications as to the way in which the above-mentioned principle must be applied. Article 6 of that instrument requires the application of the 1987 Agreement, which binds the Parties and the objective of which is, according to its title, "the demarcation of the frontier between the two countries". The Court observes that, although the aim of the 1987 Agreement is the "demarcation of the frontier between the two countries" through the installation of markers, it lays down first of all the criteria that must be applied to determine the "course" of the frontier.

The Court notes that the first two Articles of that Agreement specify the acts and documents of the French colonial administration which must be used to determine the delimitation line that existed when the two countries gained independence. It observes in this connection that it follows from that Agreement that the *Arrêté* of 31 August 1927 adopted by the Governor-General *ad interim* of FWA with a view to "fixing the boundaries of the colonies of Upper Volta and Niger", as clarified by its Erratum of 5 October 1927, is the instrument to be applied for the delimitation of the boundary. The Court states that it must be interpreted in its context, taking into account the circumstances of its enactment and implementation by the colonial authorities. As to the relationship between the *Arrêté* and its Erratum, the Court notes that, since the purpose of the Erratum is to correct the text of the *Arrêté* retroactively, it forms an integral part of the latter. For that reason, whenever reference is made to the "*Arrêté*", that will signify, unless otherwise indicated, the wording of the *Arrêté* as amended by the Erratum. The Court further observes that Article 2 of the 1987 Agreement provides for the possibility of "the *Arrêté* and Erratum not suffic[ing]" and establishes that, in that event, "the course shall be that shown on the 1:200,000-scale map of the Institut géographique national de France, 1960 edition" or resulting from "any other relevant document accepted by joint agreement of the Parties". It points out, however, that the Parties do not consider that they have accepted any relevant document other than the 1960 IGN map.

B. The course of the frontier (paras. 70-112)

1. The course of the frontier between the Tong-Tong and Tao astronomic markers (paras. 72-79)

The Court observes that the Parties agree that, in accordance with the *Arrêté*, their common frontier connects the two points at which the Tong-Tong and Tao astronomic markers are respectively situated. It points out that the Parties do not disagree on the identification or the location of these markers, but on how to connect the two points at which they are situated. It notes that Burkina Faso wants the Court to connect these two points with a straight line, whereas Niger argues in favour of two straight-line segments, one running from the Tong-Tong marker to the Vibourié marker, the other running from the Vibourié marker to the Tao marker. The Court is of the opinion that the colonial administration officials interpreted the *Arrêté* as drawing, in the sector in question, a straight line between the Tong-Tong and Tao astronomic markers. Accordingly, a straight line connecting the two markers should be regarded as constituting the frontier between Burkina Faso and Niger in the sector in question.

2. The course of the frontier between the Tao astronomic marker and the River Sirba at Bossébangou (paras. 80-99)

The Court notes that it is not possible to determine from the *Arrêté* how to connect the Tao astronomic marker to "the River Sirba at Bossébangou"; the *Arrêté* merely states that the "line . . . turns ['s'infléchit'] towards the south-east, cutting the Téra-Dori motor road at the Tao astronomic marker . . ., and reaching the River Sirba at Bossébangou". The Court observes that, in Burkina Faso's opinion, this lack of detail should be interpreted as meaning that the two above-mentioned points must be connected by a straight line. It notes that, in Niger's view, this lack of detail demonstrates, on the other hand, that "the *Arrêté* and *Erratum* [do] not suffice", within the meaning of the 1987 Agreement, making it necessary in principle to follow the line as drawn on the 1960 IGN map for the section of the frontier in question, with, however, a slight deviation to the west in two segments corresponding to the Petelkolé frontier post and to the Oussaltane encampment, so as to leave those two localities in Niger's territory, whereas the said line locates them on the Upper Volta side of the inter-colonial boundary. The Court observes that, according to Niger, this is to give precedence to the *effectivités* as observed at the critical dates of independence. It notes that,

Sketch-Map 1:
PARTIES' CLAIMS AND LINE DEPICTED ON THE 1960 IGN MAP
This sketch-map has been prepared for illustrative purposes only

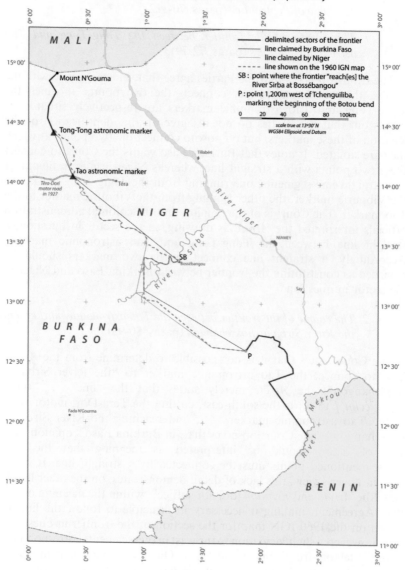

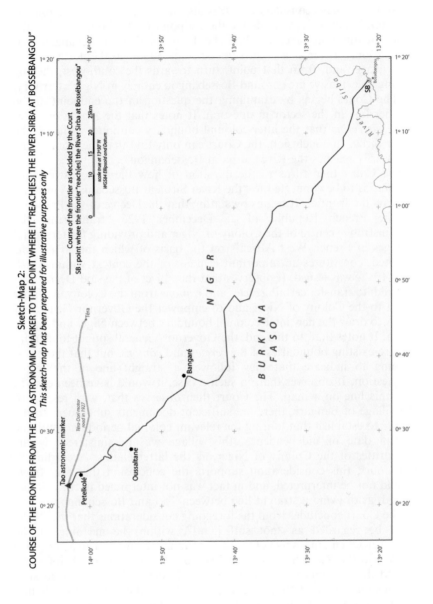

Sketch-Map 2:
COURSE OF THE FRONTIER FROM THE TAO ASTRONOMIC MARKER TO THE POINT WHERE IT "REACH[ES] THE RIVER SIRBA AT BOSSÉBANGOU"
This sketch-map has been prepared for illustrative purposes only

—— Course of the frontier as decided by the Court
SB : point where the frontier "reach[es] the River Sirba at Bossébangou"

scale true at 13°30' N
WGS84 Ellipsoid and Datum
0   5   10   15   20   25km

in addition, Niger considers that it is also necessary to deviate from the 1960 IGN map in order to define the endpoint of the frontier line in the sector in question, since the line should not end at Bossébangou, but descend only as far as a point situated some 30 km to the north-west of that village, and, from that point, turn towards the south-west, thereby leaving an extensive area around Bossébangou entirely in Niger's territory.

The Court begins by examining the question of the endpoint of the frontier line in the sector in question. It notes that the *Arrêté* provides *expressis verbis* that the inter-colonial boundary continues as far as the River Sirba. In conclusion, the Court can only find that the frontier line necessarily reaches the River Sirba at Bossébangou.

The Court then turns to the question of how the "Tao astronomic marker" is to be connected to "the River Sirba at Bossébangou" in order to draw the frontier. It begins by stating that the Decree of the President of the French Republic of 28 December 1926 "transferring the administrative centre of the Colony of Niger and providing for territorial changes in French West Africa", on the basis of which the *Arrêté* was adopted, constitutes an important element of the context within which that *Arrêté* was issued. It observes that the object of the said Decree was twofold: to transfer certain *cercles* and *cantons* from the Colony of Upper Volta to the Colony of Niger and to empower the Governor-General of FWA to draw the new inter-colonial boundary between Niger and Upper Volta. It notes that, to this end, the Governor-General sought to identify the pre-existing boundaries of the *cercles* and *cantons*, but that there was nothing to indicate that they followed a straight line in the sector in question. It observes that, in such a case, it would have been easy to plot this line on a map. The Court then observes that, with respect to the village of Bangaré, there are sufficient documents subsequent to the *Arrêté* to establish that, during the relevant colonial period and until the critical date of independence, this village was administered by the authorities of the Colony of Niger, as the latter claims. According to the Court, this consideration supports the conclusion that the *Arrêté* should not be interpreted, and in fact was not interpreted in the colonial period, as drawing a straight line between Tao and Bossébangou.

The Court concludes from the foregoing considerations that the *Arrêté* must be regarded as "not suffic[ient]", within the meaning of the 1987 Agreement, in respect of the sector running from the Tao astronomic marker to the River Sirba at Bossébangou. Recourse must therefore be had to the line appearing on the 1960 IGN map. Moreover, it declares that it cannot uphold Niger's requests that the said line be shifted slightly at the level of the localities of Petelkolé and Oussaltane, on the ground that these were purportedly administered by Niger during the colonial period. The Court considers that, once it has been concluded that the *Arrêté* is insufficient, and in so far as it is insufficient, the *effectivités* can no longer play a role in the present case. In conclusion, the Court finds that, in the sector of the frontier that runs from the Tao astronomic marker to "the River Sirba at Bossébangou", the line shown on the 1960 IGN map should be adopted.

3. The course of the frontier in the area of Bossébangou
(paras. 100-107)

The Court considers that, in order to complete the determination of the frontier line coming from the Tao astronomic marker, it is necessary to specify its endpoint where it reaches "the River Sirba at Bossébangou". It states that, according to Burkina Faso, this point is located where the straight-line segment which runs from Tao to Bossébangou intersects with the right bank of the Sirba close to that village. It notes that, for its part, Niger does not take a view on the matter, on account of its argument that the frontier line from Tao does not continue as far as the River Sirba, but turns towards the south-west at the tripoint between the *cercles* of Dori, Say and Tillabéry, some 30 km before it reaches that river.

According to the description in the *Arrêté*, it is clear, in the opinion of the Court, that the frontier line ends at the River Sirba and not at the village of Bossébangou. The endpoint of the frontier in this section must therefore be situated in the Sirba or on one of its banks. However, the use of the term "reach" *("atteindre")* in the *Arrêté* does not suggest that the frontier line crosses the Sirba completely, meeting its right bank. Moreover, the Court considers that there is no evidence before it that the River Sirba in the area of Bossébangou was attributed entirely to one of the two colonies. It notes in this regard that the requirement concerning access to water resources of all the people living in the riparian villages is better met by a frontier situated in the river than on one bank or the other. Accordingly, the Court concludes that, on the basis of the *Arrêté*, the endpoint of the frontier line in the area of Bossébangou is located in the River Sirba. This endpoint is more specifically situated on the median line because, in a non-navigable river with the characteristics of the Sirba, that line best meets the requirements of legal security inherent in the determination of a boundary.

The Court notes that, in its original wording, the *Arrêté* situated the meeting-point of the frontier line from Tao with the River Sirba further downstream and stated that this line "then joins the River Sirba". It was clear, according to that wording, that the frontier was supposed to follow that river upstream for a certain distance. The Court contends that, while the language of the Erratum is less clear, it nevertheless specifies that, after reaching the Sirba, the frontier line "almost immediately turns back up towards the north-west". It can be concluded, therefore, that the Erratum did not seek to amend the *Arrêté* entirely on this point and that it implies that the line must follow the Sirba for a short distance. For the reasons given above, the Court considers that the frontier follows the median line of the Sirba.

The Court observes that the corrected wording of the *Arrêté*, according to which the frontier line "almost immediately turns back up towards the north-west", does not establish the precise point at which that line leaves the River Sirba in order to "[turn] back up". There is no indication in the text in that regard except for the fact that the point is located close to Bossébangou. Similarly, once the frontier leaves the Sirba, its course is indicated in the *Arrêté* in a manner that makes it impossible to establish the line accurately. According to the Court, it can therefore only be concluded that the *Arrêté* does not suffice to determine the frontier line in this section and that it is thus necessary to refer to the 1960 IGN map in order to define precisely the point where the frontier line leaves the River Sirba and "turns back up towards the north-west" and the course that it must follow after that point.

The Court indicates that, according to the *Arrêté*, the frontier line, after turning up towards the north-west, "turn[s] back to the south, . . . [and] again cuts the Sirba at the level of the Say parallel". It considers that, once that place has been determined, the meridian passing through it can be followed northwards until the parallel running through the point where the line drawn on the 1960 IGN map turns back to the south. The Court observes that, whereas, in its original wording, the *Arrêté* referred to "a line starting approximately from the Sirba at the level of the Say parallel", the text of the Erratum is much more categorical in this respect and thus cannot be regarded as insufficient. It refers to the intersection between the parallel passing through Say and the River Sirba. According to the Court, it can even be deduced that this point, called point I on sketch-maps 3 and 4 (see pages 106 and 107 of this *Yearbook*), is located on the right bank of the Sirba (at the point with geographic co-ordinates 13° 06′ 12.08″ N; 00° 59′ 30.9″ E), since, according to the Erratum, the frontier line coming from the north cuts the river here before continuing towards the south-east. In the view of the Court, the frontier thus drawn from the area of Bossébangou to the point where the Say parallel cuts the River Sirba forms what might be termed a "salient", in accordance with the description contained in the *Arrêté*. Niger acknowledges that, in contrast, the frontier line which it proposes does not, for its part, "create a salient in this area".

The Court concludes that the frontier line, after reaching the median line of the River Sirba while heading towards Bossébangou, at the point with geographic co-ordinates 13° 21′ 15.9″ N; 01° 17′ 07.2″ E, called point SB on sketch-maps 1, 2, 3 and 4 (see pages 100, 101, 106 and 107 of this *Yearbook*), follows that line upstream until its intersection with the IGN line, at the point with geographic co-ordinates 13° 20′ 1.8″ N; 01° 07′ 29.3″ E, called point A on sketch-maps 3 and 4 (see pages 106 and 107 of this *Yearbook*). From that point, the frontier line follows the IGN line, turning up towards the north-west until the point, with geographic co-ordinates 13° 22′ 28.9″ N; 00° 59′ 34.8″ E, called point B on sketch-map 3 (see page 106 of this *Yearbook*), where the IGN line markedly changes direction, turning due south in a straight line. As this turning point B is situated some 200 m to the east of the meridian which passes through the intersection of the Say parallel with the River Sirba, the IGN line does not cut the River Sirba at the Say parallel. However, the Court notes, the *Arrêté* expressly requires that the boundary line cut the River Sirba at that parallel. The frontier line must therefore depart from the IGN line as from point B and, instead of turning there, continue due west in a straight line until the point, with geographic co-ordinates 13° 22′ 28.9″ N; 00° 59′ 30.9″ E, called point C on sketch-maps 3 and 4 (see pages 106 and 107 of this *Yearbook*), where it reaches the meridian which   passes through the intersection of the Say parallel with the right bank of the River Sirba. The frontier line then runs southwards along that meridian until the said intersection, at the point with geographic co-ordinates 13° 06′ 12.08″ N; 00° 59′ 30.9″ E, called point I on sketch-maps 3 and 4.

4. *The course of the southern part of the frontier* (paras. 108-112)

The Court observes that the intersection of the River Sirba with the Say parallel is the starting-point of another section of the frontier. According to the *Arrêté*, "[f]rom that point the frontier, following an east-south-east direction, continues in a straight line up to a point located 1,200 m to the west of the village of Tchenguiliba". It notes that this latter point has been identified in a consistent manner by the Parties, since it marks the start of the southern section of the already demarcated portion of the frontier. The Court recalls that the *Arrêté* specifies that, in this section, the frontier "continues in a straight line". It considers that it is precise in that it establishes that the frontier line is a straight-line segment between the intersection of the Say parallel with the Sirba and the point located 1,200 m to the west of the village of Tchenguiliba. According to the Court, it cannot therefore be said that the *Arrêté* does not suffice with respect to this section of the frontier.

The Court concludes that, in this section of the frontier, the line consists of a straight-line segment between the intersection of the Say parallel with the right bank of the River Sirba and the beginning of the Botou bend.

*

Having determined the course of the frontier between the two countries, the Court expresses its wish that each Party, in exercising its authority over the portion of the territory under its sovereignty, should have due regard to the needs of the populations concerned, in particular those of the nomadic or semi-nomadic populations, and to the necessity to overcome difficulties that may arise for them because of the frontier. The Court notes the co-operation that has already been established on a regional and bilateral basis between the Parties in this regard, in

Sketch-Map 3:
COURSE OF THE FRONTIER FROM THE POINT WHERE IT "REACH[ES] THE RIVER SIRBA AT
BOSSÉBANGOU" TO THE INTERSECTION OF THE RIVER SIRBA WITH THE SAY PARALLEL
This sketch-map has been prepared for illustrative purposes only

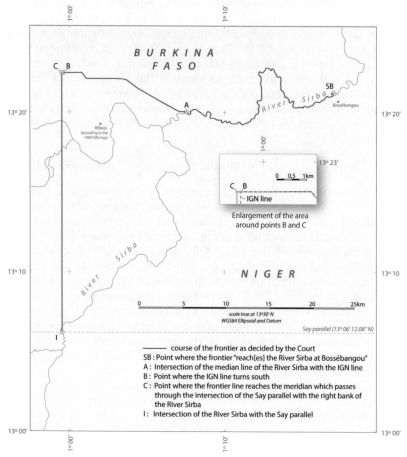

— course of the frontier as decided by the Court
SB : Point where the frontier "reach[es] the River Sirba at Bossébangou"
A : Intersection of the median line of the River Sirba with the IGN line
B : Point where the IGN line turns south
C : Point where the frontier line reaches the meridian which passes
      through the intersection of the Say parallel with the right bank of
      the River Sirba
I : Intersection of the River Sirba with the Say parallel

Sketch-Map 4:
COURSE OF THE FRONTIER AS DECIDED BY THE COURT
This sketch-map has been prepared for illustrative purposes only

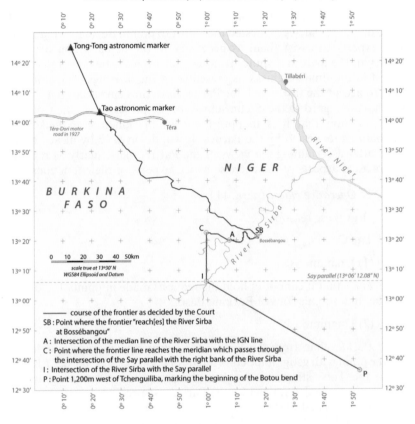

course of the frontier as decided by the Court
SB : Point where the frontier "reach[es] the River Sirba
at Bossébangou"
A : Intersection of the median line of the River Sirba with the IGN line
C : Point where the frontier line reaches the meridian which passes through
the intersection of the Say parallel with the right bank of the River Sirba
I : Intersection of the River Sirba with the Say parallel
P : Point 1,200m west of Tchenguiliba, marking the beginning of the Botou bend

particular under Chapter III of the 1987 Protocol of Agreement, and encourages them to develop it further.

IV. Nomination of experts (para. 113)

The Court observes that, in Article 7, paragraph 4, of the Special Agreement, the Parties requested the Court to nominate, in its Judgment, three experts to assist them as necessary in the demarcation of their frontier in the area in dispute. It notes that both Parties reiterated this request in the final submissions presented at the hearings. The Court is ready to accept the task which the Parties have thus entrusted to it. However, having regard to the circumstances of the present case, the Court is of the opinion that it is inappropriate at this juncture to make the nominations requested by the Parties. It will do so later by means of an order, after ascertaining the views of the Parties, particularly as regards the practical aspects of the exercise by the experts of their functions.

V. Operative clause (para. 114)

"For these reasons,

THE COURT,

(1) Unanimously,

Finds that it cannot uphold the requests made in points 1 and 3 of the final submissions of Burkina Faso;

(2) Unanimously,

Decides that, from the Tong-Tong astronomic marker, situated at the point with geographic co-ordinates 14° 24′ 53.2″ N; 00° 12′ 51.7″ E, to the Tao astronomic marker, the precise co-ordinates of which remain to be determined by the Parties as specified in paragraph 72 of the present Judgment, the course of the frontier between Burkina Faso and the Republic of Niger takes the form of a straight line;

(3) Unanimously,

Decides that, from the Tao astronomic marker, the course of the frontier follows the line that appears on the 1:200,000-scale map of the Institut géographique national (IGN) de France, 1960 edition, (hereinafter the 'IGN line') until its intersection with the median line of the River Sirba at the point with geographic co-ordinates 13° 21′ 15.9″ N; 01° 17′ 07.2″ E;

(4) Unanimously,

Decides that, from this latter point, the course of the frontier follows the median line of the River Sirba upstream until its intersection with the IGN line, at the point with geographic co-ordinates 13° 20′ 01.8″ N;

01° 07′ 29.3″ E; from that point, the course of the frontier follows the IGN line, turning up towards the north-west, until the point, with geographic co-ordinates 13° 22′ 28.9″ N; 00° 59′ 34.8″ E, where the IGN line turns south. At that point, the course of the frontier leaves the IGN line and continues due west in a straight line until the point, with geographic co-ordinates 13° 22′ 28.9″ N; 00° 59′ 30.9″ E, where it reaches the meridian which passes through the intersection of the Say parallel with the right bank of the River Sirba; it then runs southwards along that meridian until the said intersection, at the point with geographic co-ordinates 13° 06′ 12.08″ N; 00° 59′ 30.9″ E;

(5) Unanimously,

Decides that, from this last point to the point situated at the beginning of the Botou bend, with geographic co-ordinates 12° 36′ 19.2″ N; 01° 52′ 06.9″ E, the course of the frontier takes the form of a straight line;

(6) Unanimously,

Decides that it will nominate at a later date, by means of an Order, three experts in accordance with Article 7, paragraph 4, of the Special Agreement of 24 February 2009."

*

Judge Bennouna appended a declaration to the Judgment of the Court; Judges Cançado Trindade and Yusuf, as well as Judges *ad hoc* Mahiou and Daudet, appended separate opinions.

By an Order dated 12 July 2013 (see *I.C.J. Reports 2013*, p. 226), the Court nominated three experts who will assist the Parties in the operation of the demarcation of their common frontier in the disputed area. The case has thus been completed.

Four sketch-maps are attached to the Judgment of the Court. These sketch-maps are reproduced in this *Yearbook* and are titled respectively:

— Sketch-map No. 1: Parties' claims and line depicted on the 1960 IGN map;
— Sketch-map No. 2: Course of the frontier from the Tao astronomic marker to the point where it "reach[es] the River Sirba at Bossébangou";
— Sketch-map No. 3: Course of the frontier from the point where it "reach[es] the River Sirba at Bossébangou" to the intersection of the River Sirba with the Say parallel;
— Sketch-map No. 4: Course of the frontier as decided by the Court.

It is recalled that this summary, the summaries of the declaration and four individual opinions appended to the Judgment, along with the full text of the Judgment, including sketch-maps, can be found on the Court's website under "Cases/contentious cases".

By an Order dated 12 July 2013 (see *I.C.J. Reports 2013*, p. 226), the Court nominated three experts who will assist the Parties in the operation of the demarcation of their common frontier in the disputed area. The case has thus been completed.

9. *Certain Activities Carried Out by Nicaragua in the Border Area (Costa Rica v. Nicaragua)*

On 18 November 2010, the Republic of Costa Rica instituted proceedings against the Republic of Nicaragua in respect of an alleged "incursion into, occupation of and use by Nicaragua's army of Costa Rican territory as well as [alleged] breaches of Nicaragua's obligations towards Costa Rica" under a number of international treaties and conventions.

In its Application, Costa Rica claims that:

> "[b]y sending contingents of its armed forces to Costa Rican territory and establishing military camps therein, Nicaragua is not only acting in outright breach of the established boundary regime between the two States, but also of the core founding principles of the United Nations, namely the principles of territorial integrity and the prohibition of the threat or use of force against any State . . .".

Costa Rica charges Nicaragua with having occupied, in two separate incidents, the territory of Costa Rica in connection with the construction of a canal across Costa Rican territory from the San Juan River to Laguna los Portillos (also known as Harbour Head Lagoon), and with having carried out certain related works of dredging on the San Juan River. Costa Rica states that the

> "ongoing and planned dredging and the construction of the canal will seriously affect the flow of water to the Colorado River of Costa Rica, and will cause further damage to Costa Rican territory, including the wetlands and national wildlife protected areas located in the region".

The Applicant claims that Nicaragua rejected all calls for withdrawal of its armed forces from the occupied territory and all means of negotiation. Costa Rica states further that Nicaragua does not intend to comply with the resolution of 12 November 2010 of the Permanent Council of the Organization of American States calling, in particular, for the withdrawal of Nicaraguan armed forces from the border region, and requests the avoidance of the presence of military or security forces in the area, in order to create a favourable climate for dialogue between the two nations.

Costa Rica accordingly

> "requests the Court to adjudge and declare that Nicaragua is in breach of its international obligations . . . as regards the incursion

into and occupation of Costa Rican territory, the serious damage inflicted to its protected rainforests and wetlands, and the damage intended to the Colorado River, wetlands and protected ecosystems, as well as the dredging and canalization activities being carried out by Nicaragua on the San Juan River. In particular the Court is requested to adjudge and declare that, by its conduct, Nicaragua has breached:

(a) the territory of the Republic of Costa Rica, as agreed and delimited by the 1858 Treaty of Limits, the Cleveland Award and the first and second Alexander Awards;

(b) the fundamental principles of territorial integrity and the prohibition of use of force under the Charter of the United Nations and the Charter of the Organization of American States;

(c) the obligation imposed upon Nicaragua by Article IX of the 1858 Treaty of Limits not to use the San Juan River to carry out hostile acts;

(d) the obligation not to damage Costa Rican territory;

(e) the obligation not to artificially channel the San Juan River away from its natural watercourse without the consent of Costa Rica;

(f) the obligation not to prohibit the navigation on the San Juan River by Costa Rican nationals;

(g) the obligation not to dredge the San Juan River if this causes damage to Costa Rican territory (including the Colorado River), in accordance with the 1888 Cleveland Award;

(h) the obligations under the Ramsar Convention on Wetlands;

(i) the obligation not to aggravate and extend the dispute by adopting measures against Costa Rica, including the expansion of the invaded and occupied Costa Rican territory or by adopting any further measure or carrying out any further actions that would infringe Costa Rica's territorial integrity under international law."

The Court is also requested, in the Application, to determine the reparation which must be made by Nicaragua, in particular in relation to any measures of the kind referred to in the paragraph above.

As the basis for the jurisdiction of the Court, the Applicant invokes Article 36, paragraph 1, of the Statute of the Court by virtue of the operation of Article XXXI of the American Treaty on Pacific Settlement of 30 April 1948 ("Pact of Bogotá"), as well as the declarations of acceptance made by Costa Rica on 20 February 1973 and by Nicaragua on 24 September 1929 (modified on 23 October 2001), pursuant to Article 36, paragraph 2, of the Statute of the Court.

On 18 November 2010, Costa Rica also filed a request for the indication of provisional measures, in which it stated that

"Costa Rica's rights which are subject of the dispute and of this request for provisional measures are its right to sovereignty, to territorial integrity and to non-interference with its rights over the San Juan River, its lands, its environmentally protected areas, as well as the integrity and flow of the Colorado River".

Costa Rica also indicated that the protection of its rights was of real urgency and pointed out that "[t]here is a real risk that without a grant of provisional measures, action prejudicial to the rights of Costa Rica will continue and may significantly alter the factual situation on the ground before the Court has the opportunity to render its final decision".

Costa Rica accordingly

"requests the Court as a matter of urgency to order the following provisional measures so as to rectify the presently ongoing breach of Costa Rica's territorial integrity and to prevent further irreparable harm to Costa Rica's territory, pending its determination of this case on the merits:

(1) the immediate and unconditional withdrawal of all Nicaraguan troops from the unlawfully invaded and occupied Costa Rican territories;

(2) the immediate cessation of the construction of a canal across Costa Rican territory;

(3) the immediate cessation of the felling of trees, removal of vegetation and soil from Costa Rican territory, including its wetlands and forests;

(4) the immediate cessation of the dumping of sediment in Costa Rican territory;

(5) the suspension of Nicaragua's ongoing dredging programme, aimed at the occupation, flooding and damage of Costa Rican territory, as well as at the serious damage to and impairment of the navigation of the Colorado River, giving full effect to the Cleveland Award and pending the determination of the merits of this dispute;

(6) that Nicaragua shall refrain from any other action which might prejudice the rights of Costa Rica, or which may aggravate or extend the dispute before the Court."

Public hearings on the request for the indication of provisional measures submitted by Costa Rica were held from 11 to 13 January 2011.

At the close of its second round of oral observations, the Agent of Costa Rica set out the provisional measures requested by that State as follows:

"Costa Rica requests the Court to order the following provisional measures:

A. Pending the determination of this case on the merits, Nicaragua shall not, in the area comprising the entirety of Isla Portillos, that is to say, across the right bank of the San Juan River and between the banks of the Laguna los Portillos (also known as Harbour Head Lagoon) and the Taura River ('the relevant area'):

(1)   station any of its troops or other personnel;
(2)   engage in the construction or enlargement of a canal;
(3)   fell trees or remove vegetation or soil;
(4)   dump sediment.

B.   Pending the determination of this case on the merits, Nicaragua shall suspend its ongoing dredging programme in the River San Juan adjacent to the relevant area.
C.   Pending the determination of this case on the merits, Nicaragua shall refrain from any other action which might prejudice the rights of Costa Rica, or which may aggravate or extend the dispute before the Court."

At the close of its second round of oral observations, the Agent of Nicaragua presented the following submissions on behalf of his Government:

> "In accordance with Article 60 of the Rules of Court and having regard to the request for the indication of provisional measures of the Republic of Costa Rica and its oral pleadings, the Republic of Nicaragua respectfully submits that, [f]or the reasons explained during these hearings and any other reasons the Court might deem appropriate, the Republic of Nicaragua asks the Court to dismiss the request for provisional measures filed by the Republic of Costa Rica."

On 8 March 2011, the Court delivered its decision on the request for the indication of provisional measures submitted by Costa Rica (*I.C.J. Reports 2011 (I)*, p. 6). In its Order, the Court indicated the following provisional measures:

> "(1) Unanimously,
>
> Each Party shall refrain from sending to, or maintaining in the disputed territory, including the *caño* [the canal cut by Nicaragua], any personnel, whether civilian, police or security;
>
> (2) By thirteen votes to four,
>
> Notwithstanding point (1) above, Costa Rica may dispatch civilian personnel charged with the protection of the environment to the disputed territory, including the *caño*, but only in so far as it is necessary to avoid irreparable prejudice being caused to the part of the wetland where that territory is situated; Costa Rica shall consult with the Secretariat of the Ramsar Convention in regard to these actions, give Nicaragua prior notice of them and use its best endeavours to find common solutions with Nicaragua in this respect;
>
> IN FAVOUR: *President* Owada; *Vice-President* Tomka; *Judges* Koroma, Al-Khasawneh, Simma, Abraham, Keith, Bennouna, Cançado Trindade, Yusuf, Greenwood, Donoghue; *Judge* ad hoc Dugard;
>
> AGAINST: *Judges* Sepúlveda-Amor, Skotnikov, Xue; *Judge* ad hoc Guillaume;

(3) Unanimously,

Each Party shall refrain from any action which might aggravate or extend the dispute before the Court or make it more difficult to resolve;

(4) Unanimously,

Each Party shall inform the Court as to its compliance with the above provisional measures."

*

Judges Koroma and Sepúlveda-Amor appended separate opinions to the Order. Judges Skotnikov, Greenwood and Xue appended declarations to the Order. Judge *ad hoc* Guillaume appended a declaration to the Order. Judge *ad hoc* Dugard appended a separate opinion to the Order.

The full text of the Order is available on the website of the Court under "Contentious Cases". Please note that in this case, the document entitled "Summary 2011/1", available online, also provides summaries of Judges' opinions and declarations.

By an Order of 5 April 2011, the Court, taking account of the views of the Parties, fixed 5 December 2011 and 6 August 2012 respectively, as the time-limits for the filing of a Memorial by the Republic of Costa Rica and a Counter-Memorial by the Republic of Nicaragua.

Those pleadings were filed within the time-limits thus fixed.

In its Counter-Memorial, Nicaragua submitted four counter-claims. In its first counter-claim, it requested the Court to declare that Costa Rica bore responsibility to Nicaragua for "the impairment and possible destruction of navigation on the San Juan River caused by the construction of a road next to its right bank" by Costa Rica. In its second counter-claim, Nicaragua asked the Court to declare that it had become the sole sovereign over the area formerly occupied by the Bay of San Juan del Norte. In its third counter-claim, it requested the Court to find that Nicaragua had a right to free navigation on the Colorado Branch of the San Juan de Nicaragua River, until the conditions of navigability existing at the time when the 1858 Treaty was concluded were re-established. In its fourth counter-claim, Nicaragua alleged that Costa Rica had failed to implement the provisional measures indicated by the Court in its Order of 8 March 2011.

By two separate Orders dated 17 April 2013, the Court joined the proceedings in the case concerning *Certain Activities Carried Out by Nicaragua in the Border Area (Costa Rica v. Nicaragua)* (hereinafter "the *Costa Rica* v. *Nicaragua* case") and in the case concerning the *Construction of a Road in Costa Rica along the San Juan River (Nicaragua v. Costa Rica)* (hereinafter "the *Nicaragua* v. *Costa Rica* case"). In those two Orders, the Court emphasized that it had so proceeded "in conformity with the principle of the sound administration of justice and with the need for judicial economy".

By an Order dated 18 April 2013, the Court ruled on the four counter-claims submitted by Nicaragua in its Counter-Memorial filed in the *Costa Rica* v. *Nicaragua* case. In that Order, the Court found, unanimously, that there was no need for it to adjudicate on the admissibility of Nicaragua's first counter-claim as such, since that claim had become without object by reason of the fact that the proceedings in the *Costa Rica* v. *Nicaragua* and *Nicaragua* v. *Costa Rica* cases had been joined. That claim will therefore be examined as a principal claim within the context of the joined proceedings. The Court also unanimously found that the second and third counter-claims were inadmissible as such and did not form part of the current proceedings, since there was no direct connection, either in fact or in law, between those claims and the principal claims of Costa Rica. In its Order, the Court lastly found, unanimously, that there was no need for it to entertain the fourth counter-claim as such, since the question of compliance by both Parties with provisional measures may be considered in the principal proceedings, irrespective of whether or not the respondent State raised that issue by way of a counter-claim and that, consequently, the Parties could take up any question relating to the implementation of the provisional measures indicated by the Court in the further course of the proceedings.

On 23 May 2013, Costa Rica presented the Court with a request for the modification of the Order of 8 March 2011. That request made reference to Article 41 of the Statute of the Court and Article 76 of the Rules of Court.

In the first place, Costa Rica complained of "Nicaragua's sending to the disputed area . . . and maintaining thereon large numbers of persons" and, secondly, of the "activities undertaken by those persons affecting that territory and its ecology". In Costa Rica's view, those actions, which had occurred since the Court decided to indicate provisional measures, created a new situation necessitating the modification of the Order of 8 March 2011, in the form of further provisional measures, in particular so as to prevent the presence of any individual in the disputed territory other than civilian personnel sent by Costa Rica and charged with the protection of the environment.

The Court immediately communicated a copy of the said request to the Government of Nicaragua.

By letters dated 24 May 2013, the Registrar of the Court informed the Parties that the time-limit for the filing of any written observations that Nicaragua might wish to present on Costa Rica's request had been fixed as 14 June 2013.

In its written observations, filed within the time-limit thus prescribed, Nicaragua asked the Court to reject Costa Rica's request, while in its turn requesting the Court to modify or adapt the Order of 8 March 2011 on the basis of Article 76 of the Rules of Court.

Nicaragua considered that there had been a change in the factual and legal situations in question as a result of, first, the construction by Costa Rica of a 160-km-long road along the right bank of the San Juan River and, second, the joinder, by the Court, of the proceedings in the two cases. Consequently, Nicaragua asked the Court to modify its Order of 8 March 2011, in particular to allow both Parties (and not only Costa Rica) to dispatch civilian personnel charged with the protection of the environment to the disputed territory.

A copy of Nicaragua's written observations and request was transmitted to Costa Rica, which was informed that the time-limit for the filing of any written observations that it might wish to present on the said request had been fixed as 20 June 2013.

In its written observations, filed within the time-limit thus prescribed, Costa Rica asserted that no part of the road in question was in the disputed area and considered that the joinder of the proceedings in the *Costa Rica* v. *Nicaragua* and *Nicaragua* v. *Costa Rica* cases "does not mean that there is now one proceeding which should be the subject of joint Orders". Consequently, it asked the Court to reject Nicaragua's request.

In its Order of 16 July 2013 (see *I.C.J. Reports 2013*, p. 230), the Court,

> "(1) By fifteen votes to two,
>
> *[Found]* that the circumstances, as they [then] present[ed] themselves to the Court, [were] not such as to require the exercise of its power to modify the measures indicated in the Order of 8 March 2011;
>
> IN FAVOUR: *President* Tomka; *Vice-President* Sepúlveda-Amor; *Judges* Owada, Abraham, Keith, Bennouna, Skotnikov, Yusuf, Greenwood, Xue, Donoghue, Gaja, Sebutinde, Bhandari; *Judge* ad hoc Guillaume;
>
> AGAINST: *Judge* Cançado Trindade; *Judge* ad hoc Dugard;
>
> (2) Unanimously,
>
> *Reaffirm[ed]* the provisional measures indicated in its Order of 8 March 2011, in particular the requirement that the Parties 'sh[ould] refrain from any action which might aggravate or extend the dispute before the Court or make it more difficult to resolve'".

The Court reminded the Parties once again that "these measures ha[d] binding effect . . . and therefore create[d] international legal obligations which each [of them was] required to comply with". Finally, the Court underlined that its Order of 16 July 2013 was without prejudice as to any finding on the merits concerning the Parties' compliance with its Order of 8 March 2011.

*

Judge Cançado Trindade appended a dissenting opinion to the Order of the Court; Judge *ad hoc* Dugard appended a dissenting opinion to the Order of the Court.

The full text of the Order and the attached opinions are available on the website of the Court. A summary of these texts is also available online (see "Summary 2013/18").

10. *Request for Interpretation of the Judgment of 15 June 1962 in the Case concerning the* Temple of Preah Vihear (Cambodia *v.* Thailand) *(Cambodia* v. *Thailand)*

On 28 April 2011, the Kingdom of Cambodia submitted, by an Application filed in the Registry of the Court, a request for interpretation of the Judgment rendered by the Court on 15 June 1962 in the case concerning the *Temple of Preah Vihear (Cambodia* v. *Thailand)*.

In its Application, Cambodia indicates the "points in dispute as to the meaning or scope of the Judgment", as stipulated by Article 98 of the Rules of Court. It states in particular that:

"(1) according to Cambodia, the Judgment [rendered by the Court in 1962] is based on the prior existence of an international boundary established and recognized by both States;

(2) according to Cambodia, that boundary is defined by the map to which the Court refers on page 21 of its Judgment . . ., a map which enables the Court to find that Cambodia's sovereignty over the Temple is a direct and automatic consequence of its sovereignty over the territory on which the Temple is situated . . .;

(3) according to . . . [Cambodia], Thailand is under an obligation [pursuant to the Judgment] to withdraw any military or other personnel from the vicinity of the Temple on Cambodian territory. [T]his is a general and continuing obligation deriving from the statements concerning Cambodia's territorial sovereignty recognized by the Court in that region."

Cambodia asserts that "Thailand disagrees with all of these points". The Applicant seeks to base the jurisdiction of the Court on Article 60 of the Statute of the Court, which provides that "[i]n the event of dispute as to the meaning or scope of the judgment, the Court shall construe it upon the request of any party". Cambodia also invokes Article 98 of the Rules of Court.

It explains in its Application that, while "Thailand does not dispute Cambodia's sovereignty over the Temple — and only over the Temple itself", it does, however, call into question the 1962 Judgment in its entirety.

Cambodia contends that "in 1962, the Court placed the Temple under Cambodian sovereignty, because the territory on which it is situated is on the Cambodian side of the boundary", and that "[t]o refuse Cambodia's sovereignty over the area beyond the Temple as far as its 'vicinity' is to say to the Court that the boundary line which it recognized [in 1962] is wholly erroneous, *including in respect of the Temple itself*".

Cambodia emphasizes that the purpose of its request is to seek an explanation from the Court regarding the "meaning and . . . scope of its judgment, within the limit laid down by Article 60 of the Statute". It adds that such an explanation, "which would be binding on Cambodia and Thailand, . . . could then serve as a basis for a final resolution of this dispute through negotiation or any other peaceful means".

Regarding the facts underlying its Application, Cambodia recalls that it instituted proceedings against Thailand in 1959, and that certain problems arose after the Court had given judgment on the merits in 1962. It goes on to describe the more recent events which directly motivated the present Application (failure of endeavours aimed at achieving agreement between the two States on a joint interpretation of the 1962 Judgment; deterioration in relations following "discussions within UNESCO to have the Temple declared a World Heritage Site"; armed incidents between the two States in April 2011).

At the close of its Application, Cambodia asks the Court to adjudge and declare that

> "[t]he obligation incumbent upon Thailand to 'withdraw any military or police forces, or other guards or keepers, stationed by her at the Temple, or in its vicinity on Cambodian territory' [point 2 of the operative clause of the Judgment rendered by the Court in 1962] is a particular consequence of the general and continuing obligation to respect the integrity of the territory of Cambodia, that territory having been delimited in the area of the Temple and its vicinity by the line on the map [referred to on page 21 of the Judgment], on which [the Judgment] is based."

On the same day, Cambodia also filed a request for the indication of provisional measures, pursuant to Article 41 of the Statute and Article 73 of the Rules of Court. The Applicant explained that "[s]ince 22 April 2011, serious incidents have occurred in the area of the Temple of Preah Vihear, . . . as well as at several locations along that boundary between the two States, causing fatalities, injuries and the evacuation of local inhabitants".

Cambodia stated that "[s]erious armed incidents are continuing at the time of filing . . . [its] request [for interpretation], for which Thailand is entirely responsible".

According to the Applicant, "[m]easures are urgently required, both to safeguard the rights of Cambodia pending the Court's decision — rights relating to its sovereignty, its territorial integrity and to the duty of non-interference incumbent upon Thailand — and to avoid aggravation of the dispute". Cambodia further explained that, "in the unfortunate event that its request were to be rejected, and if Thailand persisted in its conduct, the damage to the Temple of Preah Vihear, as well as irremediable losses of life and human suffering as a result of these armed clashes, would become worse".

In conclusion, Cambodia:

> "respectfully [requested] the Court to indicate the following provisional measures, pending the delivery of its judgment on the request for interpretation:
>
> — an immediate and unconditional withdrawal of all Thai forces from those parts of Cambodian territory situated in the area of the Temple of Preah Vihear;
> — a ban on all military activity by Thailand in the area of the Temple of Preah Vihear;
> — that Thailand refrain from any act or action which could interfere with the rights of Cambodia or aggravate the dispute in the principal proceedings."

Furthermore, "[b]ecause of the gravity of the situation, and for the reasons expressed above, Cambodia respectfully request[ed] the Court to indicate these measures as a matter of urgency, and to fix a date as soon as possible for the subsequent proceedings".

Public hearings on the request for the indication of provisional measures filed by Cambodia were held on Monday, 30 and Tuesday, 31 May 2011.

At the close of the second round of oral observations, Cambodia reiterated its request for the indication of provisional measures; the Agent of Thailand, for his part, presented the following submissions on behalf of his Government:

> "[i]n accordance with Article 60 of the Rules of Court and having regard to the Request for the indication of provisional measures of the Kingdom of Cambodia and its oral pleadings, the Kingdom of Thailand respectfully requests the Court to remove the case introduced by the Kingdom of Cambodia on 28 April 2011 from the General List".

On 18 July 2011, the Court delivered its Order (*I.C.J. Reports 2011 (II)*, p. 537) on the request for the indication of provisional measures submitted by Cambodia.

The operative part of the Order reads as follows:

> "For these reasons,
>
> THE COURT,
>
> (A) Unanimously,
>
> *Rejects* the Kingdom of Thailand's request to remove the case introduced by the Kingdom of Cambodia on 28 April 2011 from the General List of the Court;

(B) *Indicates* the following provisional measures:

(1) By eleven votes to five,

Both Parties shall immediately withdraw their military personnel currently present in the provisional demilitarized zone, as defined in paragraph 62 of the present Order, and refrain from any military presence within that zone and from any armed activity directed at that zone;

IN FAVOUR: *Vice-President* Tomka; *Judges* Koroma, Simma, Abraham, Keith, Bennouna, Skotnikov, Cançado Trindade, Yusuf, Greenwood; *Judge* ad hoc Guillaume;

AGAINST: *President* Owada; *Judges* Al-Khasawneh, Xue, Donoghue; *Judge* ad hoc Cot;

(2) By fifteen votes to one,

Thailand shall not obstruct Cambodia's free access to the Temple of Preah Vihear or Cambodia's provision of fresh supplies to its non-military personnel in the Temple;

IN FAVOUR: *President* Owada; *Vice-President* Tomka; *Judges* Koroma, Al-Khasawneh, Simma, Abraham, Keith, Bennouna, Skotnikov, Cançado Trindade, Yusuf, Greenwood, Xue; *Judges* ad hoc Guillaume, Cot;

AGAINST: *Judge* Donoghue;

(3) By fifteen votes to one,

Both Parties shall continue the co-operation which they have entered into within ASEAN and, in particular, allow the observers appointed by that organization to have access to the provisional demilitarized zone;

IN FAVOUR: *President* Owada; *Vice-President* Tomka; *Judges* Koroma, Al-Khasawneh, Simma, Abraham, Keith, Bennouna, Skotnikov, Cançado Trindade, Yusuf, Greenwood, Xue; *Judges* ad hoc Guillaume, Cot;

AGAINST: *Judge* Donoghue;

(4) By fifteen votes to one,

Both Parties shall refrain from any action which might aggravate or extend the dispute before the Court or make it more difficult to resolve;

IN FAVOUR: *President* Owada; *Vice-President* Tomka; *Judges* Koroma, Al-Khasawneh, Simma, Abraham, Keith, Bennouna, Skotnikov, Cançado Trindade, Yusuf, Greenwood, Xue; *Judges* ad hoc Guillaume, Cot;

AGAINST: *Judge* Donoghue;

(C) By fifteen votes to one,

Decides that each Party shall inform the Court as to its compliance with the above provisional measures;

IN FAVOUR: *President* Owada; *Vice-President* Tomka; *Judges* Koroma, Al-Khasawneh, Simma, Abraham, Keith, Bennouna, Skotnikov, Cançado Trindade, Yusuf, Greenwood, Xue; *Judges* ad hoc Guillaume, Cot;

AGAINST: *Judge* Donoghue;

(D) By fifteen votes to one,

Decides that, until the Court has rendered its judgment on the request for interpretation, it shall remain seised of the matters which form the subject of this Order.

IN FAVOUR: *President* Owada; *Vice-President* Tomka; *Judges* Koroma, Al-Khasawneh, Simma, Abraham, Keith, Bennouna, Skotnikov, Cançado Trindade, Yusuf, Greenwood, Xue; *Judges* ad hoc Guillaume, Cot;

AGAINST: *Judge* Donoghue."

*

President Owada appended a dissenting opinion to the Order of the Court; Judge Koroma appended a declaration to the Order of the Court; Judge Al-Khasawneh appended a dissenting opinion to the Order of the Court; Judge Cançado Trindade appended a separate opinion to the Order of the Court; Judges Xue and Donoghue appended dissenting opinions to the Order of the Court; Judge *ad hoc* Guillaume appended a declaration to the Order of the Court; Judge *ad hoc* Cot appended a dissenting opinion to the Order of the Court.

The full text of the Order and a summary are available on the website of the Court under the case name. Annexed to this summary (entitled "Summary 2011/5") are summaries of declarations and individual opinions.

By letters dated 24 November 2011, the Registrar of the Court informed the Parties that the Court had decided to afford them the opportunity of furnishing further written explanations, pursuant to Article 98, paragraph 4, of the Rules of Court, and had fixed 8 March 2012 and 21 June 2012 as the respective time-limits for the filing by Cambodia and Thailand of such explanations. The further written explanations were filed within the time-limits thus fixed.

Public hearings on the merits of the case were held from 15 to 19 April 2013.

At the conclusion of those hearings, the Parties presented the following final submissions to the Court:

On behalf of Cambodia:

"Rejecting the submissions of the Kingdom of Thailand, and on the basis of the foregoing, Cambodia respectfully asks the Court, under Article 60 of its Statute, to respond to Cambodia's Request for interpretation of its Judgment of 15 June 1962.

In Cambodia's view: 'the Temple of Preah Vihear is situated in territory under the sovereignty of Cambodia' (first paragraph of the operative clause), which is the legal consequence of the fact that the Temple is situated on the Cambodian side of the frontier, as that frontier was recognized by the Court in its Judgment. Therefore, the obligation incumbent upon Thailand to 'withdraw any military or police forces, or other guards or keepers, stationed by her at the Temple, or in its vicinity on Cambodian territory' (second paragraph of the operative clause) is a particular consequence of the general and continuing obligation to respect the integrity of the territory of Cambodia, that territory having been delimited in the region of the Temple and its vicinity by the line on the Annex I map, on which the Judgment of the Court is based."

On behalf of Thailand:

"In accordance with Article 60 of the Rules of Court and having regard to the Request for interpretation of the Kingdom of Cambodia and its written and oral pleadings, and in view of the written and oral pleadings of the Kingdom of Thailand, the Kingdom of Thailand requests the Court to adjudge and declare:

— that the Request of the Kingdom of Cambodia asking the Court to interpret the Judgment of 15 June 1962 in the case concerning the *Temple of Preah Vihear (Cambodia v. Thailand)* under Article 60 of the Statute of the Court does not satisfy the conditions laid down in that Article and that, consequently, the Court has no jurisdiction to respond to that Request and/or that the Request is inadmissible;

— in the alternative, that there are no grounds to grant Cambodia's Request to construe the Judgment and that there is no reason to interpret the Judgment of 1962; and

— to formally declare that the 1962 Judgment does not determine with binding force the boundary line between the Kingdom of Thailand and the Kingdom of Cambodia, nor does it fix the limit of the vicinity of the Temple."

The Court will deliver its Judgment on the merits of the case at a public sitting, the date of which will be announced in due course.

11. Construction of a Road in Costa Rica along the San Juan River (Nicaragua v. Costa Rica)

On 22 December 2011, the Republic of Nicaragua instituted proceedings against the Republic of Costa Rica with regard to "violations of Nicaraguan sovereignty and major environmental damages to its territory". Nicaragua contends that Costa Rica is carrying out major construction works along most of the border area between the two countries with grave environmental consequences.

In its Application, Nicaragua claims *inter alia* that "Costa Rica's unilateral actions . . . threaten to destroy the San Juan de Nicaragua River and its fragile ecosystem, including the adjacent biosphere reserves and internationally protected wetlands that depend upon the clean and uninterrupted flow of the river for their survival". According to the Applicant, "[t]he most immediate threat to the river and its environment is posed by Costa Rica's construction of a road running parallel and in extremely close proximity to the southern bank of the river, and extending for a distance of at least 120 kilometres, from Los Chiles in the west to Delta in the east". It is also stated in the Application that "[t]hese works have already caused and will continue to cause significant economic damage to Nicaragua".

Nicaragua accordingly:

"requests the Court to adjudge and declare that Costa Rica has breached:

   (a) its obligation not to violate Nicaragua's territorial integrity as delimited by the 1858 Treaty of Limits, the Cleveland Award of 1888 and the five Awards of the Umpire EP Alexander of 30 September 1897, 20 December 1897, 22 March 1898, 26 July 1899 and 10 March 1900;
   (b) its obligation not to damage Nicaraguan territory;
   (c) its obligations under general international law and the relevant environmental conventions, including the Ramsar Convention on Wetlands, the Agreement over the Border Protected Areas between Nicaragua and Costa Rica (International System of Protected Areas for Peace [SI-A-PAZ] Agreement), the Convention on Biological Diversity and the Convention for the Conservation of the Biodiversity and Protection of the Main Wild Life Sites in Central America."

Furthermore, Nicaragua requests the Court to adjudge and declare that Costa Rica must:

   "(a) restore the situation to the *status quo ante*;
   (b) pay for all damages caused including the costs added to the dredging of the San Juan River;
   (c) not undertake any future development in the area without an appropriate transboundary Environmental Impact Assessment and that this assessment must be presented in a timely fashion to Nicaragua for its analysis and reaction."

Finally, Nicaragua requests the Court to adjudge and declare that Costa Rica must:

> "(a) cease all the constructions underway that affect or may affect the rights of Nicaragua;
> (b) produce and present to Nicaragua an adequate Environmental Impact Assessment with all the details of the works."

As the basis for the jurisdiction of the Court, the Applicant invokes Article 36, paragraph 1, of the Statute of the Court by virtue of the operation of Article XXXI of the American Treaty on Pacific Settlement of 30 April 1948 (Pact of Bogotá), as well as the declarations of acceptance made by Nicaragua on 24 September 1929 (modified on 23 October 2001) and by Costa Rica on 20 February 1973, pursuant to Article 36, paragraph 2, of the Statute of the Court.

Nicaragua asserts that Costa Rica has repeatedly refused to give Nicaragua appropriate information on the construction works it is undertaking and has denied that it has any obligation to prepare and provide to Nicaragua an Environmental Impact Assessment, which would allow for an evaluation of the works. The Applicant therefore requests the Court to order Costa Rica to produce such a document and to communicate it to Nicaragua. It adds that "in all circumstances and particularly if this request does not produce results, [it] reserves its right to formally request provisional measures".

Nicaragua also states that as "the legal and factual grounds of the [Application] are connected to the ongoing case concerning *Certain Activities Carried Out by Nicaragua in the Border Area (Costa Rica v. Nicaragua)*", it "reserves its rights to consider in a subsequent phase of the present proceedings . . . whether to request that the proceedings in both cases should be joined".

By an Order of 23 January 2012, the Court fixed 19 December 2012 and 19 December 2013 as the respective time-limits for the filing of a Memorial by Nicaragua and a Counter-Memorial by Costa Rica.

The Memorial of Nicaragua was filed within the time-limit thus fixed.

By two separate Orders dated 17 April 2013 (see *I.C.J. Reports 2013*, pp. 166 and 184), the Court joined the proceedings in the *Costa Rica v. Nicaragua* and the *Nicaragua v. Costa Rica* cases. In those two Orders, the Court emphasized that it had so "in conformity with the principle of the sound administration of justice and with the need for judicial economy".

In the context of those joined proceedings, the Court, by an Order dated 18 April 2013 (see *I.C.J. Reports 2013*, p. 200), ruled on the counter-claims submitted by Nicaragua in its Counter-Memorial filed in the *Costa Rica v. Nicaragua case*.

In those same joined proceedings, the Court, by an Order dated 16 July 2013, (see *ibid.*, p. 230), ruled on the requests made by Costa Rica and

Nicaragua, respectively, for the modification of the provisional measures indicated by the Court on 8 March 2011 in the *Costa Rica* v. *Nicaragua* case.

12. *Obligation to Negotiate Access to the Pacific Ocean* (*Bolivia* v. *Chile*)

On 24 April 2013, Bolivia instituted proceedings against Chile concerning a dispute in relation to "Chile's obligation to negotiate in good faith and effectively with Bolivia in order to reach an agreement granting Bolivia a fully sovereign access to the Pacific Ocean".

Bolivia's Application contains a summary of the facts — starting from the independence of that country in 1825 and continuing until the present day — which, according to Bolivia, constitute "the main relevant facts on which [its] claim is based".

In its Application, Bolivia stated that the subject of the dispute lies in: "*(a)* the existence of [the above-mentioned] obligation, *(b)* the non-compliance with that obligation by Chile and *(c)* Chile's duty to comply with the said obligation".

Bolivia asserted, *inter alia*, that "beyond its general obligations under international law, Chile has committed itself, more specifically through agreements, diplomatic practice and a series of declarations attributable to its highest-level representatives, to negotiate a sovereign access to the sea for Bolivia". According to Bolivia, "Chile has not complied with this obligation and . . . denies the existence of its obligation".

Bolivia accordingly requested the Court "to adjudge and declare that:

> *(a)* Chile has the obligation to negotiate with Bolivia in order to reach an agreement granting Bolivia a fully sovereign access to the Pacific Ocean;
>
> *(b)* Chile has breached the said obligation;
>
> *(c)* Chile must perform the said obligation in good faith, promptly, formally, within a reasonable time and effectively, to grant Bolivia a fully sovereign access to the Pacific Ocean."

As the basis for the jurisdiction of the Court, the Applicant invokes Article XXXI of the American Treaty on Pacific Settlement ("Pact of Bogotá") of 30 April 1948, to which both States are parties.

At the end of its Application, Bolivia "reserve[d] the right to request that an arbitral tribunal be established in accordance with the obligation under Article XII of the Treaty of Peace and Friendship concluded with Chile on 20 October 1904 and the Protocol of 16 April 1907, in the case of any claims arising out of the said Treaty".

By an Order dated 18 June 2013, the Court fixed 17 April 2014 and 18 February 2015 as the respective time-limits for the filing of the Memorial of Bolivia and the Counter-Memorial of Chile. The subsequent procedure was reserved for further decision.

II. ACTION PURSUANT TO DECISIONS OF THE COURT

The present heading contains the information received in the Registry between 1 August 2012 and 31 July 2013 concerning action taken pursuant to certain decisions of the Court. The Registry, which does not take the initiative of seeking such information, publishes it without comment as and when it is received and can accept no responsibility in connection with it.

Legality of the Threat or Use of Nuclear Weapons

By a note dated 15 October 1996 the Secretary-General of the United Nations transmitted the text of the Advisory Opinion given by the Court on 8 July 1996 to the General Assembly (United Nations doc. A/51/218).

In December of that year, and every year since, this text has been the subject of a new General Assembly resolution, of which the full text has been reproduced in the relevant *I.C.J. Yearbook*. The history of these resolutions (1996-2012) can be found in Annex 29, page 220 of this *Yearbook*.

The latest resolution (A/RES/67/33), on the subject of this Advisory Opinion was rendered by the General Assembly during its 48th plenary meeting of its 67th session held on 3 December 2012. The General Assembly adopted the resolution by a recorded vote of 135 in favour to 22 against, with 26 abstentions (see press release GA/11321 published by the General Assembly on 3 December 2012). The full text of resolution 67/33 can be found in Annex 30, page 221 of this *Yearbook*.

III. VISITS AND EVENTS

A. Visits

1. Visit by Mr. Ivan Gašparovič, President of Slovakia

On 21 November 2012, the Court was visited by Mr. Ivan Gašparovič, President of Slovakia, accompanied by a sizeable delegation. Mr. Gašparovič and his delegation were welcomed on their arrival by the President of the Court, Judge Peter Tomka, and by the Registrar, Mr. Philippe Couvreur. The President of Slovakia and his delegation were then given a tour of the Peace Palace, and, in particular, of the refurbished Great Hall of Justice, after which an exchange of views took place focusing on the functioning and jurisprudence of the Court.

2. Visit by Ms Anouchka van Miltenburg, President of the House of Representatives of the Netherlands

On 18 March 2013, Ms Anouchka van Miltenburg, President of the House of Representatives of the Netherlands, paid a visit to the Court.

She was accompanied by the Mayor of The Hague, Mr. Jozias van Aartsen. During their meeting with President Tomka and the Registrar, they addressed such topics as future trends in international justice, the role of the Court and the support received by the Court from the host country's authorities.

3. Visit by Prince Bander bin Salman Al Saud from Saudi Arabia

On 28 March 2013, the Court was visited by Prince Bander bin Salman Al Saud from Saudi Arabia and his seven-member delegation. The Prince and his delegation had a meeting with the President and the Registrar on the functioning of the Court and the prospects for co-operation between the Court and Saudi Arabia. The Prince put forward the idea of having the Court's judgments translated into Arabic by Saudi translators. This proposal was welcomed by his hosts.

4. Visit by the Secretary-General of the United Nations, Mr. Ban Ki-moon

On 7 April 2013, the Court received the Secretary-General of the United Nations, Mr. Ban Ki-moon, for a working dinner. He was accompanied, in particular, by Ms Patricia O'Brien, Under-Secretary-General for Legal Affairs. President Tomka, Vice-President Bernardo Sepúlveda-Amor, Judge Dalveer Bhandari and the Registrar of the Court, Mr. Couvreur, were present at that dinner. Conversation focused on the mission and functioning of the Court, the cases brought before it and its most recent decisions. The Secretary-General used the occasion to reaffirm his complete confidence in the Court's contribution to peace and international justice. He also expressed his firm belief that justice is an essential prerequisite to any form of lasting peace. At the close of the meeting, the Secretary-General signed the Court's Visitors' Book.

5. Visit by Mr. Joachim Gauck, President of the Federal Republic of Germany

On 30 May 2013, the Court received a visit from Mr. Joachim Gauck, President of the Federal Republic of Germany, accompanied by a large delegation. He was welcomed by Vice-President Sepúlveda-Amor, Acting President, and by the Registrar of the Court, Mr. Couvreur. Mr. Gauck and his delegation then held discussions with the Vice-President, other Members of the Court and the Registrar in the Chamber in which the Court meets prior to hearings. Questions addressed included, in particular, the Court's contribution to the promotion of human rights. Following this exchange of views, President Gauck signed the Court's Visitors' Book.

6. Other Visits

In addition, during the period under review, the President and Members of the Court, as well as the Registrar and Registry officials, welcomed a large number of dignitaries, including members of governments, diplomats, parliamentary representatives, presidents and members of judicial bodies and other senior officials, to the seat of the Court.

There were also many visits by researchers, academics, lawyers and other members of the legal profession, and journalists, among others. Presentations on the Court were made during several of these visits.

B. Events

1. The International Day of Peace

On Friday, 21 September 2012, the International Day of Peace was celebrated at the Peace Palace in The Hague, seat of the International Court of Justice. The ceremony, organized by the City of The Hague and the Carnegie Foundation, was attended by H.E. Judge Bernardo Sepúlveda-Amor, Vice-President of the International Court of Justice, H.E. Mr. Philippe Couvreur, Registrar of the Court, ambassadors, representatives of the Dutch authorities, officials from various international organizations and hundreds of children from local schools. During the ceremony, speeches were made by Judge Bernardo Sepúlveda-Amor, the Mayor of The Hague, Mr. Jozias van Aartsen, and the Chairman of the Board of Directors of the Carnegie Foundation, which owns the Peace Palace, Mr. Bernard Bot. At the end of the ceremony, the schoolchildren released white balloons into the air and the Mayor of The Hague gave the starting signal for a "Peace Walk" through the streets of The Hague, igniting the Torch of Peace.

2. Fifth "Open Day" at the Court

On Sunday, 23 September 2012, the Court welcomed several hundreds of visitors as part of "The Hague International Day". This was the fifth time that the Court had taken part in this event, organized in conjunction with the Municipality of The Hague and aimed at introducing the general public to the international organizations based in the city and surrounding area. The Information Department screened (in English and in French) the film about the Court produced by the Registry, gave presentations and answered visitors' questions (in English, French and Dutch). It also distributed various information brochures.

IV. ANNUAL REPORT AND REPRESENTATION OF THE COURT AT THE SEAT OF THE UNITED NATIONS

During the period under review, the President of the Court, Judge Peter Tomka, addressed representatives of the United Nations Member States assembled in New York for the 29th plenary meeting of the Sixty-Seventh Session of the General Assembly on 1 November 2012. He was accompanied by the Registrar of the Court. President Tomka presented the Court's *Annual Report* for the period 1 August 2011 to 31 July 2012 (A/67/4).

In his address, President Tomka informed the General Assembly that over the last 12 months the Court had "continued to fulfil its role as the international community of States' forum of choice for the peaceful settlement of every kind of international dispute over which it has jurisdiction". He added that the Court had "made every effort to meet the expectations of the parties appearing before it in a timely manner" and noted in that regard that, "since the Court has been able to clear its backlog of cases, States thinking of submitting cases to the principal judicial organ of the United Nations can be confident that, as soon as they have finished their written exchanges, the Court will be able to move to the hearings without delay".

As is traditional, during the President's speech, he presented a brief overview of the judicial activities of the Court over the last 12 months, pointing out that during the period under review as many as 15 contentious cases and one advisory procedure were pending before it and that the Court had delivered four Judgments and an Advisory Opinion and had held public hearings in four cases. President Tomka also confirmed that the next hearings to be held by the Court would begin on 3 December 2012.

The President then reported on the key findings in the four Judgments and one Advisory Opinion rendered by the Court during the period under review.

President Tomka moved on to the subject of the refurbishment of the Great Hall of Justice in the Peace Palace, which he explained was "the first major renovation of th[e] Hall in 100 years". "No renovation on the scale of the current project has previously been envisaged" he said, adding that "the newly-renovated Great Hall of Justice will be equipped with improved modern technical facilities offering a wide range of possibilities". He assured those present that the Court would "continue to hear cases submitted to [it] faithfully and impartially, as required by the noble judicial mission entrusted to [it]". He further underlined that the Court was "also modernizing the setting in which [it] exercise[d] this function" thus putting the "funds mobilized by the United Nations General Assembly to good use".

President Tomka expressed his hope that "he had conveyed [to those present] the extent to which the Court seeks to meet the expectations of the international community as a whole". He noted that "the Court must do its utmost to serve the noble purposes and goals of the United Nations using limited resources, since Member States award it less than 1 per cent of the Organization's regular budget". "[T]he recent contributions of the Court are not to be measured in terms of the financial resources that sustain it, but against the great progress made by it in the advancement of international justice and the peaceful settlement of disputes between States", he concluded.

The full text of President Tomka's speech can be found in Annex 27 on page 193 of this *Yearbook*. This text, as well as the Court's *Annual Report* for the judicial year 2011-2012, are available on the Court's website, under the heading "The Court" (click on "Presidency" and "Annual Reports").

Following the presentation of the Court's Report by its President, representatives of a number of United Nations Member States made statements before the General Assembly (in the order in which these declarations were made): Iran (also speaking on behalf of the Movement of Non-Aligned Countries), Australia (also speaking on behalf of Canada and New Zealand), India, Romania, Peru, Singapore, Philippines, Japan, Italy and Norway.

A summary of these statements can be found online (www.un.org) in the press release published by the General Assembly on 1 November 2012 (GA/11305).

On 2 November 2012, President Tomka was invited to speak before the Sixth Committee of the General Assembly.

The text of this speech can be found in Annex 28 on page 203 of this *Yearbook* and on the website of the Court under "The Court/Presidency/Statements by the President".

The *Annual Report* of the Court covered by this *Yearbook* (from 1 August 2012 to 31 July 2013) will be presented by President Tomka to the General Assembly on the occasion of its sixty-eighth session, in October 2013.

V. Other Speeches, Conferences and Publications on the Work of the Court

During the period under review, the President of the Court delivered numerous speeches and addresses and made a number of official visits. He most notably delivered the following speeches:

— Statement at the conference entitled "The Judge and International Custom", organized by the Ministry of Foreign Affairs of France and the Committee of Legal Advisers on Public International Law (CAHDI) of the Council of Europe, 21 September 2012, Paris.

— Statement at the breakfast meeting hosted by the Dutch Government on the occasion of the United Nations High-Level Meeting on the Rule of Law, 24 September 2012, New York.

— Statement at the United Nations High-Level Meeting on the Rule of Law, 24 September 2012, New York.

— Statement on the occasion of the launch of the book entitled *Foreign Policy: From Conception to Diplomatic Practice* (Nijhoff, 2013) by Ambassador Ernest Petrič, 26 March 2013, Historic Reading Room at the Peace Palace.

— Statement entitled "The Role of the International Court of Justice in the Inter-State Legal Order" to students of the St. Petersburg University, 14 May 2013, St. Petersburg.

— Statement entitled "Competition and Co-operation between Legal Systems: The Role of Law in Ensuring the Development of Society, the State, and the Economy" at the plenary session

of the St. Petersburg International Legal Forum, 15 May 2013, St. Petersburg.
— Statement on the panel entitled "The Hague: International City of Peace and Justice", St. Petersburg International Legal Forum, 16 May 2013, St. Petersburg.
— Remarks and chairing panel on "Evidentiary Issues before International Tribunals" at the St. Petersburg International Legal Forum, 16 May 2013, St. Petersburg.
— Statement on the occasion of the international conference marking the closing of the public debate over Romania's possible recognition of the jurisdiction of the International Court of Justice as compulsory, 14 June 2013, Bucharest (Romanian Ministry of Foreign Affairs).
— Speech at the Sixty-Fifth Session of the International Law Commission, 18 July 2013, Geneva.

The President, Members of the Court and the Registrar regularly record video conferences on various subjects relating to international law, and the Court in particular. Produced by the Codification Division of the United Nations Office of Legal Affairs, these recordings are available to view free of charge on the website of the Audiovisual Library of International Law (www.un.org/law/avl). To find a particular speaker, click on "Faculty Directory", and the letter corresponding to the speaker's name.

VI. PEACE PALACE MUSEUM

On 17 May 1999, the Secretary-General of the United Nations, H.E. Mr. Kofi Annan, inaugurated the museum created by the International Court of Justice and situated in the south wing of the Peace Palace. Its collection presents an overview of the theme "Peace through Justice", highlighting the history of the Hague Peace Conferences of 1899 and 1907; the creation at that time of the Permanent Court of Arbitration; the subsequent construction of the Peace Palace as a seat for international justice; as well as the establishment and the functioning of the Permanent Court of International Justice and the present Court (different displays showcase the genesis of the United Nations; the Court and its Registry; the judges on the Bench; the provenance of judges and cases; the procedure of the Court; the world's legal systems; the case law of the Court; and prominent visitors).

ANNEXES

ANNEX 1

Revisions to the Rules of Court

The first Rules of Court were adopted on 6 May 1946, and were published in the volume *I.C.J. Acts and Documents No. 1* (second edition, pp. 54-83). They were based on the latest text of the Rules of the Permanent Court, that of 11 March 1936, with certain changes, formal and substantive, a list of which was given in *I.C.J. Yearbook 1946-1947* (pp. 102-103).

Although the Rules remained unchanged from 1946 to 1972, a revision was undertaken by the Court in 1967. On 10 May 1972, the Court adopted some amendments of immediate interest, involving, in particular, the partial renumbering of certain articles (a table of concordance was published in *I.C.J. Yearbook 1971-1972*, pp. 3-11). The amended and partly renumbered Rules came into force on 1 September 1972 (published in the volume *I.C.J. Acts and Documents No. 3*, pp. 93-149).

The work of revision was subsequently resumed, and culminated on 14 April 1978 in the adoption of a new set of Rules, which came into force on 1 July 1978. They were first published in *I.C.J. Acts and Documents No. 4* concurrently with the *I.C.J. Background Note V*, entitled *Note by the Registry on the Revised Rules of Court (1978)*, indicating those articles modified and containing a table of concordance comparing the new Rules to those of 1972 (published in the *I.C.J. Acts and Documents No. 3* (1972)). For additional background information, the reader is referred to pages 111-119 of the *I.C.J. Yearbook 1977-1978*, which contains an analytical table comparing the structure of the new set of Rules to those of the 1946 and 1972 sets, and a table of concordance between the specific articles of the 1946, 1972 and 1978 Rules of Court.

It was not until 2000 that the Court amended the Rules of Court again. On that occasion, two articles were amended, namely Article 79, relating to preliminary objections, and Article 80, relating to counterclaims. They came into force on 1 February 2001. The Rules of Court as adopted in 1978 have continued to apply to all cases submitted to the Court prior to 1 February 2001, and all phases of those cases.

In 2005, the Court again amended the Rules, first Article 52 and subsequently Article 43. That same year, the Court adopted a new procedure for the promulgation of modifications to its Rules (see *I.C.J. Acts and Documents No. 6*, p. 91).

ANNEX 2

The original text of the Practice Directions was made up of six Directions (numbered I to VI). It was supplemented in 2002 by the adoption of Practice Directions VII and VIII in February of that year and by Direction IX in April.

In July 2004, wishing to further enhance its productivity, the Court adopted Directions X, XI and XII. It also modified Direction V.

Two years later, in 2006, two new Directions were adopted (numbered IX*bis* and IX*ter*) and two others were amended (IX and XI).

In January 2009, the Court adopted Practice Direction XIII, also the date when it modified Practice Directions III and VI.

Changes to the text of the Practice Directions are set out in detail in the *Yearbooks* corresponding to the date of their adoption. The full text of the Practice Directions currently in force can be found on the Court's website under the headings "Basic Documents/Practice Directions" (with a note of any temporal reservations).

ANNEX 3

Chronological Survey of Proceedings before the Court since 1947

The following list provides all of the proceedings brought before the Court since 1947. In the case of proceedings instituted by means of a special agreement, the names of the parties are separated by an oblique stroke.

Title	Dates
(a) Contentious cases[1]	
Corfu Channel (United Kingdom v. *Albania)*	1947-1949
Fisheries (United Kingdom v. *Norway)*	1949-1951
Protection of French Nationals and Protected Persons in Egypt (France v. *Egypt)*	1949-1950
Asylum (Colombia/Peru)	1949-1950
Rights of Nationals of the United States of America in Morocco (France v. *United States of America)*	1950-1952
Request for Interpretation of the Judgment of 20 November 1950 in the Asylum Case (Colombia v. *Peru)*	1950
Haya de la Torre (Colombia v. *Peru)*	1950-1951
Ambatielos (Greece v. *United Kingdom)*	1951-1953
Anglo-Iranian Oil Co. (United Kingdom v. *Iran)*	1951-1952
Minquiers and Ecrehos (France/United Kingdom)	1951-1953
Nottebohm (Liechtenstein v. *Guatemala)*	1951-1955
Monetary Gold Removed from Rome in 1943 (Italy v. *France, United Kingdom and United States of America)*	1953-1954
Electricité de Beyrouth Company (France v. *Lebanon)*	1953-1954
Treatment in Hungary of Aircraft and Crew of United States of America (United States of America v. *Hungary)*	1954

---

[1] Although the total number of contentious cases that have been entered in the General List of the Court is 126, the present List shows only 124, the Court having joined the proceedings in a number of cases. This involved, firstly, the two *South West Africa* cases *(Ethiopia* v. *South Africa; Liberia* v. *South Africa)*, which were entered in the General List on 4 November 1960, under separate numbers (46 and 47, respectively); these proceedings were joined by Order of the Court on 20 May 1961, the Court having found that the submissions in the Applications and Memorials filed by the Applicant Governments were *mutatis mutandis* identical and that they were accordingly in the same interest. The Court also joined the proceedings in two cases concerning the *North Sea Continental Shelf (Federal Republic of Germany/Denmark; Federal Republic of Germany/Netherlands)*. These cases were entered in the General List of the Court on 20 February 1967 under separate numbers (51 and 52, respectively), but the proceedings were joined by Order of the Court on 26 April 1968, Denmark and the Netherlands having decided that their Applications were in the same interest.

Title	Dates
Treatment in Hungary of Aircraft and Crew of United States of America (United States of America v. *USSR)*	1954
Aerial Incident of 10 March 1953 (United States of America v. *Czechoslovakia)*	1955-1956
Antarctica (United Kingdom v. *Argentina)*	1955-1956
Antarctica (United Kingdom v. *Chile)*	1955-1956
Aerial Incident of 7 October 1952 (United States of America v. *USSR)*	1955-1956
Certain Norwegian Loans (France v. *Norway)*	1955-1957
Right of Passage over Indian Territory (Portugal v. *India)*	1955-1960
Application of the Convention of 1902 Governing the Guardianship of Infants (Netherlands v. *Sweden)*	1957-1958
Interhandel (Switzerland v. *United States of America)*	1957-1959
Aerial Incident of 27 July 1955 (Israel v. *Bulgaria)*	1957-1959
Aerial Incident of 27 July 1955 (United States of America v. *Bulgaria)*	1957-1960
Aerial Incident of 27 July 1955 (United Kingdom v. *Bulgaria)*	1957-1959
Sovereignty over Certain Frontier Land (Belgium/ Netherlands)	1957-1959
Arbitral Award Made by the King of Spain on 23 December 1906 (Honduras v. *Nicaragua)*	1958-1960
Aerial Incident of 4 September 1954 (United States of America v. *USSR)*	1958
Barcelona Traction, Light and Power Company, Limited (Belgium v. *Spain)*	1958-1961
Compagnie du Port, des Quais et des Entrepôts de Beyrouth and Société Radio-Orient (France v. *Lebanon)*	1959-1960
Aerial Incident of 7 November 1954 (United States of America v. *USSR)*	1959
Temple of Preah Vihear (Cambodia v. *Thailand)*	1959-1962
South West Africa (Ethiopia v. *South Africa; Liberia* v. *South Africa)*	1960-1966
Northern Cameroons (Cameroon v. *United Kingdom)*	1961-1963
Barcelona Traction, Light and Power Company, Limited (New Application: 1962) (Belgium v. *Spain)*	1962-1970
North Sea Continental Shelf (Federal Republic of Germany/Denmark; Federal Republic of Germany/ Netherlands)	1967-1969
Appeal Relating to the Jurisdiction of the ICAO Council (India v. *Pakistan)*	1971-1972
Fisheries Jurisdiction (United Kingdom v. *Iceland)*	1972-1974

Title	Dates
Fisheries Jurisdiction (Federal Republic of Germany v. *Iceland)*	1972-1974
Nuclear Tests (Australia v. *France)*	1973-1974
Nuclear Tests (New Zealand v. *France)*	1973-1974
Trial of Pakistani Prisoners of War (Pakistan v. *India)*	1973
Aegean Sea Continental Shelf (Greece v. *Turkey)*	1976-1978
Continental Shelf (Tunisia/Libyan Arab Jamahiriya)	1978-1982
United States Diplomatic and Consular Staff in Tehran (United States of America v. *Iran)*	1979-1981
Delimitation of the Maritime Boundary in the Gulf of Maine Area (Canada/United States of America) [case referred to a Chamber]	1981-1984
Continental Shelf (Libyan Arab Jamahiriya/Malta)	1982-1985
Frontier Dispute (Burkina Faso/Republic of Mali) [case referred to a Chamber]	1983-1986
Military and Paramilitary Activities in and against Nicaragua (Nicaragua v. *United States of America)*	1984-1991
Application for Revision and Interpretation of the Judgment of 24 February 1982 in the Case concerning the Continental Shelf (Tunisia/Libyan Arab Jamahiriya) *(Tunisia* v. *Libyan Arab Jamahiriya)*	1984-1985
Border and Transborder Armed Actions (Nicaragua v. *Costa Rica)*	1986-1987
Border and Transborder Armed Actions (Nicaragua v. *Honduras)*	1986-1992
Land, Island and Maritime Frontier Dispute (El Salvador/Honduras: Nicaragua intervening) [case referred to a Chamber] [the intervention of Nicaragua was admitted on 13 September 1990 (see *I.C.J. Yearbook 1990-1991*, pp. 160-174).]	1986-1992
Elettronica Sicula S.p.A. (ELSI) (United States of America v. *Italy)* [case referred to a Chamber]	1987-1989
Maritime Delimitation in the Area between Greenland and Jan Mayen (Denmark v. *Norway)*	1988-1993
Aerial Incident of 3 July 1988 (Islamic Republic of Iran v. *United States of America)*	1989-1996
Certain Phosphate Lands in Nauru (Nauru v. *Australia)*	1989-1993
Arbitral Award of 31 July 1989 (Guinea-Bissau v. *Senegal)*	1989-1991
Territorial Dispute (Libyan Arab Jamahiriya/Chad)	1990-1994
East Timor (Portugal v. *Australia)*	1991-1995
Maritime Delimitation between Guinea-Bissau and Senegal (Guinea-Bissau v. *Senegal)*	1991-1995
Passage through the Great Belt (Finland v. *Denmark)*	1991-1992
Maritime Delimitation and Territorial Questions between Qatar and Bahrain (Qatar v. *Bahrain)*	1991-2001

Title	Dates
Questions of Interpretation and Application of the 1971 Montreal Convention arising from the Aerial Incident at Lockerbie (Libyan Arab Jamahiriya v. *United Kingdom)*	1992-2003
Questions of Interpretation and Application of the 1971 Montreal Convention arising from the Aerial Incident at Lockerbie (Libyan Arab Jamahiriya v. *United States of America)*	1992-2003
Oil Platforms (Islamic Republic of Iran v. *United States of America)*	1992-2003
Application of the Convention on the Prevention and Punishment of the Crime of Genocide (Bosnia and Herzegovina v. *Serbia and Montenegro)*	1993-2007
Gabčíkovo-Nagymaros Project (Hungary/Slovakia)[1]	1993-
Land and Maritime Boundary between Cameroon and Nigeria (Cameroon v. *Nigeria: Equatorial Guinea intervening)* [The intervention of Equatorial Guinea was admitted on 21 October 1999 (see *I.C.J. Yearbook 1999-2000*, p. 218).]	1994-2002
Fisheries Jurisdiction (Spain v. *Canada)*	1995-1998
Request for an Examination of the Situation in Accordance with Paragraph 63 of the Court's Judgment of 20 December 1974 in the Nuclear Tests (New Zealand *v.* France) *Case*	1995
Kasikili/Sedudu Island (Botswana/Namibia)	1996-1999
Vienna Convention on Consular Relations (Paraguay v. *United States of America)*	1998
Request for Interpretation of the Judgment of 11 June 1998 in the Case concerning the Land and Maritime Boundary between Cameroon and Nigeria (Cameroon *v.* Nigeria), Preliminary Objections *(Nigeria* v. *Cameroon)*	1998-1999
Sovereignty over Pulau Ligitan and Pulau Sipadan (Indonesia/Malaysia)	1998-2002

---

[1] The Court delivered its Judgment in the case concerning the *Gabčíkovo-Nagymaros Project (Hungary/Slovakia)* on 25 September 1997. The case nevertheless technically remains pending, given the fact that, in September 1998, Slovakia filed a request for an additional Judgment. Hungary filed a written statement of its position on the request made by Slovakia within the time-limit of 7 December 1998 fixed by the President of the Court. The Parties have subsequently resumed negotiations over the implementation of the 1997 Judgment and have informed the Court on a regular basis of the progress made.

Title	Dates
Ahmadou Sadio Diallo (Republic of Guinea v. Democratic Republic of the Congo)	1998-2012
LaGrand (Germany v. United States of America)	1999-2001
Legality of Use of Force (Serbia and Montenegro v. Belgium)	1999-2004
Legality of Use of Force (Serbia and Montenegro v. Canada)	1999-2004
Legality of Use of Force (Serbia and Montenegro v. France)	1999-2004
Legality of Use of Force (Serbia and Montenegro v. Germany)	1999-2004
Legality of Use of Force (Serbia and Montenegro v. Italy)	1999-2004
Legality of Use of Force (Serbia and Montenegro v. Netherlands)	1999-2004
Legality of Use of Force (Serbia and Montenegro v. Portugal)	1999-2004
Legality of Use of Force (Yugoslavia v. Spain)	1999
Legality of Use of Force (Serbia and Montenegro v. United Kingdom)	1999-2004
Legality of Use of Force (Yugoslavia v. United States of America)	1999
Armed Activities on the Territory of the Congo (Democratic Republic of the Congo v. Burundi)	1999-2001
Armed Activities on the Territory of the Congo (Democratic Republic of the Congo v. Uganda)[1]	1999-
Armed Activities on the Territory of the Congo (Democratic Republic of the Congo v. Rwanda)	1999-2001
Application of the Convention on the Prevention and Punishment of the Crime of Genocide (Croatia v. Serbia)	1999-
Aerial Incident of 10 August 1999 (Pakistan v. India)	1999-2000
Territorial and Maritime Dispute between Nicaragua and Honduras in the Caribbean Sea (Nicaragua v. Honduras)	1999-2007
Arrest Warrant of 11 April 2000 (Democratic Republic of the Congo v. Belgium)	2000-2002
Arrest Warrant of 11 April 2000 (Democratic Republic of the Congo v. Belgium)	2000-2002

---

[1] The Court delivered its Judgment in this case on 19 December 2005. This case also technically remains pending, in the sense that the Parties could again turn to the Court, as they are entitled to do under the Judgment, to decide the question of reparation if they are unable to agree on this point.

Title	Dates
Application for Revision of the Judgment of 11 July 1996 in the Case concerning Application of the Convention on the Prevention and Punishment of the Crime of Genocide (Bosnia and Herzegovina *v.* Yugoslavia), Preliminary Objections *(Yugoslavia* v. *Bosnia and Herzegovina)*	2001-2003
Certain Property (Liechtenstein v. *Germany)*	2001-2005
Territorial and Maritime Dispute (Nicaragua v. *Colombia)*	2001-2012
Frontier Dispute (Benin/Niger) [case referred to a Chamber]	2002-2005
Armed Activities on the Territory of the Congo (New Application: 2002) (Democratic Republic of the Congo v. *Rwanda)*	2002-2006
Application for Revision of the Judgment of 11 September 1992 in the Case concerning the Land, Island and Maritime Frontier Dispute (El Salvador/ Honduras: Nicaragua intervening) *(El Salvador* v. *Honduras)* [case referred to a Chamber]	2002-2003
Avena and Other Mexican Nationals (Mexico v. *United States of America)*	2003-2004
Certain Criminal Proceedings in France (Republic of the Congo v. *France)*	2003-2010
Sovereignty over Pedra Branca/Pulau Batu Puteh, Middle Rocks and South Ledge (Malaysia/Singapore)	2003-2008
Maritime Delimitation in the Black Sea (Romania v. *Ukraine)*	2004-2009
Dispute regarding Navigational and Related Rights (Costa Rica v. *Nicaragua)*	2005-2009
Status vis-à-vis the Host State of a Diplomatic Envoy to the United Nations (Commonwealth of Dominica v. *Switzerland)*	2006
Pulp Mills on the River Uruguay (Argentina v. *Uruguay)*	2006-2010
Certain Questions of Mutual Assistance in Criminal Matters (Djibouti v. *France)*	2006-2008
Maritime Dispute (Peru v. *Chile)*	2008-
Aerial Herbicide Spraying (Ecuador v. *Colombia)*	2008-
Request for Interpretation of the Judgment of 31 March 2004 in the Case concerning Avena and Other Mexican Nationals (Mexico *v.* United States of America) *(Mexico* v. *United States of America)*	2008-2009
Application of the Interim Accord of 13 September 1995 (the former Yugoslav Republic of Macedonia v. *Greece)*	2008-2011

Title	Dates
Jurisdictional Immunities of the State (Germany v. *Italy: Greece intervening)*. On 4 July 2011, the Court authorized Greece to intervene in the case as a non-party (see *I.C.J. Yearbook 2010-2011*)	2008-2012
Questions relating to the Obligation to Prosecute or Extradite (Belgium v. *Senegal)*	2009-2012
Certain Questions concerning Diplomatic Relations (Honduras v. *Brazil)*	2009
Jurisdiction and Enforcement of Judgments in Civil and Commercial Matters (Belgium v. *Switzerland)*	2009-2011
Whaling in the Antarctic (Australia v. *Japan: New Zealand intervening)*. On 6 February 2013, the Court authorized New Zealand to intervene in the case.	2010-
Frontier Dispute (Burkina Faso/Niger)	2010-
Certain Activities Carried Out by Nicaragua in the Border Area (Costa Rica v. *Nicaragua)*	2010-
Request for Interpretation of the Judgment of 15 June 1962 in the Case concerning the Temple of Preah Vihear (Cambodia *v.* Thailand) *(Cambodia* v. *Thailand)*	2011-
Construction of a Road in Costa Rica along the San Juan River (Nicaragua v. *Costa Rica)*	2011-
Obligation to Negotiate Access to the Pacific Ocean (Bolivia v. *Chile)*	2013-

(b) Advisory Proceedings

Title	Dates
Conditions of Admission of a State to Membership in the United Nations (Article 4 of the Charter)	1947-1948
Reparation for Injuries Suffered in the Service of the United Nations	1948-1949
Interpretation of Peace Treaties with Bulgaria, Hungary and Romania	1949-1950
Competence of the General Assembly for the Admission of a State to the United Nations	1949-1950
International Status of South West Africa	1949-1950
Reservations to the Convention on the Prevention and Punishment of the Crime of Genocide	1950-1951
Effect of Awards of Compensation Made by the United Nations Administrative Tribunal	1953-1954
Voting Procedure on Questions relating to Reports and Petitions concerning the Territory of South West Africa	1954-1955

Title	Dates
Judgments of the Administrative Tribunal of the ILO upon Complaints Made against Unesco	1955-1956
Admissibility of Hearings of Petitioners by the Committee on South West Africa	1955-1956
Constitution of the Maritime Safety Committee of the Inter-Governmental Maritime Consultative Organization	1959-1960
Certain Expenses of the United Nations (Article 17, paragraph 2, of the Charter)	1961-1962
Legal Consequences for States of the Continued Presence of South Africa in Namibia (South West Africa) notwithstanding Security Council Resolution 276 (1970)	1970-1971
Application for Review of Judgement No. 158 of the United Nations Administrative Tribunal	1972-1973
Western Sahara	1974-1975
Interpretation of the Agreement of 25 March 1951 between the WHO and Egypt	1980
Application for Review of Judgement No. 273 of the United Nations Administrative Tribunal	1981-1982
Application for Review of Judgement No. 333 of the United Nations Administrative Tribunal	1984-1987
Applicability of the Obligation to Arbitrate under Section 21 of the United Nations Headquarters Agreement of 26 June 1947	1988
Applicability of Article VI, Section 22, of the Convention on the Privileges and Immunities of the United Nations	1989
Legality of the Use by a State of Nuclear Weapons in Armed Conflict	1993-1996
Legality of the Threat or Use of Nuclear Weapons	1994-1996
Difference Relating to Immunity from Legal Process of a Special Rapporteur of the Commission on Human Rights	1998-1999
Legal Consequences of the Construction of a Wall in the Occupied Palestinian Territory	2003-2004
Accordance with International Law of the Unilateral Declaration of Independence in Respect of Kosovo	2008-2010
Judgment No. 2867 of the Administrative Tribunal of the International Labour Organization upon a Complaint Filed against the International Fund for Agricultural Development	2010-2012

ANNEX 4

FORMER PRESIDENTS AND VICE-PRESIDENTS OF THE COURT

The following list contains the names of all judges who have served as President or Vice-President prior to the present holders of those offices:

1946-1949, J. G. Guerrero and J. Basdevant;

1949-1952, J. Basdevant and J. G. Guerrero[1];

1952-1955, Sir Arnold McNair and J. G. Guerrero[1];

1955-1958, G. H. Hackworth and A. H. Badawi[2];

1958-1961, H. Klaestad and Sir Muhammad Zafrulla Khan;

1961-1964, B. Winiarski and R. J. Alfaro;

1964-1967, Sir Percy Spender and V. K. Wellington Koo;

1967-1970, J. L. Bustamante y Rivero and V. M. Koretsky;

1970-1973, Sir Muhammad Zafrulla Khan and F. Ammoun[3];

1973-1976, M. Lachs and F. Ammoun[3];

1976-1979, E. Jiménez de Aréchaga and Nagendra Singh;

1979-1982, Sir Humphrey Waldock[4] and T. O. Elias[5];

---

[1] While he was Vice-President of the Court, Judge Guerrero acted as President, by virtue of Article 13, paragraphs 1 and 2, of the 1946 Rules, in the following cases: *Corfu Channel (United Kingdom* v. *Albania); Protection of French Nationals and Protected Persons in Egypt (France* v. *Egypt); Rights of Nationals of the United States of America in Morocco (France* v. *United States of America); Ambatielos (Greece* v. *United Kingdom); Anglo-Iranian Oil Co. (United Kingdom* v. *Iran); Minquiers and Ecrehos (France/United Kingdom); Monetary Gold Removed from Rome in 1943 (Italy* v. *France, United Kingdom and United States of America).*

[2] While he was Vice-President of the Court, Judge Badawi acted as President, by virtue of Article 13, paragraph 1, of the 1946 Rules, in the cases concerning *Interhandel (Switzerland* v. *United States of America), Interim Protection* and *Aerial Incident of 27 July 1955 (United States of America* v. *Bulgaria).*

[3] While he was Vice-President of the Court, Judge Ammoun acted as President, by virtue of Article 11 and Article 13, paragraph 1, of the then Rules of Court, in *Appeal Relating to the Jurisdiction of the ICAO Council (India* v. *Pakistan), Nuclear Tests (Australia* v. *France), Interim Protection* and *Nuclear Tests (New Zealand* v. *France), Interim Protection.*

[4] Sir Humphrey Waldock died on 15 August 1981. The functions of the Presidency were thereafter exercised by T. O. Elias, by virtue of Article 13, paragraph 1, and Article 14 of the 1978 Rules of Court.

[5] Vice-President Elias was for a time Acting President in *Continental Shelf (Tunisia/Libyan Arab Jamahiriya)* and in the proceedings relating to the Orders made on 20 January and 1 February 1982 in *Delimitation of the Maritime Boundary in the Gulf of Maine Area (Canada/United States of America).*

1982-1985, T. O. Elias[1] and J. Sette-Camara;

1985-1988, Nagendra Singh and G. Ladreit de Lacharrière[2];

1988-1991, J. M. Ruda and K. Mbaye;

1991-1994, Sir Robert Jennings and S. Oda[3];

1994-1997, M. Bedjaoui and S. M. Schwebel;

1997-2000, S. M. Schwebel and C. G. Weeramantry[4];

2000-2003, G. Guillaume and Shi Jiuyong;

2003-2006, Shi Jiuyong and R. Ranjeva;

2006-2009, Dame R. Higgins[5] and A. S. Al-Khasawneh[5];

2009-2012, H. Owada and P. Tomka[6].

---

[1] Judge Elias continued to act as President in *Continental Shelf (Libyan Arab Jamahiriya/Malta)* after 5 February 1985, by virtue of Article 32, paragraph 2, of the 1978 Rules of Court.

[2] Judge Ladreit de Lacharrière died on 10 March 1987. On 6 May 1987, the Court elected Judge Mbaye to be its Vice-President for the remainder of his predecessor's term.

[3] While he was President of the Court, Sir Robert Jennings, being a national of one of the Parties, did not, in accordance with Article 32 of the Rules of Court, preside in the case concerning *Questions of Interpretation and Application of the 1971 Montreal Convention arising from the Aerial Incident at Lockerbie (Libyan Arab Jamahiriya* v. *United Kingdom)*. Vice-President Oda exercised the functions of the Presidency in that case, as well as in the case concerning *Questions of Interpretation and Application of the 1971 Montreal Convention arising from the Aerial Incident at Lockerbie (Libyan Arab Jamahiriya* v. *United States of America)*. (See *I.C.J. Yearbook 1991-1992*, p. 198.)

[4] While he was President of the Court, Judge Schwebel, being a national of one of the Parties, did not, in accordance with Article 32 of the Rules of Court, preside in the cases concerning *Questions of Interpretation and Application of the 1971 Montreal Convention arising from the Aerial Incident at Lockerbie (Libyan Arab Jamahiriya* v. *United States of America), Oil Platforms (Islamic Republic of Iran* v. *United States of America), Vienna Convention on Consular Relations (Paraguay* v. *United States of America), LaGrand (Germany* v. *United States of America)* and *Legality of Use of Force (Yugoslavia* v. *United States of America)*. Although Article 32 was not applicable in the cases concerning *Questions of Interpretation and Application of the 1971 Montreal Convention arising from the Aerial Incident at Lockerbie (Libyan Arab Jamahiriya* v. *United Kingdom)* and *Legality of Use of Force (Serbia and Montenegro* v. *Belgium) (Serbia and Montenegro* v. *Canada) (Serbia and Montenegro* v. *France) (Serbia and Montenegro* v. *Germany) (Serbia and Montenegro* v. *Italy) (Serbia and Montenegro* v. *Netherlands) (Serbia and Montenegro* v. *Portugal) (Yugoslavia* v. *Spain) (Serbia and Montenegro* v. *United Kingdom)*, he did not think it appropriate to exercise the functions of the Presidency in those cases either. It was therefore the Vice-President, Judge Weeramantry, who, in accordance with Article 13, paragraph 1, of the Rules, exercised those functions.

[5] Prior to her election as President of the Court, Dame Higgins, referring to Article 17, paragraph 2, of the Statute, recused herself from participating in the case concerning *Sovereignty over Pedra Branca/Pulau Batu Puteh, Middle Rocks and South Ledge (Malaysia/Singapore)*. It therefore fell upon the Vice-President, Judge Al-Khasawneh, to exercise from 6 February 2006 onwards the functions of the Presidency for the purpose of the case, in accordance with Article 13, paragraphs 1 and 2, of the Rules of Court.

[6] During his term as Vice-President of the Court, Judge Tomka acted as President, by virtue of Article 13 of the Rules of Court, in the case concerning *Pulp Mills on the River Uruguay (Argentina* v. *Uruguay)* and *Whaling in the Antarctic (Australia* v. *Japan)*.

ANNEX 5

The following list contains the names of all judges who have previously served as Members of the Court (the names of deceased judges are preceded by an asterisk):

	Country	Period of Office
* R. Ago	Italy	1979-1995
* A. Aguilar-Mawdsley	Venezuela	1991-1995
Prince B. A. Ajibola	Nigeria	1991-1994
* R. J. Alfaro	Panama	1959-1964
* A. Alvarez	Chile	1946-1955
A. S. Al-Khasawneh	Jordan	2000-2011
* F. Ammoun	Lebanon	1965-1976
* E. C. Armand-Ugon	Uruguay	1952-1961
* Ph. Azevedo	Brazil	1946-1951
* A. H. Badawi	Egypt	1946-1965
* J. Basdevant	France	1946-1964
* R. R. Baxter	United States	1979-1980
M. Bedjaoui	Algeria	1982-2001
* C. Bengzon	Philippines	1967-1976
Th. Buergenthal	United States	2000-2010
* J. L. Bustamante y Rivero	Peru	1961-1970
* L. F. Carneiro	Brazil	1951-1955
* F. de Castro	Spain	1970-1979
* R. Córdova	Mexico	1955-1964
* Ch. De Visscher	Belgium	1946-1952
* H. C. Dillard	United States	1970-1979
N. Elaraby	Egypt	2001-2006
* A. El-Erian	Egypt	1979-1981
* T. O. Elias	Nigeria	1976-1991
A. El-Khani	Syria	1981-1985
* J. Evensen	Norway	1985-1994
* I. Fabela	Mexico	1946-1952
L. Ferrari Bravo	Italy	1995-1997
* Sir Gerald Fitzmaurice	United Kingdom	1960-1973
* C.-A. Fleischhauer	Germany	1994-2003
* I. Forster	Senegal	1964-1982
* S. A. Golunsky	USSR	1952-1953
* A. Gros	France	1964-1984
* J. G. Guerrero	El Salvador	1946-1958
G. Guillaume	France	1987-2005
* G. H. Hackworth	United States	1946-1961

	Country	Period of Office
* G. Herczegh	Hungary	1993-2003
Dame Rosalyn Higgins	United Kingdom	1995-2009
* Hsu Mo	China	1946-1956
* L. Ignacio-Pinto	Benin	1970-1979
* Sir Robert Yewdall Jennings	United Kingdom	1982-1995
* P. C. Jessup	United States	1961-1970
* E. Jiménez de Aréchaga	Uruguay	1970-1979
* H. Klaestad	Norway	1946-1961
* F. I. Kojevnikov	USSR	1953-1961
* P. H. Kooijmans	Netherlands	1997-2006
* V. M. Koretsky	USSR	1961-1970
A. G. Koroma	Sierra Leone	1994-2012
* S. B. Krylov	USSR	1946-1952
* M. Lachs	Poland	1967-1993
* G. Ladreit de Lacharrière	France	1982-1987
* Sir Hersch Lauterpacht	United Kingdom	1955-1960
* K. Mbaye	Senegal	1982-1991
* Sir Arnold McNair	United Kingdom	1946-1955
* G. Morelli	Italy	1961-1970
* L. M. Moreno Quintana	Argentina	1955-1964
* P. D. Morozov	USSR	1970-1985
* H. Mosler	Fed. Rep. of Germany	1976-1985
* Nagendra Singh	India	1973-1988
* Ni Zhengyu	China	1985-1994
S. Oda	Japan	1976-2003
* C. D. Onyeama	Nigeria	1967-1976
* L. Padilla Nervo	Mexico	1964-1973
G. Parra-Aranguren	Venezuela	1996-2009
* R. S. Pathak	India	1989-1991
* S. Petrén	Sweden	1967-1976
R. Ranjeva	Madagascar	1991-2009
* Sir Benegal Rau	India	1952-1953
* J. E. Read	Canada	1946-1958
F. Rezek	Brazil	1997-2006
* J. M. Ruda	Argentina	1973-1991
S. M. Schwebel	United States	1981-2000
* J. Sette-Camara	Brazil	1979-1988
M. Shahabuddeen	Guyana	1988-1997
Shi Jiuyong	China	1994-2010
B. Simma	Germany	2003-2012
* Sir Percy C. Spender	Australia	1958-1967
* J. Spiropoulos	Greece	1958-1967
* K. Tanaka	Japan	1961-1970
* N. K. Tarassov	Russian Federation	1985-1995

	Country	Period of Office
* S. Tarazi	Syria	1976-1980
V. S. Vereshchetin	Russian Federation	1995-2006
* Sir Humphrey Waldock	United Kingdom	1973-1981
C. G. Weeramantry	Sri Lanka	1991-2000
* V. K. Wellington Koo	China	1957-1967
* B. Winiarski	Poland	1946-1967
* Sir Muhammad Zafrulla Khan	Pakistan	1954-1961 and 1964-1973
* M. Zoričić	Yugoslavia	1946-1958

ANNEX 6

The following list contains, in chronological order from date of filing on the General List, the names of all cases in which judges *ad hoc* have been appointed. This list includes cases still pending (unless otherwise indicated, judges *ad hoc* held the nationality of the appointing party)[1]:

Corfu Channel (United Kingdom v. *Albania)*. Albania chose Mr. I. Daxner (Czechoslovakia), who sat upon the Bench when the preliminary objection was heard, and Mr. B. Ečer (Czechoslovakia), who sat when the case was heard on the merits and also for the assessment of amount of compensation.

Asylum (Colombia/Peru), *Request for Interpretation of the Judgment of 20 November 1950 in the Asylum Case (Colombia* v. *Peru)* and *Haya de la Torre (Colombia* v. *Peru)*. Mr. J. J. Caicedo Castilla was chosen by Colombia and Mr. L. Alayza y Paz Soldán by Peru.

Ambatielos (Greece v. *United Kingdom)*. Mr. J. Spiropoulos was chosen by Greece.

Anglo-Iranian Oil Co. (United Kingdom v. *Iran)*. Mr. K. Sandjabi was chosen by Iran.

Nottebohm (Liechtenstein v. *Guatemala)*. Mr. P. Guggenheim (Switzerland) was chosen by Liechtenstein. The Government of Guatemala had first chosen as judge *ad hoc* Mr. J. C. Herrera and subsequently Mr. J. Matos, before choosing Mr. García Bauer.

Monetary Gold Removed from Rome in 1943 (Italy v. *France, United Kingdom and United States of America)*. Mr. G. Morelli was chosen by Italy.

Right of Passage over Indian Territory (Portugal v. *India)*. Mr. M. Fernandes was chosen by Portugal and the Hon. M. A. C. Chagla by India.

Application of the Convention of 1902 Governing the Guardianship of Infants (Netherlands v. *Sweden)*. Mr. J. Offerhaus was chosen by the Netherlands and Mr. F. J. C. Sterzel by Sweden.

Interhandel (Switzerland v. *United States of America)*. Mr. P. Carry was chosen by Switzerland.

Aerial Incident of 27 July 1955 (Israel v. *Bulgaria)*. Mr. D. Goitein was chosen by Israel and Mr. J. Zourek (Czechoslovakia) by Bulgaria.

Aerial Incident of 27 July 1955 (United States of America v. *Bulgaria)*. Mr. J. Zourek (Czechoslovakia) was chosen by Bulgaria.

---

[1] The full list of judges *ad hoc* (in alphabetical order) can be found on the Court's website under "The Court/Judges *ad hoc*".

Arbitral Award Made by the King of Spain on 23 December 1906 (Honduras v. Nicaragua). Mr. R. Ago (Italy) was chosen by Honduras and Mr. F. Urrutia Holguín (Colombia) by Nicaragua.

Barcelona Traction, Light and Power Company, Limited (Belgium v. Spain). Mr. W. J. Ganshof van der Meersch was chosen by Belgium and Mr. F. de Castro by Spain. The case was removed from the List before the Court had occasion to sit.

South West Africa (Ethiopia v. South Africa; Liberia v. South Africa). The Governments of Ethiopia and Liberia had first chosen as judge *ad hoc* the Hon. J. Chesson, subsequently Sir Muhammad Zafrulla Khan (Pakistan) and then Sir Adetokunboh A. Ademola (Nigeria), before choosing Sir Louis Mbanefo (Nigeria). South Africa chose the Hon. J. T. van Wyk.

Northern Cameroons (Cameroon v. United Kingdom). Mr. P. Beb a Don was chosen by Cameroon.

Barcelona Traction, Light and Power Company, Limited (New Application: 1962) (Belgium v. Spain). Belgium chose Mr. W. J. Ganshof van der Meersch, who sat upon the Bench when the preliminary objections were heard, and Mr. W. Riphagen (Netherlands), who sat in the second phase. Spain chose Mr. E. C. Armand-Ugon (Uruguay).

North Sea Continental Shelf (Federal Republic of Germany/Denmark; Federal Republic of Germany/Netherlands). Mr. H. Mosler was chosen by the Federal Republic of Germany and Mr. M. Sørensen (Denmark) by Denmark and the Netherlands.

Appeal Relating to the Jurisdiction of the ICAO Council (India v. Pakistan). Mr. Nagendra Singh was chosen by India.

Nuclear Tests (Australia v. France). Sir Garfield Barwick was chosen by Australia.

Nuclear Tests (New Zealand v. France). Sir Garfield Barwick (Australia) was chosen by New Zealand.

Trial of Pakistani Prisoners of War (Pakistan v. India). Pakistan chose Sir Muhammad Zafrulla Khan, who sat in the proceedings on the request for interim measures up to 2 July 1973, and Mr. Muhammad Yaqub Ali Khan. This case was removed from the List before the Court had occasion to hear argument on the question of its jurisdiction.

Western Sahara. Mr. A. Boni (Ivory Coast) was chosen by Morocco.

Aegean Sea Continental Shelf (Greece v. Turkey). Mr. M. Stassinopoulos was chosen by Greece.

Continental Shelf (Tunisia/Libyan Arab Jamahiriya). Mr. E. Jiménez de Aréchaga (Uruguay) was chosen by the Libyan Arab Jamahiriya and Mr. J. Evensen (Norway) by Tunisia.

Delimitation of the Maritime Boundary in the Gulf of Maine Area (Canada/United States of America) (case referred to a Chamber). Mr. M. Cohen was chosen by Canada.

Continental Shelf (Libyan Arab Jamahiriya/Malta). Mr. E. Jiménez de Aréchaga (Uruguay) was chosen by the Libyan Arab Jamahiriya.

Mr. J. Castañeda (Mexico) was chosen by Malta and sat in the proceedings culminating in the Judgment on Italy's Application for permission to intervene. Mr. N. Valticos (Greece) was chosen by Malta to sit when the case was heard on the merits.

Frontier Dispute (Burkina Faso/Republic of Mali) (case referred to a Chamber). Mr. F. Luchaire (France) was chosen by Burkina Faso and Mr. G. Abi-Saab (Egypt) by the Republic of Mali.

Military and Paramilitary Activities in and against Nicaragua (Nicaragua v. *United States of America)*. Mr. C.-A. Colliard (France) was chosen by Nicaragua.

Application for Revision and Interpretation of the Judgment of 24 February 1982 in the Case concerning the Continental Shelf (Tunisia/Libyan Arab Jamahiriya) *(Tunisia* v. *Libyan Arab Jamahiriya)*. Mrs. S. Bastid (France) was chosen by Tunisia and Mr. E. Jiménez de Aréchaga (Uruguay) by the Libyan Arab Jamahiriya.

Land, Island and Maritime Frontier Dispute (El Salvador/Honduras: Nicaragua intervening) (case referred to a Chamber). Mr. N. Valticos (Greece) was chosen by El Salvador and Mr. M. Virally (France) was chosen by Honduras. Following the death of Mr. Virally, Mr. S. Torres Bernárdez (Spain) was chosen by Honduras.

Maritime Delimitation in the Area between Greenland and Jan Mayen (Denmark v. *Norway)*. Mr. P. H. Fischer was chosen by Denmark.

Aerial Incident of 3 July 1988 (Islamic Republic of Iran v. *United States of America)*. Mr. M. Aghahosseini was chosen by the Islamic Republic of Iran. The case was removed from the List before the Court had occasion to hear argument on the preliminary objections raised by the United States.

Arbitral Award of 31 July 1989 (Guinea-Bissau v. *Senegal)*. Mr. H. Thierry (France) was chosen by Guinea-Bissau. Following the expiry of Judge Mbaye's term of office on 5 February 1991, Senegal no longer had a judge of its nationality on the Bench. It therefore chose Mr. K. Mbaye to sit as judge *ad hoc*.

Territorial Dispute (Libyan Arab Jamahiriya/Chad). Mr. J. Sette-Camara (Brazil) was chosen by the Libyan Arab Jamahiriya and Mr. G. M. Abi-Saab (Egypt) by Chad.

East Timor (Portugal v. *Australia)*. Mr. A. de Arruda Ferrer-Correia was chosen by Portugal. Following his resignation, on 14 July 1994, Mr. K. J. Skubiszewski (Poland) was chosen by Portugal. Sir Ninian Stephen was chosen by Australia.

Passage through the Great Belt (Finland v. *Denmark)*. Mr. B. Broms was chosen by Finland and Mr. P. H. Fischer by Denmark.

Maritime Delimitation and Territorial Questions between Qatar and Bahrain (Qatar v. *Bahrain)*. Mr. J. M. Ruda (Argentina) was chosen by Qatar. Following the death of Mr. Ruda, Mr. S. Torres Bernárdez (Spain) was chosen by Qatar. Mr. N. Valticos (Greece) was chosen by Bahrain. He resigned for health reasons as from the end of the jurisdiction and admissibility phase of the case. Bahrain subsequently chose Mr. M. Shaha-buddeen (Guyana). After the resignation of Mr. Shahabuddeen, Bahrain chose Mr. Yves L. Fortier (Canada) to sit as judge *ad hoc.*

Questions of Interpretation and Application of the 1971 Montreal Convention arising from the Aerial Incident at Lockerbie (Libyan Arab Jamahiriya v. *United Kingdom).* Mr. A. S. El-Kosheri (Egypt) was chosen by the Libyan Arab Jamahiriya. Dame Rosalyn Higgins having recused herself, the United Kingdom chose Sir Robert Jennings to sit as judge *ad hoc.* The latter has been sitting as such in the phase of the proceedings concerning jurisdiction and admissibility.

Questions of Interpretation and Application of the 1971 Montreal Convention arising from the Aerial Incident at Lockerbie (Libyan Arab Jamahiriya v. *United States of America).* Mr. A. S. El-Kosheri (Egypt) was chosen by the Libyan Arab Jamahiriya.

Oil Platforms (Islamic Republic of Iran v. *United States of America).* Mr. F. Rigaux (Belgium) was chosen by the Islamic Republic of Iran.

Application of the Convention on the Prevention and Punishment of the Crime of Genocide (Bosnia and Herzegovina v. *Serbia and Montenegro).* Sir Elihu Lauterpacht (United Kingdom) was chosen by Bosnia and Herzegovina. Following his resignation, on 22 February 2002, Mr. Ahmed Mahiou (Algeria) was chosen by Bosnia and Herzegovina. Mr. M. Kreća was chosen by Serbia and Montenegro.

Gabčíkovo-Nagymaros Project (Hungary/Slovakia). H.E. K. J. Skubiszewski (Poland) was chosen by Slovakia. Professor Skubiszewski, President of the Iran/US Claims Tribunal and judge *ad hoc* at the Court died on 8 February 2010, while the case was still pending.

Land and Maritime Boundary between Cameroon and Nigeria (Cameroon v. *Nigeria: Equatorial Guinea intervening).* Mr. K. Mbaye (Senegal) was chosen by Cameroon and Prince B. A. Ajibola by Nigeria.

Fisheries Jurisdiction (Spain v. *Canada).* Mr. S. Torres Bernárdez was chosen by Spain and Mr. M. Lalonde by Canada.

Request for an Examination of the Situation in Accordance with Paragraph 63 of the Court's Judgment of 20 December 1974 in the Nuclear Tests (New Zealand *v.* France) *Case.* Sir Geoffrey Palmer was chosen by New Zealand.

Request for Interpretation of the Judgment of 11 June 1998 in the Case concerning the Land and Maritime Boundary between Cameroon and Nigeria (Cameroon *v.* Nigeria), Preliminary Objections *(Nigeria* v. *Cameroon).* Prince B. A. Ajibola was chosen by Nigeria and Mr. K. Mbaye (Senegal) by Cameroon.

Sovereignty over Pulau Ligitan and Pulau Sipadan (Indonesia/Malaysia). Mr. M. Shahabuddeen (Guyana) was chosen by Indonesia. Following the resignation of Mr. Shahabuddeen, Mr. Thomas Franck (United States of America) was chosen by Indonesia. Mr. C. G. Weeramantry (Sri Lanka) was chosen by Malaysia.

Ahmadou Sadio Diallo (Republic of Guinea v. *Democratic Republic of the Congo).* Mr. Mohammed Bedjaoui (Algeria) was chosen by the Republic of Guinea and Mr. Auguste Mampuya Kanunk'A-Tshiabo by the Democratic Republic of the Congo. Following the resignation of Mr. Bedjaoui, on 10 September 2002, Mr. Ahmed Mahiou (Algeria) was chosen by the Republic of Guinea.

Legality of Use of Force (Serbia and Montenegro v. *Belgium) (Serbia and Montenegro* v. *Canada) (Serbia and Montenegro* v. *France) (Serbia and Montenegro* v. *Germany) (Serbia and Montenegro* v. *Italy) (Serbia and Montenegro* v. *Netherlands) (Serbia and Montenegro* v. *Portugal) (Yugoslavia* v. *Spain) (Serbia and Montenegro* v. *United Kingdom) (Yugoslavia* v. *United States of America).* In all ten cases Serbia and Montenegro [Yugoslavia] chose Mr. M. Kreća; in the case of *Serbia and Montenegro* v. *Belgium,* Mr. P. Duinslaeger was chosen by Belgium; in the case of *Serbia and Montenegro* v. *Canada,* Mr. M. Lalonde was chosen by Canada; in the case of *Serbia and Montenegro* v. *Italy,* Mr. G. Gaja was chosen by Italy and in the case of *Yugoslavia* v. *Spain,* Mr. S. Torres Bernárdez was chosen by Spain. These have been sitting as such during the examination of Serbia and Montenegro's requests for the indication of provisional measures. In March 2000 Portugal indicated its intention to appoint a judge *ad hoc.* With regard to the phase of the procedure concerning the preliminary objections, the Court, taking into account the presence upon the Bench of judges of British, Dutch and French nationality, decided that the judges *ad hoc* chosen by the respondent States should not sit during that phase. The Court observed that this decision did not in any way prejudice the question whether, if the Court should reject the preliminary objections of the respondents, judges *ad hoc* might sit in subsequent stages of the cases.

Armed Activities on the Territory of the Congo (Democratic Republic of the Congo v. *Burundi) (Democratic Republic of the Congo* v. *Uganda) (Democratic Republic of the Congo* v. *Rwanda).* In all three cases Mr. Joe Verhoeven (Belgium) was chosen by the Democratic Republic of the Congo; in the case of *Democratic Republic of the Congo* v. *Burundi,* Mr. J. J. A. Salmon (Belgium) was chosen by Burundi; in the case of *Democratic Republic of the Congo* v. *Uganda,* Mr. James L. Kateka (Tanzania) was chosen by Uganda. Following the election of Ms Julia Sebutinde, of Ugandan nationality, as a Member of the Court with effect from 6 February 2012, the term of office of Mr. Kateka came to an end; and, in the case of *Democratic Republic of the Congo* v. *Rwanda,* Mr. C. J. R. Dugard (South Africa) was chosen by Rwanda.

Application of the Convention on the Prevention and Punishment of the Crime of Genocide (Croatia v. *Serbia).* Mr. B. Vukas was chosen by Croatia and Mr. M. Kreća by Serbia.

Aerial Incident of 10 August 1999 (Pakistan v. *India).* Mr. S. S. U. Pirzada was chosen by Pakistan and Mr. B. P. J. Reddy by India.

Territorial and Maritime Dispute between Nicaragua and Honduras in the Caribbean Sea (Nicaragua v. Honduras). Mr. Giorgio Gaja (Italy) was chosen by Nicaragua and Mr. Julio González Campos (Spain) by Honduras. Following the resignation of Mr. González Campos, Honduras chose Santiago Torres Bernárdez (Spain).

Arrest Warrant of 11 April 2000 (Democratic Republic of the Congo v. Belgium). Mr. Sayeman Bula-Bula was chosen by the Democratic Republic of the Congo and Mrs. Christine Van den Wyngaert by Belgium.

Application for Revision of the Judgment of 11 July 1996 in the Case concerning Application of the Convention on the Prevention and Punishment of the Crime of Genocide (Bosnia and Herzegovina *v.* Yugoslavia), Preliminary Objections *(Yugoslavia v. Bosnia and Herzegovina)*. Mr. Vojin Dimitrijević was chosen by Yugoslavia. Mr. Sead Hodžić was chosen by Bosnia and Herzegovina. Following the resignation of Mr. Hodžić, on 9 April 2002, Bosnia and Herzegovina chose Mr. Ahmed Mahiou (Algeria).

Certain Property (Liechtenstein v. Germany). Mr. Ian Brownlie (United Kingdom) was chosen by Liechtenstein. Following his resignation, on 25 April 2002, Sir Franklin Berman (United Kingdom) was chosen by Liechtenstein. Mr. Carl-August Fleischhauer was chosen by Germany, Judge Simma being disqualified from sitting.

Territorial and Maritime Dispute (Nicaragua v. Colombia). Nicaragua chose Mohammed Bedjaoui. Following the latter's resignation, it chose Giorgio Gaja (Algeria). In view of that choice, Judge Gaja considered that it seemed appropriate for him, as the former judge *ad hoc* chosen by Nicaragua, not to take part in any further proceedings concerning the case. Following Mr. Gaja's election as a Member of the Court, it chose Thomas A. Mensah. In view of Nicaragua's choice, Colombia chose Yves L. Fortier. Following the latter's resignation, it chose Jean-Pierre Cot.

Frontier Dispute (Benin/Niger). Mr. Mohamed Bennouna (Morocco) was chosen by Benin and Mr. Mohammed Bedjaoui (Algeria) by Niger.

Armed Activities on the Territory of the Congo (New Application: 2002) (Democratic Republic of the Congo v. Rwanda). Mr. Jean-Pierre Mavungu Mvumbi-di-Ngoma was chosen by the Democratic Republic of the Congo and Mr. John Dugard (South Africa) by Rwanda.

Application for Revision of the Judgment of 11 September 1992 in the Case concerning the Land, Island and Maritime Frontier Dispute (El Salvador/Honduras: Nicaragua intervening) *(El Salvador v. Honduras)*. Mr. Felipe H. Paolillo (Uruguay) was chosen by El Salvador and Mr. Santiago Torres Bernárdez (Spain) by Honduras.

Avena and Other Mexican Nationals (Mexico v. United States of America). Mr. Bernardo Sepúlveda-Amor was chosen by Mexico.

Certain Criminal Proceedings in France (Republic of the Congo v. France). Mr. Jean-Yves De Cara (France) was chosen by the Republic of the Congo. Judge Abraham having recused himself under Article 24 of the Statute of the Court, Mr. Gilbert Guillaume was chosen by France.

Sovereignty over Pedra Branca/Pulau Batu Puteh, Middle Rocks and South Ledge (Malaysia/Singapore). Mr. Christopher J. Dugard (South Africa) was chosen by Malaysia and Mr. P. Sreenivasa Rao (India) by Singapore.

Maritime Delimitation in the Black Sea (Romania v. Ukraine). Mr. Jean-Pierre Cot (France) was chosen by Romania and Mr. Bernard H. Oxman (United States) by Ukraine.

Dispute regarding Navigational and Related Rights (Costa Rica v. Nicaragua). Mr. Antônio Augusto Cançado Trindade (Brazil) was chosen as judge *ad hoc* by Costa Rica. Mr. Cançado Trindade was later elected as a Member of the Court, as of 6 February 2009. He continued to sit on that case until its conclusion on 13 July 2009. Mr. Gilbert Guillaume (France) was chosen by Nicaragua.

Pulp Mills on the River Uruguay (Argentina v. Uruguay). Mr. Raúl Emilio Vinuesa was chosen by Argentina and Mr. Santiago Torres Bernárdez (Spain) by Uruguay.

Certain Questions of Mutual Assistance in Criminal Matters (Djibouti v. France). Mr. Abdulqawi Ahmed Yusuf (Somalia) was chosen by Djibouti. Judge Abraham having recused himself under Article 24 of the Statute of the Court, Mr. Gilbert Guillaume was chosen by France.

Maritime Dispute (Peru v. Chile). Mr. Gilbert Guillaume (France) was chosen by Peru. Mr. Francisco Orrego Vicuña was chosen by Chile.

Aerial Herbicide Spraying (Ecuador v. Colombia). Mr. Raúl Emilio Vinuesa (Argentina) was chosen by Ecuador. Mr. Jean-Pierre Cot (France) was chosen by Colombia.

Application of the International Convention on the Elimination of All Forms of Racial Discrimination (Georgia v. Russian Federation). Mr. Giorgio Gaja (Italy) was chosen by Georgia.

Application of the Interim Accord of 13 September 1995 (the former Yugoslav Republic of Macedonia v. Greece). Mr. Budislav Vukas (Croatia) was chosen by Macedonia and Mr. Emmanuel Roucounas was chosen by Greece.

Jurisdictional Immunities of the State (Germany v. Italy: Greece intervening). Mr. Giorgio Gaja was chosen by Italy.

Questions relating to the Obligation to Prosecute or Extradite (Belgium v. Senegal). Mr. Philippe Kirsch (Belgium/Canada) was chosen by Belgium and Mr. Serge Sur (France) was chosen by Senegal.

Jurisdiction and Enforcement of Judgments in Civil and Commercial Matters (Belgium v. Switzerland). Mr. Fausto Pocar (Italy) was chosen by Belgium and Mr. Andreas Bucher was chosen by Switzerland.

Whaling in the Antarctic (Australia v. Japan: New Zealand intervening). Ms Hilary Charlesworth was chosen by Australia.

Frontier Dispute (Burkina Faso/Niger). Burkina Faso chose Mr. Jean-Pierre Cot (France). Following the latter's resignation, Burkina Faso chose Yves Daudet. Niger chose Mr. Ahmed Mahiou (Algeria).

Certain Activities Carried Out by Nicaragua in the Border Area (Costa Rica v. Nicaragua). Costa Rica chose Mr. John Dugard (South Africa) and Nicaragua chose Mr. Gilbert Guillaume (France).

Request for Interpretation of the Judgment of 15 June 1962 in the Case concerning the Temple of Preah Vihear (Cambodia v. Thailand) *(Cambodia v. Thailand)*. Cambodia chose Mr. Gilbert Guillaume (France) and Thailand chose Mr. Jean-Pierre Cot (France).

Construction of a Road in Costa Rica along the San Juan River (Nicaragua v. Costa Rica). Nicaragua chose Gilbert Guillaume (France) and Costa Rica chose Bruno Simma (Germany). Further to the Court's decision to join the proceedings in this case and in that concerning *Certain Activities Carried Out by Nicaragua in the Border Area (Costa Rica v. Nicaragua)*, Mr. Simma resigned.

ANNEX 7

The Statute (Art. 26, para. 2) provides that the Court may form a chamber to deal with a particular case, the number of judges constituting such a chamber being determined by the Court with the approval of the parties. The following list includes the six cases in which chambers of this kind have been formed at the joint request of the parties. The case title, members of each chamber and the dates that the chambers were dissolved are given below.

Delimitation of the Maritime Boundary in the Gulf of Maine Area (Canada/ United States of America): constituted on 20 January 1982; *Judges* Ago *(President)*, Gros, Mosler, Schwebel; *Judge* ad hoc Cohen. The judgment on the merits was rendered on 12 October 1984, after which the Chamber formed to hear that case was dissolved.

Frontier Dispute (Burkina Faso/Republic of Mali): constituted on 3 April 1985; *Judges* Bedjaoui *(President)*, Lachs, Ruda; *Judges* ad hoc Luchaire, Abi-Saab. The judgment on the merits was rendered on 22 December 1986, after which the Chamber formed to hear that case was dissolved.

Elettronica Sicula S.p.A. (ELSI) (United States of America v. Italy): constituted on 2 March 1987 with the following composition — *Judges* Nagendra Singh *(President)*, Oda, Ago, Schwebel, Sir Robert Jennings. Following the death of Judge Nagendra Singh, the Court, on 20 December 1988, elected President Ruda to succeed him as member and (ex officio) President of the Chamber. The judgment on the merits was rendered on 20 July 1989, after which the Chamber formed to hear that case was dissolved.

Land, Island and Maritime Frontier Dispute (El Salvador/Honduras: Nicaragua intervening) [as from 13 September 1990]: constituted on 8 May 1987 with the following composition — *Judges* Oda, Sette-Camara, Sir Robert Jennings; *Judges* ad hoc Valticos, Virally. The Chamber elected Judge Sette-Camara to be its *President*. After the death of Judge Virally, Mr. Torres Bernárdez was chosen to sit as judge *ad hoc* in his place, and on 13 December 1989 the Court declared the Chamber to be composed as follows: *Judges* Sette-Camara *(President)*, Oda, Sir Robert Jennings; *Judges* ad hoc Valticos, Torres Bernárdez. On 7 February 1991 Judges Sir Robert Jennings and Oda exchanged places in the order of precedence within the Chamber owing to their election to be, respectively, the Court's President and Vice-President. The judgment on the merits was rendered on 11 September 1992, after which the Chamber formed to hear that case was dissolved.

Frontier Dispute (Benin/Niger): constituted on 27 November 2002 with the following composition — *Judges* Guillaume *(President)*, Ranjeva, Kooijmans; *Judges* ad hoc Bedjaoui, Bennouna. Following an election held on 16 February 2005 to fill the vacancy left by the resignation of Judge Guillaume, the composition of that Chamber was as follows: *Judges* Ranjeva *(President)*, Kooijmans, Abraham; *Judges* ad hoc Bedjaoui, Bennouna. The judgment on the merits was rendered on 12 July 2005, after which the Chamber formed to hear that case was dissolved.

Application for Revision of the Judgment of 11 September 1992 in the Case concerning the Land, Island and Maritime Frontier Dispute (El Salvador/Honduras: Nicaragua intervening) *(El Salvador v. Honduras)*: constituted on 27 November 2002 with the following composition — *Judges* Guillaume *(President)*, Rezek, Buergenthal; *Judges* ad hoc Torres Bernárdez, Paolillo. The judgment on the admissibility of the Application filed by El Salvador was rendered on 18 December 2003, after which the Chamber formed to hear that case was dissolved.

ANNEX 8

CASES SUBMITTED BY SPECIAL AGREEMENT

The following 17 cases were submitted by means of special agreement:

— *Asylum (Colombia/Peru);*
— *Minquiers and Ecrehos (France/United Kingdom);*
— *Sovereignty over Certain Frontier Land (Belgium/Netherlands);*
— *North Sea Continental Shelf (Federal Republic of Germany/Denmark; Federal Republic of Germany/Netherlands);*
— *Continental Shelf (Tunisia/Libyan Arab Jamahiriya);*
— *Delimitation of the Maritime Boundary in the Gulf of Maine Area (Canada/United States of America)* [case referred to a Chamber];
— *Continental Shelf (Libyan Arab Jamahiriya/Malta);*
— *Frontier Dispute (Burkina Faso/Republic of Mali)* [case referred to a Chamber];
— *Land, Island and Maritime Frontier Dispute (El Salvador/Honduras: Nicaragua intervening)* [case referred to a Chamber];
— *Territorial Dispute (Libyan Arab Jamahiriya/Chad);*
— *Gabčíkovo-Nagymaros Project (Hungary/Slovakia);*
— *Kasikili/Sedudu Island (Botswana/Namibia);*
— *Sovereignty over Pulau Ligitan and Pulau Sipadan (Indonesia/Malaysia);*
— *Frontier Dispute (Benin/Niger)* [case referred to a Chamber];
— *Sovereignty over Pedra Branca/Pulau Batu Puteh, Middle Rocks and South Ledge (Malaysia/Singapore);*
— *Frontier Dispute (Burkina Faso/Niger).*

It should be noted that in the *Corfu Channel (United Kingdom* v. *Albania)* case the Parties made a special agreement after delivery of the Judgment on the preliminary objection, and that the case concerning the *Arbitral Award Made by the King of Spain on 23 December 1906 (Honduras* v. *Nicaragua)* was submitted by means of an Application, but the Parties had previously concluded an agreement on the procedure to be followed in submitting the dispute to the Court.

ANNEX 9 (A)

Cases which the Court found it could take no further steps upon an Application in which it was admitted that the opposing party did not accept its jurisdiction (prior to the present Rules of Court coming into force on 1 July 1978, when Article 38, paragraph 5, was introduced):

— *Treatment in Hungary of Aircraft and Crew of United States of America (United States of America* v. *Hungary) (United States of America* v. *USSR);*
— *Aerial Incident of 10 March 1953 (United States of America* v. *Czechoslovakia);*
— *Antarctica (United Kingdom* v. *Argentina) (United Kingdom* v. *Chile);*
— *Aerial Incident of 7 October 1952 (United States of America* v. *USSR);*
— *Aerial Incident of 4 September 1954 (United States of America* v. *USSR);*
— *Aerial Incident of 7 November 1954 (United States of America* v. *USSR).*

ANNEX 9 (B)

QUESTIONS OF CONSENT: AFTER THE INTRODUCTION
OF ARTICLE 38, PARAGRAPH 5, OF THE RULES

In the following ten Applications, the provisions of Article 38, paragraph 5, were invoked by the Applicant, but the jurisdiction of the Court was not accepted by the Respondent:

— An Application filed by Hungary on 23 October 1992, instituting proceedings against the Czech and Slovak Republic, but no action was taken, the party against which the Application was filed having not consented to the Court's jurisdiction;

— An Application filed by the Federal Republic of Yugoslavia on 16 March 1994, instituting proceedings against the Member States of NATO, but no action was taken, the party against which the Application was filed having not consented to the Court's jurisdiction;

— In the cases concerning *Legality of Use of Force (Serbia and Montenegro* v. *France) (Serbia and Montenegro* v. *Germany) (Serbia and Montenegro* v. *Italy) (Serbia and Montenegro* v. *United States of America)*, Serbia and Montenegro (formerly called Yugoslavia) referred to Article IX of the Genocide Convention and to Article 38, paragraph 5, of the Rules of Court as bases for the jurisdiction of the Court. The cases were entered in the General List on the basis of the reference to Article IX of the Genocide Convention. No action was taken, the party against which the action was filed having not consented to the Court's jurisdiction;

— An Application filed by Eritrea on 16 February 1999, instituting proceedings against Ethiopia, but no action was taken, the party against which the Application was filed having not consented to the Court's jurisdiction;

— An Application filed by Liberia on 4 August 2003, instituting proceedings against Sierra Leone, but no action was taken, the party against which the Application was filed having not consented to the Court's jurisdiction;

— An Application filed by the Republic of Rwanda on 18 April 2007, instituting proceedings against France. As far as this Application is concerned, in accordance with Article 38, paragraph 5, of the Rules of Court, the Application by the Republic of Rwanda, to which was appended a request for the indication of provisional measures, was transmitted to the French Government. However, no action was taken in the proceedings as France did not consent to the Court's jurisdiction in the case;

— An Application filed by Equatorial Guinea on 25 September 2012, to which was annexed a request for provisional measures. In accordance with the Rules of Court, a copy of the above-mentioned document has been transmitted to the Government of France. No action shall be taken in the proceedings and the case shall not be entered in the General List unless and until France consents to the Court's jurisdiction in this case.

*

It should be noted that press releases were published announcing the filing of the above ten Applications. These press releases are filed by date of publication and can be found on the website of the Court under "Press Room".

ANNEX 10

ACCEPTANCE OF THE COURT'S JURISDICTION IN VIRTUE
OF ARTICLE 38, PARAGRAPH 5, OF THE RULES

In the following two Applications, the provisions of Article 38, paragraph 5, of the Rules of Court were invoked by the Applicant and accepted by the Respondent (the Court thus had jurisdiction as of the date of acceptance in virtue of the rule of *forum prorogatum*):

— An Application filed by the Republic of the Congo on 9 December 2002, instituting proceedings against France. As far as this Application is concerned, the Respondent consented to the Court's jurisdiction on 11 April 2003. That consent led to the case being entered into the General List with effect from the date of receipt of the consent as *Certain Criminal Proceedings (Republic of the Congo* v. *France)*;

— An Application filed by the Republic of Djibouti on 10 January 2006, instituting proceedings against France. As far as this Application is concerned, the Respondent consented to the Court's jurisdiction on 9 August 2006. That consent led to the case being entered into the General List with effect from the date of receipt of the consent as *Certain Questions of Mutual Assistance in Criminal Matters (Djibouti* v. *France)*.

ANNEX 11

REQUESTS FOR INTERPRETATION

Requests for interpretation of judgments of the Court were made on the following five occasions (the two cases accepted, at least in part by the Court, are shown with an asterisk):

— By Colombia in respect of the Judgment delivered by the Court on 20 November 1950 in the *Asylum (Colombia/Peru)* case;
— By Tunisia (along with an Application for revision) in respect of the Judgment delivered by the Court on 24 February 1982 in the case concerning the *Continental Shelf (Tunisia/Libyan Arab Jamahiriya)**;
— By Nigeria in respect of the Court's Judgment on preliminary objections of 11 June 1998 in the case concerning the *Land and Maritime Boundary between Cameroon and Nigeria (Cameroon v. Nigeria)*;
— By Mexico in respect of the Judgment delivered by the Court on 31 March 2004 in the case concerning *Avena and Other Mexican Nationals (Mexico v. United States of America)*;
— By Cambodia in respect of the Judgment delivered by the Court on 15 June 1962 in the case concerning *Temple of Preah Vihear (Cambodia v. Thailand)**.

ANNEX 12

Applications for the revision of judgments of the Court were made on the following three occasions:

— An Application for revision (along with a request for interpretation) of the Judgment of 24 February 1982 in the case concerning the *Continental Shelf (Tunisia/Libyan Arab Jamahiriya)* was filed by Tunisia;
— An Application for revision of the Court's Judgment on preliminary objections of 11 July 1996 in the case concerning *Application of the Convention on the Prevention and Punishment of the Crime of Genocide (Bosnia and Herzegovina v. Yugoslavia)* was filed by Yugoslavia;
— An Application for revision of the Judgment of 11 September 1992 in the case concerning the *Land, Island and Maritime Frontier Dispute (El Salvador/Honduras: Nicaragua intervening)* was filed by El Salvador.

*

No Applications for revision have to date been accepted by the Court.

ANNEX 13 (A)

The list that follows contains all organs and institutions within the United Nations system authorized to request advisory opinions of the Court, along with a list of the requests made by each of the organs and institutions concerned.

It is recalled that this information is also available on the website of the Court under "Jurisdiction/Advisory Jurisdiction", and the list of advisory opinions requested can be found under "Cases/Advisory proceedings".

(a) United Nations Organizations:

General Assembly

The General Assembly has requested 15 advisory opinions of the Court. For the list of these proceedings see Annex 13 (B), page 168.

Security Council

The Security Council requested an advisory opinion of the Court concerning the *Legal Consequences for States of the Continued Presence of South Africa in Namibia (South West Africa) notwithstanding Security Council Resolution 276 (1970))*.

Economic and Social Council

The Economic and Social Council requested an advisory opinion of the Court on two occasions: *Applicability of Article VI, Section 22, of the Convention on the Privileges and Immunities of the United Nations* and *Difference Relating to Immunity from Legal Process of a Special Rapporteur of the Commission on Human Rights*.

Trusteeship Council;
Interim Committee of the General Assembly;

(b) Specialized Agencies:

International Labour Organization;
Food and Agriculture Organization of the United Nations;
United Nations Educational, Scientific and Cultural Organization

The Executive Board of UNESCO requested an advisory opinion of the Court concerning *Judgments of the Administrative Tribunal of the ILO upon Complaints Made against Unesco*;

World Health Organization

The World Health Assembly requested an advisory opinion of the Court on two occasions: *Interpretation of the Agreement of*

25 March 1951 between the WHO and Egypt and *Legality of the Use by a State of Nuclear Weapons in Armed Conflict*;

International Bank for Reconstruction and Development;
International Finance Corporation;
International Development Association;
International Monetary Fund;
International Civil Aviation Organization;
International Telecommunication Union;
International Fund for Agricultural Development

> The International Fund for Agricultural Development requested an advisory opinion on *Judgment No. 2867 of the Administrative Tribunal of the International Labour Organization upon a Complaint Filed against the International Fund for Agricultural Development*;

World Meteorological Organization;
International Maritime Organization

> The Assembly of this organization requested an advisory opinion of the Court concerning the *Constitution of the Maritime Safety Committee of the Inter-Governmental Maritime Consultative Organization*;

World Intellectual Property Organization;
United Nations Industrial Development Organization;

(c) Related Organizations:

International Atomic Energy Agency.

The International Refugee Organization, which had been authorized to request advisory opinions of the Court, ceased to exist in 1952. The Havana Charter for an International Trade Organization, which provides for the jurisdiction of the Court in proceedings in regard to advisory opinions, has not entered into force.

ANNEX 13 (B)

ADVISORY OPINIONS

The following fifteen Advisory Opinions were requested by the General Assembly with the year of the Application noted in parentheses:

— *Conditions of Admission of a State to Membership in the United Nations (Article 4 of the Charter)* (1947);
— *Reparation for Injuries Suffered in the Service of the United Nations* (1948);
— *Interpretation of Peace Treaties with Bulgaria, Hungary and Romania, First Phase;* ibid., *Second Phase* (1949);
— *Competence of the General Assembly for the Admission of a State to the United Nations* (1949);
— *International Status of South West Africa* (1949);
— *Reservations to the Convention on the Prevention and Punishment of the Crime of Genocide* (1950);
— *Effect of Awards of Compensation Made by the United Nations Administrative Tribunal* (1953);
— *Voting Procedure on Questions relating to Reports and Petitions concerning the Territory of South West Africa* (1954);
— *Admissibility of Hearings of Petitioners by the Committee on South West Africa* (1955);
— *Certain Expenses of the United Nations (Article 17, paragraph 2, of the Charter)* (1961);
— *Western Sahara* (1974);
— *Applicability of the Obligation to Arbitrate under Section 21 of the United Nations Headquarters Agreement of 26 June 1947* (1988);
— *Legality of the Threat or Use of Nuclear Weapons* (1995);
— *Legal Consequences of the Construction of a Wall in the Occupied Palestinian Territory* (2003);
— *Accordance with International Law of the Unilateral Declaration of Independence in Respect of Kosovo* (2008).

Please note that a list of requests for Advisory Opinions are available on the Court's website under "Cases/Advisory Opinions".

ANNEX 13 (C)

This Annex lists the instruments governing the relationship of organs of the United Nations and international organizations with the Court in relation to its advisory jurisdiction, including: constitutional texts of public international organizations; agreements concluded between the United Nations and other international organizations; authorizations accorded by the General Assembly of the United Nations to other organs of the United Nations or to international organizations by virtue of Article 96, paragraph 2, of the Charter. By resolution 957 (X) of 8 November 1955 the General Assembly, amending the Statute of the United Nations Administrative Tribunal (Art. 11), authorized the Committee on Applications for Review of Judgments of the United Nations Administrative Tribunal to request advisory opinions of the International Court of Justice. By resolution 50/54 of 11 December 1995, the General Assembly amended the Tribunal's Statute again, *inter alia*, deleting Article 11 with respect to judgments rendered after 31 December 1995; multilateral conventions relating to the privileges and immunities of world-wide international organizations; agreements concluded by international organizations with States.

The present list is compiled from the information available to the Registry. It takes into account, so far as the Registry is informed of them, any amendments to those instruments which have affected their provisions concerning the jurisdiction of the Court. The inclusion or omission of any instrument should not be regarded as an indication of any view entertained by the Registry, or *a fortiori* by the Court, regarding the nature, scope or validity of the instrument in question.

1. United Nations

Authorization to the *General Assembly* and the *Security Council* to request advisory opinions of the International Court of Justice: Charter, Article 96, paragraph 1.

Authorization to the *Economic and Social Council* to request advisory opinions of the International Court of Justice: resolution 89 (I) of the General Assembly, 11 December 1946.

Authorization to the *Trusteeship Council* to request advisory opinions of the International Court of Justice: resolution 171 (II) of the General Assembly, 14 November 1947, paragraph B.

Authorization to the *Interim Committee of the General Assembly* to request advisory opinions of the International Court of Justice: resolution 196 (III) of the General Assembly, 3 December 1948, paragraph 3. The mandate of the Interim Committee was extended indefinitely by resolution 295 (IV) of the General Assembly of 21 November 1949, paragraph 3, of which preserved its authority to request advisory opinions of the Court.

Convention on the privileges and immunities of the United Nations, adopted by the General Assembly on 13 February 1946, Article VIII, Section 30 (United Nations, *Treaty Series*, I, No. 4, Vol. 1).

Agreement between the United Nations and the United States of America regarding the Headquarters of the United Nations, 26 June 1947, Article VIII, Section 21 (United Nations, *Treaty Series*, I, No. 147, Vol. 11).

Agreement between Chile and the United Nations Economic Commission for Latin America regulating conditions for the operation, in Chile, of the Headquarters of the Commission, 16 February 1953, Article XI, Section 21 (United Nations, *Treaty Series*, I, No. 4541, Vol. 314).

Agreement between the United Nations and Thailand relating to the Headquarters of the Economic Commission for Asia and the Far East in Thailand, 26 May 1954, Article XIII, Section 26 (United Nations, *Treaty Series*, I, No. 3703, Vol. 260).

Agreement between the United Nations and Ethiopia regarding the Headquarters of the United Nations Economic Commission for Africa, 18 June 1958, Article IX (United Nations, *Treaty Series*, I, No. 4597, Vol. 317).

Agreement between the United Nations and Japan regarding the Headquarters of the United Nations University, 14 May 1976, Section 22 (United Nations, *Treaty Series*, I, No. 14839, Vol. 1009).

Agreement between the United Nations and Greece regarding the Headquarters of the Co-ordinating Unit for the Mediterranean Action Plan, 11 February 1982, Section 26 (United Nations, *Treaty Series*, I, No. 20736, Vol. 1261).

2. Specialized Agencies

Convention on the privileges and immunities of specialized agencies approved by the General Assembly of the United Nations on 21 November 1947, Article VII, Section 24, and Article IX, Section 32 (United Nations, *Treaty Series*, I, No. 521, Vol. 33).

(a) *International Labour Organization*

Instrument for the amendment of the Constitution of the International Labour Organization, 9 October 1946, Articles 29, 31-34 and 37 (United Nations, *Treaty Series*, I, No. 229, Vol. 15).

Agreement between the United Nations and the International Labour Organization, approved by the General Assembly of the United Nations on 14 December 1946, Article IX (United Nations, *Treaty Series*, II, No. 9, Vol. 1).

Statute of the Administrative Tribunal of the International Labour Organization, adopted by the International Labour Conference on 9 October 1946 and modified by the Conference on 29 June 1949, Article XII. The jurisdiction of this Tribunal, which is open to officials of the International Labour Organization or other persons claiming under the terms of appointment of an official, has been recognized also by the following international organizations, which are authorized to request advisory opinions: Food and Agriculture Organization of the United Nations; United Nations Educational, Scientific and Cultural Organization; World Health Organization; International Telecommunication Union; World Meteorological Organization; World Intellectual Property Organization; International Atomic Energy Agency.

(b) *Food and Agriculture Organization of the United Nations*

Constitution of the Food and Agriculture Organization of the United Nations, 16 October 1945, as amended in 1957, Article XVII (Food and Agriculture Organization of the United Nations, *Basic Texts*, Vol. I, 1968).

Agreement between the United Nations and the Food and Agriculture Organization of the United Nations, approved by the General Assembly of the United Nations on 14 December 1946, Article IX (United Nations, *Treaty Series*, II, No. 10, Vol. 1).

Terms of appointment of the Director General of the Food and Agriculture Organization of the United Nations: recommendation by the Conference of the Organization, 27 October 1945, paragraph 3 (Food and Agriculture Organization of the United Nations, *Report of the First Session of the Conference*, 16 October-1 November 1945).

(c) *United Nations Educational, Scientific and Cultural Organization*

Constitution of the United Nations Educational, Scientific and Cultural Organization, 16 November 1945, Articles V, paragraph 11 (adopted in 1952), and XIV, paragraph 2 (United Nations, *Treaty Series*, I, No. 52, Vol. 4). See also Rules of Procedure of the General Conference of UNESCO, Rule 33, and the Protocol of 10 December 1962 instituting a Conciliation and Good Offices Commission to be responsible for seeking the settlement of any disputes which may arise between States parties to the Convention against Discrimination in Education, Article 18 (UNESCO document 12C/Resolutions).

Agreement between the United Nations and the United Nations Educational, Scientific and Cultural Organization, approved by the General Assembly of the United Nations on 14 December 1946, as revised and approved by the General Assembly of the United Nations on 8 December 1962, Article X (Article XI before the revision of 1962)

(United Nations, *Treaty Series*, II, No. 11, Vol. 1; *ibid.*, General Assembly, resolution 1786 (XVII)).

Agreement between the United Nations Educational, Scientific and Cultural Organization and France regarding the Headquarters of UNESCO and the privileges and immunities of the Organization on French territory, 2 July 1954, Article 29 (United Nations, *Treaty Series*, I, No. 5103, Vol. 357).

(d) *World Health Organization*

Constitution of the World Health Organization, 22 July 1946, Articles 75-77 (United Nations, *Treaty Series*, I, No. 221, Vol. 14).

Agreement between the United Nations and the World Health Organization, approved by the General Assembly of the United Nations on 15 November 1947, Article X (United Nations, *Treaty Series*, II, No. 115, Vol. 19).

(e) *International Bank for Reconstruction and Development, International Finance Corporation and International Development Association*

Agreement between the United Nations and the International Bank for Reconstruction and Development, approved by the General Assembly of the United Nations on 15 November 1947, Article VIII (United Nations, *Treaty Series*, II, No. 109, Vol. 16).

Agreement on relationship between the United Nations and the International Finance Corporation, approved by the General Assembly of the United Nations on 20 February 1957, paragraph I (United Nations, *Treaty Series*, II, No. 546, Vol. 265).

Agreement on relationship between the United Nations and the International Development Association, approved by the General Assembly of the United Nations on 27 March 1961, Article I (United Nations, *Treaty Series*, II, No. 582, Vol. 394).

(f) *International Monetary Fund*

Agreement between the United Nations and the International Monetary Fund, approved by the General Assembly of the United Nations on 15 November 1947, Article VIII (United Nations, *Treaty Series*, II, No. 108, Vol. 16).

(g) *International Civil Aviation Organization*

Convention on International Civil Aviation, 7 December 1944, Articles 84-86 (United Nations, *Treaty Series*, I, No. 10612, Vol. 740; ICAO, *Convention on International Civil Aviation*, 1969).

Agreement between the United Nations and the International Civil Aviation Organization, approved by the General Assembly of the United Nations on 14 December 1946, Article X (United Nations, *Treaty Series*, II, No. 45, Vol. 8).

Agreement between the International Civil Aviation Organization and Canada regarding the Headquarters of the Organization, 14 April 1951,

Article VII, Section 31 (United Nations, *Treaty Series*, I, No. 1335, Vol. 96).

(h) *International Telecommunication Union*

Agreement between the United Nations and the International Telecommunication Union, approved by the General Assembly of the United Nations on 15 November 1947, Article VII (United Nations, *Treaty Series*, II, No. 175, Vol. 30).

(i) *World Meteorological Organization*

Agreement between the United Nations and the World Meteorological Organization, approved by the General Assembly of the United Nations on 20 December 1951, Article VII (United Nations, *Treaty Series*, II, No. 415, Vol. 123).

(j) *International Maritime Organization*

Convention on the Inter-Governmental Maritime Consultative Organization, 6 March 1948, entered into force on 17 March 1958, Articles 55 and 56 (United Nations, *Treaty Series*, I, No. 4214, Vol. 289). As from 22 May 1982 the Inter-Governmental Maritime Consultative Organization (IMCO) became the International Maritime Organization (IMO); the name of the organization was changed in the title of the 1948 Convention and the relevant articles of the Convention were renumbered 69 and 70.

Agreement between the United Nations and the Inter-Governmental Maritime Consultative Organization, approved by the General Assembly of the United Nations on 18 November 1948, entered into force on 13 January 1959, Article IX (United Nations, *Treaty Series*, II, No. 553, Vol. 324).

(k) *World Intellectual Property Organization*

Agreement between the United Nations and the World Intellectual Property Organization, approved by the General Assembly of the United Nations on 17 December 1974, Article 12 (United Nations, *Treaty Series*, II, No. 729).

(l) *International Fund for Agricultural Development*

Agreement between the United Nations and the International Fund for Agricultural Development, approved by the General Assembly of the United Nations on 15 December 1977, Article XIII (United Nations, *Treaty Series*, II, No. 806, Vol. 1080).

(m) *United Nations Industrial Development Organization*

Constitution of the United Nations Industrial Development Organization, 8 April 1979, Article 22 (United Nations, *Treaty Series*, I, No. 23432, Vol. 1401).

Agreement between the United Nations Organization and the United Nations Industrial Development Organization, approved by the General Assembly of the United Nations on 17 December 1985, Article 12.

3. Related Organizations

International Atomic Energy Agency

Statute of the International Atomic Energy Agency, 26 October 1956, Article XVII (United Nations, *Treaty Series*, I, No. 3988, Vol. 276).

Agreement concerning the relationship between the United Nations and the International Atomic Energy Agency, approved by the General Assembly of the United Nations on 14 November 1957, Article X (United Nations, *Treaty Series*, II, No. 548, Vol. 281).

Authorization to the International Atomic Energy Agency to request advisory opinions of the International Court of Justice: resolution 1146 (XII) of the General Assembly of the United Nations, 14 November 1957.

Agreement on the privileges and immunities of the International Atomic Energy Agency, approved by the Board of Governors of the Agency on 1 July 1959, Article X, Section 34 (United Nations, *Treaty Series*, I, No. 5334, Vol. 374).

Agreement between the International Atomic Energy Agency and Iraq, Lebanon, Libya, Tunisia, United Arab Republic, etc., for the establishment in Cairo of a Middle Eastern regional radio-isotope centre for the Arab countries, approved by the Board of Governors of the Agency on 14 September 1962, Article XVI (United Nations, *Treaty Series*, I, No. 7236, Vol. 494).

Nordic Mutual Emergency Assistance Agreement in connection with radiation accidents, signed on 17 October 1963 by the International Atomic Energy Agency, Denmark, Finland, Norway and Sweden, Article IX (United Nations, *Treaty Series*, I, No. 7585, Vol. 525).

ANNEX 14

Staff members of the Registry are subject to Instructions for the Registry and Staff Regulations for the Registry.

The Instructions for the Registry, established by the Registry and approved by the Court in October 1946, were amended in March 1947 and again in September 1949. The Court adopted a revised version of the Instructions in March 2012.

According to Article 28, paragraph 4, of the Rules of Court, the Staff Regulations, established by the Registry and approved by the Court, must be "so far as possible in conformity with the United Nations Staff Regulations and Staff Rules".

Before 1979, staff members of the Registry were subject to Staff Regulations adopted by the President and approved by the Court in March 1947 in accordance with Article 18, paragraph 2, of the 1946 Rules of Court; these Staff Regulations were amended in February and March 1950 and in June 1951.

On 7 March 1979, the Court adopted new Staff Regulations for the Registry. These Staff Regulations were amended in November 1987, July 1996, April 1997, December 2000, September 2002, May 2006, June 2009 and March 2012.

The text of the Instructions for the Registry and the Staff Regulations for the Registry can be found on the website of the Court (www.icj-cij.org) under "Registry/Texts Governing the Registry".

ANNEX 15

Former Registrars of the Court:

— E. Hambro (1946-1953),
— J. López-Oliván (1953-1960),
— J. Garnier-Coignet (1960-1966),
— S. Aquarone (1966-1980),
— S. Torres Bernárdez (1980-1986),
— E. Valencia-Ospina (1987-2000).

Former Deputy-Registrars of the Court:

— J. Garnier-Coignet (1946-1960),
— S. Aquarone (1960-1966),
— W. Tait (1966-1976),
— A. Pillepich (1977-1984),
— E. Valencia-Ospina (1984-1987),
— B. Noble (1987-1994),
— J. J. Arnaldez (1994-2008),
— T. de Saint-Phalle (2008-2013).

ANNEX 16

Approved Budget for the Biennium 2012-2013

Approved budget (revised appropriation) for the biennium 2012-2013 (United States dollars):

Programme		
Members of the Court		
0311025	Allowances for various expenses[1]	1,534,300
0311023	Pensions	3,850,700
0393909	Duty allowance: judges *ad hoc*	1,233,400
2042302	Travel on official business	52,900
0393902	Emoluments	7,825,200
Subtotal		**14,496,500**
Registry		
0110000	Established posts	17,518,200
0170000	Temporary posts for the biennium	199,300
0200000	Common staff costs	6,652,000
1540000	(Medical and associated costs, after suspension of services)	317,900
0211014	Representation allowance	7,200
1210000	Temporary assistance for meetings	1,508,100
1310000	General temporary assistance	264,500
1410000	Consultants[2]	170,400
1510000	Overtime	101,800
2042302	Official travel	49,400
0454501	Hospitality	20,500
Subtotal		**26,809,300**

---

[1] Including a total of US$410,000 pursuant to the General Assembly resolution on unforeseen expenses.

[2] Including a total of US$11,900 pursuant to the General Assembly resolution on unforeseen expenses.

Programme		
Programme Support		
3030000	External translation	446,100
3050000	Printing	635,200
3070000	Data-processing services	670,600
4010000	Rental/maintenance of premises	3,375,900
4030000	Rental of furniture and equipment	246,800
4040000	Communications	210,900
4060000	Maintenance of furniture and equipment	111,900
4090000	Miscellaneous services	48,900
5000000	Supplies and materials	277,400
5030000	Library books and supplies	244,000
6000000	Furniture and equipment	201,000
6025041	Acquisition of office automation equipment	80,000
6025042	Replacement of office automation equipment	135,100
Subtotal		**6,683,800**
Total		**47,989,600**

ANNEX 17

EMOLUMENTS OF MEMBERS OF THE COURT

The emoluments of Members of the Court are made up of an annual salary, which may not be decreased during the period of office (Statute of the Court, Art. 32, paras. 1 and 5). By its resolution 61/262 of 4 April 2007, the General Assembly decided that the annual salaries of the Members of the Court would comprise an annual base salary with a corresponding post adjustment per index point equal to 1 per cent of the net base salary to which would be applied a post adjustment multiplier for the Netherlands. With effect from 1 January 2012, the annual base salary of Members of the Court is fixed at $169,098.

Under Article 32, paragraphs 2 and 3, of the Statute, the President of the Court and the Vice-President (for every day on which he/she acts as President) receive special allowances in addition. The rates, fixed by resolution 40/257 of 18 December 1985, were revised by resolution 65/258 of 16 March 2011 and amount to $25,000 per annum for the President of the Court and $156 for the Vice-President for every day on which he/she acts as President up to a maximum amount of $15,600 per annum.

Article 32, paragraph 7, of the Statute provides: "Regulations made by the General Assembly shall fix the conditions under which retirement pensions may be given to Members of the Court." The General Assembly first adopted the Pensions Scheme Regulations for Members of the International Court of Justice in its resolution 86 (I) of 11 December 1946 and modifications were made over the years. The detailed conditions of the current pension scheme for Members of the Court are provided on pages 368-370 of the *I.C.J. Yearbook 2009-2010*.

By its resolution 65/258, the General Assembly decided that the pension scheme of Members of the Court will next be reviewed at its sixty-sixth session, including options for defined benefit and defined contribution pensions schemes, and in this regard, requested the Secretary-General to ensure that, in that review, the expertise available within the United Nations is taken full advantage of. The General Assembly further decided, by its resolution 66/638, to defer the review of the pension scheme of Members of the Court to its sixty-eighth session.

By its resolutions 40/257 of 18 December 1985, 61/262 of 4 April 2007 and 63/251 of 24 December 2008, the General Assembly determined the conditions of education grants applicable to Members of the Court, which remain unchanged to the present day.

By virtue of Article 32, paragraph 7, of the Statute, regulations made by the General Assembly fix the conditions under which Members of the Court have their travelling expenses refunded. The General Assembly adopted the first Travel and Subsistence Regulations of the International Court of Justice by its resolution 85 (I) of 11 December 1946, which were subsequently amended by resolution 37/240 of 21 December 1982 and are still in force. The provisions of these regulations are set out in the *I.C.J. Yearbook 1982-1983*, pp. 164-167.

ANNEX 18

Witnesses and/or experts have been called in the following 11 cases:

— *Corfu Channel (United Kingdom* v. *Albania)* where the Court heard witnesses and experts presented by each of the Parties, appointed experts by Order and prescribed an enquiry on the spot;

— *Temple of Preah Vihear (Cambodia* v. *Thailand)* where the Court heard witnesses and experts presented by each of the Parties;

— *South West Africa (Ethiopia* v. *South Africa; Liberia* v. *South Africa)* where the Court heard witnesses and experts presented by one Party;

— *Continental Shelf (Tunisia/Libyan Arab Jamahiriya)* where the Court heard an expert presented by one Party;

— *Delimitation of the Maritime Boundary in the Gulf of Maine Area (Canada/United States of America)* where the Chamber constituted heard an expert presented by one Party and itself appointed, by Order, at the request of the Parties and in accordance with the Special Agreement concluded between them, a technical expert to assist it in its work;

— *Continental Shelf (Libyan Arab Jamahiriya/Malta)* where the Court heard experts presented by each of the Parties;

— *Military and Paramilitary Activities in and against Nicaragua (Nicaragua* v. *United States of America)* where the Court heard witnesses presented by one Party;

— *Elettronica Sicula S.p.A. (ELSI) (United States of America* v. *Italy)* where the Chamber constituted heard witnesses presented by one of the Parties and experts presented by each of them;

— *Land, Island and Maritime Frontier Dispute (El Salvador/Honduras: Nicaragua intervening)* where the Court heard a witness presented by one Party;

— *Application of the Convention on the Prevention and Punishment of the Crime of Genocide (Bosnia and Herzegovina* v. *Serbia and Montenegro)* where the Court heard witnesses, experts and witness-experts presented by both Parties.

ANNEX 19

Provisional measures have been requested in the following cases:

— *Anglo-Iranian Oil Co. (United Kingdom* v. *Iran);*
— *Interhandel (Switzerland* v. *United States of America);*
— *Fisheries Jurisdiction (United Kingdom* v. *Iceland) (Federal Republic of Germany* v. *Iceland);*
— *Nuclear Tests (Australia* v. *France) (New Zealand* v. *France);*
— *Trial of Pakistani Prisoners of War (Pakistan* v. *India);*
— *Aegean Sea Continental Shelf (Greece* v. *Turkey);*
— *United States Diplomatic and Consular Staff in Tehran (United States of America* v. *Iran);*
— *Military and Paramilitary Activities in and against Nicaragua (Nicaragua* v. *United States of America);*
— *Frontier Dispute (Burkina Faso/Republic of Mali)* (case referred to a Chamber);
— *Border and Transborder Armed Actions (Nicaragua* v. *Honduras)* (in this case the request was withdrawn);
— *Arbitral Award of 31 July 1989 (Guinea-Bissau* v. *Senegal);*
— *Passage through the Great Belt (Finland* v. *Denmark);*
— *Questions of Interpretation and Application of the 1971 Montreal Convention arising from the Aerial Incident at Lockerbie (Libyan Arab Jamahiriya* v. *United Kingdom) (Libyan Arab Jamahiriya* v. *United States of America);*
— *Application of the Convention on the Prevention and Punishment of the Crime of Genocide (Bosnia and Herzegovina* v. *Serbia and Montenegro)* (in this case two requests were made by Bosnia and Herzegovina and one by Serbia and Montenegro);
— *Land and Maritime Boundary between Cameroon and Nigeria (Cameroon* v. *Nigeria);*
— *Request for an Examination of the Situation in Accordance with Paragraph 63 of the Court's Judgment of 20 December 1974 in the* Nuclear Tests (New Zealand *v.* France) *Case;*
— *Vienna Convention on Consular Relations (Paraguay* v. *United States of America);*
— *LaGrand (Germany* v. *United States of America);*
— *Legality of Use of Force (Serbia and Montenegro* v. *Belgium) (Serbia and Montenegro* v. *Canada) (Serbia and Montenegro* v. *France) (Serbia and Montenegro* v. *Germany) (Serbia and Montenegro* v. *Italy) (Serbia and Montenegro* v. *Netherlands) (Serbia and Montenegro* v. *Portugal) (Yugoslavia* v. *Spain) (Serbia and Montenegro* v. *United Kingdom) (Yugoslavia* v. *United States of America);*

— *Armed Activities on the Territory of the Congo (Democratic Republic of the Congo* v. *Uganda);*
— *Arrest Warrant of 11 April 2000 (Democratic Republic of the Congo* v. *Belgium);*
— *Armed Activities on the Territory of the Congo (New Application: 2002) (Democratic Republic of the Congo* v. *Rwanda);*
— *Avena and Other Mexican Nationals (Mexico* v. *United States of America);*
— *Certain Criminal Proceedings in France (Republic of the Congo* v. *France);*
— *Pulp Mills on the River Uruguay (Argentina* v. *Uruguay)* (in this case, a request was made by Argentina and another was made by Uruguay);
— *Request for Interpretation of the Judgment of 31 March 2004 in the Case concerning* Avena and Other Mexican Nationals (Mexico *v.* United States of America) *(Mexico* v. *United States of America);*
— *Application of the International Convention on the Elimination of All Forms of Racial Discrimination (Georgia* v. *Russian Federation);*
— *Questions relating to the Obligation to Prosecute or Extradite (Belgium* v. *Senegal);*
— *Certain Activities Carried Out by Nicaragua in the Border Area (Costa Rica* v. *Nicaragua)*. On 18 November 2010, Costa Rica submitted a request for the indication of provisional measures. By an Order of 8 March 2011, the Court had indicated certain provisional measures to both Parties. It should be noted that on 23 May 2013, Costa Rica also filed a request asking the Court to modify the measures indicated in its Order of 8 March 2011 (that request makes reference to Article 41 of the Statute of the Court and Article 76 of its Rules). Nicaragua asked the Court to reject Costa Rica's request, while in turn requesting the Court to modify or adapt the Order of 8 March 2011 on the basis of Article 76 of the Rules of Court. By an Order dated 16 July 2013, the Court ruled on the requests submitted by Costa Rica and Nicaragua respectively.
— *Request for Interpretation of the Judgment of 15 June 1962 in the Case concerning the* Temple of Preah Vihear (Cambodia *v.* Thailand) *(Cambodia* v. *Thailand).*

It is recalled that an Application, to which was appended a request for the indication of provisional measures, was filed by the Republic of Guinea against France on 25 September 2012. In accordance with Article 38, paragraph 5, of the Rules of Court, the Application was transmitted to the French Government. However, no action will be taken in the proceedings unless and until France consents to the Court's jurisdiction in the case.

ANNEX 20

PRELIMINARY OBJECTIONS

The Court gave its decision on the preliminary objections raised in the following 34 cases:

— *Corfu Channel (United Kingdom* v. *Albania);*
— *Ambatielos (Greece* v. *United Kingdom);*
— *Anglo-Iranian Oil Co. (United Kingdom* v. *Iran);*
— *Nottebohm (Liechtenstein* v. *Guatemala);*
— *Monetary Gold Removed from Rome in 1943 (Italy* v. *France, United Kingdom and United States of America);*
— *Certain Norwegian Loans (France* v. *Norway);*
— *Right of Passage over Indian Territory (Portugal* v. *India);*
— *Interhandel (Switzerland* v. *United States of America);*
— *Aerial Incident of 27 July 1955 (Israel* v. *Bulgaria);*
— *Temple of Preah Vihear (Cambodia* v. *Thailand);*
— *South West Africa (Ethiopia* v. *South Africa; Liberia* v. *South Africa);*
— *Northern Cameroons (Cameroon* v. *United Kingdom);*
— *Barcelona Traction, Light and Power Company, Limited (New Application: 1962) (Belgium* v. *Spain);*
— *Elettronica Sicula S.p.A. (ELSI) (United States of America* v. *Italy);*
— *Certain Phosphate Lands in Nauru (Nauru* v. *Australia);*
— *Questions of Interpretation and Application of the 1971 Montreal Convention arising from the Aerial Incident at Lockerbie (Libyan Arab Jamahiriya* v. *United Kingdom) (Libyan Arab Jamahiriya* v. *United States of America);*
— *Oil Platforms (Islamic Republic of Iran* v. *United States of America);*
— *Application of the Convention on the Prevention and Punishment of the Crime of Genocide (Bosnia and Herzegovina* v. *Serbia and Montenegro);*
— *Land and Maritime Boundary between Cameroon and Nigeria (Cameroon* v. *Nigeria);*
— *Aerial Incident of 10 August 1999 (Pakistan* v. *India);*
— *Legality of Use of Force (Serbia and Montenegro* v. *Belgium) (Serbia and Montenegro* v. *Canada) (Serbia and Montenegro* v. *France) (Serbia and Montenegro* v. *Germany) (Serbia and Montenegro* v. *Italy) (Serbia and Montenegro* v. *Netherlands) (Serbia and Montenegro* v. *Portugal) (Serbia and Montenegro* v. *United Kingdom);*
— *Certain Property (Liechtenstein* v. *Germany);*
— *Ahmadou Sadio Diallo (Republic of Guinea* v. *Democratic Republic of the Congo);*
— *Territorial and Maritime Dispute (Nicaragua* v. *Colombia);*
— *Application of the Convention on the Prevention and Punishment of the Crime of Genocide (Croatia* v. *Serbia);*

— *Application of the International Convention on the Elimination of All Forms of Racial Discrimination (Georgia* v. *Russian Federation).*

In another seven cases the Court was not called upon to give a decision on the preliminary objections, either because they were withdrawn:

— *Rights of Nationals of the United States of America in Morocco (France* v. *United States of America);*

or as the result of a discontinuance by the respondent party:

— *Aerial Incident of 27 July 1955 (United States of America* v. *Bulgaria);*
— *Barcelona Traction, Light and Power Company, Limited (Belgium* v. *Spain)* (first application);
— *Compagnie du Port, des Quais et des Entrepôts de Beyrouth and Société Radio-Orient (France* v. *Lebanon);*
— *Trial of Pakistani Prisoners of War (Pakistan* v. *India);*
— *Aerial Incident of 3 July 1988 (Islamic Republic of Iran* v. *United States of America);*
— *Armed Activities on the Territory of the Congo (Democratic Republic of the Congo* v. *Burundi) (Democratic Republic of the Congo* v. *Rwanda).*

ANNEX 21

QUESTIONS OF JURISDICTION AND/OR ADMISSIBILITY

The Court has ruled on questions of jurisdiction and/or admissibility in a number of cases, a list of which can be found below (classed in order of their entry in the General List of the Court):

— *Nottebohm (Liechtenstein* v. *Guatemala);*
— *South West Africa (Ethiopia* v. *South Africa; Liberia* v. *South Africa);*
— *Appeal Relating to the Jurisdiction of the ICAO Council (India* v. *Pakistan);*
— *Fisheries Jurisdiction (United Kingdom* v. *Iceland) (Federal Republic of Germany* v. *Iceland);*
— *Nuclear Tests (Australia* v. *France) (New Zealand* v. *France);*
— *Aegean Sea Continental Shelf (Greece* v. *Turkey);*
— *United States Diplomatic and Consular Staff in Tehran (United States of America* v. *Iran);*
— *Military and Paramilitary Activities in and against Nicaragua (Nicaragua* v. *United States of America);*
— *Border and Transborder Armed Actions (Nicaragua* v. *Honduras);*
— *Maritime Delimitation and Territorial Questions between Qatar and Bahrain (Qatar* v. *Bahrain);*
— *East Timor (Portugal* v. *Australia);*
— *Application of the Convention on the Prevention and Punishment of the Crime of Genocide (Bosnia and Herzegovina* v. *Serbia and Montenegro).* After the Court gave its decision on preliminary objections, it dealt once more with questions of jurisdiction in its judgment on the merits in the case;
— *Fisheries Jurisdiction (Spain* v. *Canada);*
— *LaGrand (Germany* v. *United States of America);*
— *Arrest Warrant of 11 April 2000 (Democratic Republic of the Congo* v. *Belgium);*
— *Certain Criminal Proceedings in France (Republic of the Congo v. France);*
— *Avena and Other Mexican Nationals (Mexico v. United States of America);*
— *Request for Interpretation of the Judgment of 31 March 2004 in the Case concerning* Avena and Other Mexican Nationals (Mexico *v.* United States of America) *(Mexico* v. *United States of America);*
— *Application of the Interim Accord of 13 September 1995 (the former Yugoslav Republic of Macedonia* v. *Greece);*
— *Jurisdictional Immunities of the State (Germany* v. *Italy: Greece intervening);*
— *Questions relating to the Obligation to Prosecute or Extradite (Belgium* v. *Senegal);*
— *Whaling in the Antarctic (Australia* v. *Japan: New Zealand intervening);*
— *Frontier Dispute (Burkina Faso/Niger);*
— *Request for Interpretation of the Judgment of 15 June 1962 in the Case concerning the* Temple of Preah Vihear (Cambodia *v.* Thailand) *(Cambodia* v. *Thailand).*

ANNEX 22

COUNTER-CLAIMS (RULES, ARTICLE 80)

Counter-claims were made by the respondent States and admitted by the Court in the following four cases:

— *Application of the Convention on the Prevention and Punishment of the Crime of Genocide (Bosnia and Herzegovina v. Serbia and Montenegro).* In an Order of 10 September 2001, the Court placed on record the withdrawal of the counter-claims submitted by the respondent State in this case;

— *Oil Platforms (Islamic Republic of Iran v. United States of America);*

— *Land and Maritime Boundary between Cameroon and Nigeria (Cameroon v. Nigeria);*

— *Armed Activities on the Territory of the Congo (Democratic Republic of the Congo v. Uganda).*

*

It is recalled that on 4 February 2010, the Court directed the submission of a Reply by the Republic of Croatia and a Rejoinder by the Republic of Serbia in respect of the claims presented by the Parties in the case concerning *Application of the Convention on the Prevention and Punishment of the Crime of Genocide (Croatia v. Serbia).* The Court took account of the fact that the Counter-Memorial filed by Serbia on 4 January 2010 contains counter-claims (a summary of this request can be found in press release No. 2010/3, available online). Given the absence of objections by Croatia to the admissibility of the above-mentioned counter-claims, the Court did not consider that it was required to rule definitively at this stage on the question of whether the said claims fulfilled the conditions set forth in Article 80, paragraph 1, of the Rules of Court.

In order to protect the rights which third States entitled to appear before the Court derive from the Statute, the Court instructed the Registrar to transmit to them a copy of the Order. The Court stated that it was also appropriate, "in order to ensure strict equality between the Parties, to reserve the right for Croatia to express its views for a second time in writing within a reasonable time-limit on Serbia's counter-claims, in an additional pleading whose submission may be dealt with in a subsequent Order". By its Order of 23 January 2012, the Court authorized the submission by the Republic of Croatia of an additional pleading relating solely to the counter-claims submitted by the Republic of Serbia. The Court made this Order following an indication by Croatia that it wished to present its views for a second time in writing, in an additional pleading, on Serbia's counter-claims, and taking account of the views of the Parties.

ANNEX 23

Applications for permission to intervene under Articles 62 and/or declarations of intervention under Article 63 of the Statute were submitted in the following 12 cases:

— *Haya de la Torre (Colombia* v. *Peru);*
— *Nuclear Tests* cases *(Australia* v. *France) (New Zealand* v. *France);*
— *Continental Shelf (Tunisia/Libyan Arab Jamahiriya);*
— *Continental Shelf (Libyan Arab Jamahiriya/Malta);*
— *Land, Island and Maritime Frontier Dispute (El Salvador/Honduras);*
— *Request for an Examination of the Situation in Accordance with Paragraph 63 of the Court's Judgment of 20 December 1974 in the* Nuclear Tests (New Zealand *v.* France) *Case* (in this case, several States filed a document entitled "Application for Permission to Intervene under Article 62/Declaration of Intervention under Article 63");
— *Land and Maritime Boundary between Cameroon and Nigeria (Cameroon* v. *Nigeria);*
— *Sovereignty over Pulau Ligitan and Pulau Sipadan (Indonesia/Malaysia);*
— *Military and Paramilitary Activities in and against Nicaragua (Nicaragua* v. *United States of America)* (in this case a Declaration of Intervention under Article 63 was submitted);
— *Territorial and Maritime Dispute (Nicaragua* v. *Colombia);*
— *Jurisdictional Immunities of the State (Germany* v. *Italy);*
— *Whaling in the Antarctic (Australia* v. *Japan).*

ANNEX 24

Twelve Judgments and Orders were delivered in the absence of one of the parties in the following twelve cases:

— *Corfu Channel (United Kingdom* v. *Albania), Assessment of Amount of Compensation;*
— *Anglo-Iranian Oil Co. (United Kingdom* v. *Iran), Interim Protection;*
— *Nottebohm (Liechtenstein* v. *Guatemala), Preliminary Objection;*
— *Fisheries Jurisdiction (United Kingdom* v. *Iceland) (Federal Republic of Germany* v. *Iceland), Interim Protection, Jurisdiction of the Court* and *Merits;*
— *Nuclear Tests (Australia* v. *France) (New Zealand* v. *France), Interim Protection* and *Second Phase;*
— *Trial of Pakistani Prisoners of War (Pakistan* v. *India), Interim Protection;*
— *Aegean Sea Continental Shelf (Greece* v. *Turkey), Interim Protection* and *Jurisdiction of the Court;*
— *United States Diplomatic and Consular Staff in Tehran (United States of America* v. *Iran), Provisional Measures* and *Merits;*
— *Military and Paramilitary Activities in and against Nicaragua (Nicaragua* v. *United States of America), Merits;*
— *Maritime Delimitation and Territorial Questions between Qatar and Bahrain (Qatar* v. *Bahrain), Jurisdiction and Admissibility.*

ANNEX 25

Discontinuance (Rules, Articles 88-89)

The following 21 cases were discontinued:

— *Protection of French Nationals and Protected Persons in Egypt (France* v. *Egypt);*
— *Electricité de Beyrouth Company (France* v. *Lebanon);*
— *Aerial Incident of 27 July 1955 (United States of America* v. *Bulgaria) (United Kingdom* v. *Bulgaria);*
— *Barcelona Traction, Light and Power Company, Limited (Belgium* v. *Spain)* (first application);
— *Compagnie du Port, des Quais et des Entrepôts de Beyrouth and Société Radio-Orient (France* v. *Lebanon);*
— *Trial of Pakistani Prisoners of War (Pakistan* v. *India);*
— *Border and Transborder Armed Actions (Nicaragua* v. *Costa Rica);*
— *Border and Transborder Armed Actions (Nicaragua* v. *Honduras);*
— *Passage through the Great Belt (Finland* v. *Denmark);*
— *Certain Phosphate Lands in Nauru (Nauru* v. *Australia);*
— *Maritime Delimitation between Guinea-Bissau and Senegal (Guinea-Bissau* v. *Senegal);*
— *Aerial Incident of 3 July 1988 (Islamic Republic of Iran* v. *United States of America);*
— *Vienna Convention on Consular Relations (Paraguay* v. *United States of America);*
— *Armed Activities on the Territory of the Congo (Democratic Republic of the Congo* v. *Burundi) (Democratic Republic of the Congo* v. *Rwanda);*
— *Questions of Interpretation and Application of the 1971 Montreal Convention arising from the Aerial Incident at Lockerbie (Libyan Arab Jamahiriya* v. *United Kingdom) (Libyan Arab Jamahiriya* v. *United States of America);*
— *Status vis-à-vis the Host State of a Diplomatic Envoy to the United Nations (Commonwealth of Dominica* v. *Switzerland);*
— *Certain Questions concerning Diplomatic Relations (Honduras* v. *Brazil);*
— *Certain Criminal Proceedings in France (Republic of the Congo* v. *France).*

The following two cases ended in discontinuance as regarded the question of reparation which the judgment had left to be settled.

— *United States Diplomatic and Consular Staff in Tehran (United States of America* v. *Iran);*
— *Military and Paramilitary Activities in and against Nicaragua (Nicaragua* v. *United States of America).*

ANNEX 26

<small>Occasional Functions Entrusted to the President of the Court</small>

Below is a general description of the appointing powers occasionally exercised by the President. Specific appointments requested and made in the course of the reporting year are not listed.

1. International Instruments Providing for Appointment of Arbitrators, etc.

There are many international instruments which provide that in certain eventualities the President of the Court may be requested by the contracting parties to appoint arbitrators, umpires, members of conciliation commissions, etc.

States proposing to insert such a provision in a treaty should consult the President as to his willingness to accept such a task, and submit the draft provision to him. This frequently provides that, if the President is of the nationality of one of the parties to the dispute, the appointment should be made either by the Vice-President or by the senior Member of the Court not so disqualified.

Such a provision is found, for instance, in bilateral agreements relating to air transport, social security, reparations or guarantees, loans, technical co-operation and the protection of investments; in multilateral treaties; in conventions or agreements concerning the constitution, status or privileges and immunities of international organizations; and in agreements or contracts concluded between States and international organs.

2. Other Requests for Appointment of Arbitrators

The President of the Court is sometimes requested to appoint arbitrators under the terms of contracts concluded between a State and a corporation or between corporations. The President should not be called upon to perform this function in regard to transnational arbitration agreements dealing with matters in which public international law does not find its place.

The President should be consulted in advance and a draft contract should be submitted to him. It is usually provided that if the President is of the same nationality as one of the parties to the contract, the appointment should be made either by the Vice-President or by the senior Member of the Court not so disqualified.

3. Other Appointments

The President has also at times been requested by States or international organizations to appoint persons to fill other offices.

Such appointments are, for instance, provided for in texts such as Article 12 of the Protocol of 23 June 1953 for limiting and regulating the cultivation of the poppy plant, the production of, international and wholesale trade in, and use of opium, or Article 4 of the Regulations for the execution of the Convention of 14 May 1954 for the protection of cultural property in the event of armed conflict or, again, Rule 109.1 *(a)* of the Staff Rules of the United Nations and Regulation 9.1.1 of the Staff Regulations of the United Nations Educational, Scientific and Cultural Organization.

————————

ANNEX 27

It is recalled that the speech reproduced below, along with the other principal speeches made by the President, are available on the website of the Court, under the headings "The Court/Presidency/Speeches of the President".

"Mr. President,
Excellencies,
Ladies and Gentlemen,

I would first like to take this opportunity to congratulate His Excellency Mr. Vuk Jeremić on his election as President of the Sixty-Seventh Session of the United Nations General Assembly. I wish him every success in this distinguished office.

In accordance with a well-established tradition, which reflects the interest in and support for the Court shown by your eminent Assembly, I would like to present a brief review of the judicial activities of the Court over the last 12 months. During this period, the Court continued to fulfil its role as the international community of States' forum of choice for the peaceful settlement of every kind of international dispute over which it has jurisdiction. It made every effort to meet the expectations of the parties appearing before it in a timely manner. It should be noted in this regard that, since the Court has been able to clear its backlog of cases, States thinking of submitting cases to the principal judicial organ of the United Nations can be confident that, as soon as they have finished their written exchanges, the Court will be able to move to the hearings without delay.

During the period under review, as many as 15 contentious cases and one advisory procedure were pending before the Court; 11 contentious cases remained so on 31 July 2012. During the same period, one new contentious case was submitted to the Court by Nicaragua, relating to the *Construction of a Road in Costa Rica along the San Juan River (Nicaragua* v. *Costa Rica)*. During the year 2011-2012, the Court held public hearings in turn in the following three cases: *Jurisdictional Immunities of the State (Germany* v. *Italy: Greece intervening)*; *Questions relating to the Obligation to Prosecute or Extradite (Belgium* v. *Senegal)*; and the *Territorial and Maritime Dispute (Nicaragua* v. *Colombia)*. The Court is now deliberating in this last case and intends on delivering its Judgment during this month. It also held hearings in the case concerning the *Frontier Dispute*

(Burkina Faso/Niger) from 8 to 17 October 2012 and has begun its deliberation. Lastly, hearings will begin in the case concerning the *Maritime Dispute (Peru* v. *Chile)* on 3 December.

During the reporting period, the Court delivered four Judgments in the following cases: *Application of the Interim Accord of 13 September 1995 (the former Yugoslav Republic of Macedonia* v. *Greece)*; *Jurisdictional Immunities of the State (Germany* v. *Italy: Greece intervening)*; *Ahmadou Sadio Diallo (Republic of Guinea* v. *Democratic Republic of the Congo)*, on the question of compensation owed to Guinea; and *Questions relating to the Obligation to Prosecute or Extradite (Belgium* v. *Senegal)*. The Court also delivered an Advisory Opinion concerning *Judgment No. 2867 of the Administrative Tribunal of the International Labour Organization upon a Complaint Filed against the International Fund for Agricultural Development*.

*

As is traditional, I will report briefly on the four Judgments and the Advisory Opinion rendered by the Court during the period under review. I shall deal with these decisions in chronological order.

On 5 December 2011, the Court delivered its Judgment in the case concerning the *Application of the Interim Accord of 13 September 1995 (the former Yugoslav Republic of Macedonia* v. *Greece)*. The case had been brought on 17 November 2008 by the former Yugoslav Republic of Macedonia against Greece for what it described as 'a flagrant violation of [Greece's] obligations under Article 11' of the Interim Accord signed by the Parties on 13 September 1995. After asking the Court, in its Application,

> 'to protect its rights under the Interim Accord and to ensure that it is allowed to exercise its rights as an independent State acting in accordance with international law, including the right to pursue membership of relevant international organizations',

the former Yugoslav Republic of Macedonia requested the Court to order Greece to 'immediately take all necessary steps to comply with its obligations under Article 11, paragraph 1' and

> 'to cease and desist from objecting in any way, whether directly or indirectly, to the Applicant's membership of the North Atlantic Treaty Organization and/or of any other 'international, multilateral and regional organizations and institutions' of which [Greece] is a member . . .'.

Greece, for its part, considered that the case brought by the Applicant did not fall within the jurisdiction of the Court and that the Applicant's claims were inadmissible; it argued, in the alternative, that, were the Court to find that it had jurisdiction and that the claims were admissible, those claims were without foundation.

With regard to the Respondent's objections as to the jurisdiction of the Court and the admissibility of the Applicant's claims, the Court ruled that it not only had jurisdiction to entertain the Application filed by the former Yugoslav Republic of Macedonia, but also that the Application was admissible. As for the second part of the Applicant's claims, the Court found that the Hellenic Republic, by objecting to the admission of the former Yugoslav Republic of Macedonia to NATO, had violated its obligation under Article 11, paragraph 1, of the Interim Accord. The Court rejected all other submissions made by the former Yugoslav Republic of Macedonia.

*

On 3 February 2012, the Court rendered its judgment in the case concerning *Jurisdictional Immunities of the State (Germany v. Italy: Greece intervening)*. It was Germany which, on 23 December 2008, filed an Application instituting proceedings against Italy, whereby it requested the Court to find that Italy had failed to respect the jurisdictional immunity enjoyed by Germany under international law by allowing civil claims to be brought against it in the Italian courts, seeking reparation for injuries caused by violations of international humanitarian law committed by the German Reich during the Second World War; that Italy had also violated Germany's immunity by taking measures of constraint against Villa Vigoni, German State property situated in Italian territory; and that Italy had further breached Germany's jurisdictional immunity by declaring enforceable in Italy decisions of Greek civil courts rendered against Germany on the basis of acts similar to those which had given rise to the claims brought before Italian courts. Consequently, Germany requested the Court to adjudge and declare that Italy's international responsibility was engaged; that Italy must, by means of its own choosing, take any and all steps to ensure that all the decisions of its courts and other judicial authorities infringing Germany's sovereign immunity became unenforceable; and that Italy must take any and all steps to ensure that in the future Italian courts did not entertain legal actions against Germany founded on the above-mentioned occurrences.

In its Judgment, the Court found that Italy had violated its obligation to respect the immunity which Germany enjoys under international law by allowing civil claims to be brought against it based on violations of international humanitarian law committed by the German Reich between 1943 and 1945; that Italy had violated its obligation to respect the immunity which Germany enjoys under international law by taking measures of constraint against Villa Vigoni; and that Italy had violated its obligation to respect the immunity which Germany enjoys under international law by declaring enforceable in Italy decisions of Greek courts based on violations of international humanitarian law committed in Greece by the German Reich. The Court also found that Italy must, by enacting appropriate legislation, or by resorting to other methods of its choosing, ensure that the decisions of its courts and those of other judicial authorities infringing the immunity which Germany enjoys under international law cease to have effect.

Last September, the Italian Minister for Foreign Affairs and Minister of Justice, in agreement with the Minister of Economy and Finance, presented draft legislation to the Italian Chamber of Deputies providing for the authorization of ratification by Italy of the United Nations Convention on Jurisdictional Immunities of States and Their Property, and its implementation. Furthermore, the draft law also addresses the effect in the Italian legal system of the Judgment of the Court in the aforementioned case, so as to ensure compliance with that decision.

*

It was on 19 June 2012 that the Court delivered its third Judgment during the period under review, namely in the case concerning *Ahmadou Sadio Diallo (Republic of Guinea* v. *Democratic Republic of the Congo)*. That Judgment concerned the question of compensation owed by the DRC to Guinea. It should be recalled that, in the Judgment on the merits on 30 November 2010, the Court had found, amongst other things, that the DRC had violated certain international obligations as a result of Mr. Diallo, a Guinean national, being continuously detained in Congolese territory for 66 days, from 5 November 1995 until 10 January 1996 and being detained for a second time between 25 and 31 January 1996, that is, for a total of 72 days. In that connection, the Court had found that Guinea had failed to demonstrate that Mr. Diallo had been subjected to inhuman or degrading treatment during his detentions. In addition, it had observed that Mr. Diallo had been expelled by the DRC on 31 January 1996 and that he had received notice of his expulsion on the same day. Accordingly, the Court had stated that the DRC was required to compensate Guinea for breaches of its obligations under certain human rights conventions, namely the International Covenant on Civil and Political Rights and the African Charter on Human and Peoples' Rights. Under the terms of the Judgment on the merits, it followed that the amount of compensation to be paid by the DRC had to be set 'for the injury flowing from the wrongful detentions and expulsion of Mr. Diallo in 1995-1996, including the resulting loss of his personal belongings'.

In the final stage of the proceedings, Guinea sought compensation amounting to eleven million five hundred and ninety thousand one hundred and forty-eight American dollars (US$11,590,148), not including statutory default interest, under four heads of damage: non-material injury (referred to by Guinea as 'mental and moral damage'); and three heads of material damage: alleged loss of personal property; alleged loss of professional remuneration (referred to by Guinea as 'loss of earnings') during Mr. Diallo's detentions and after his expulsion; and alleged deprivation of 'potential earnings'. Guinea also requested the Court to order the DRC not only to pay all the costs, but also to pay it the amount of US$500,000 for costs which it had been forced to incur in the proceedings. The DRC, for its part, requested the Court to adjudge that compensation in an amount of US$30,000, payable within a time-limit of six months from the date of the Court's Judgment, was due to Guinea to make good the non-pecuniary injury suffered by Mr. Diallo as a result of his wrongful detentions and expulsion in 1995-1996; the DRC rejected all other claims by Guinea.

In ruling on the non-material injury alleged by Guinea, the Court considered that the amount of US$85,000 would provide appropriate compensation for the damage suffered by Mr. Diallo. With regard to the compensation for material injury, the Court, relying on the jurisprudence of regional human rights courts, awarded the sum of US$10,000 for the loss of Mr. Diallo's personal property. Having then found that Guinea had not proven to the satisfaction of the Court that Mr. Diallo had suffered a loss of professional remuneration during his detentions and following his expulsion, the Court decided to award no compensation for that injury; lastly, the Court decided to award no compensation to Guinea in respect of its claim relating to the 'potential earnings' of Mr. Diallo, in so far as such a claim, which was beyond the scope of those proceedings, amounted to a claim relating to the injuries alleged to have been caused to Africom-Zaire and Africontainers-Zaire, while the Court had already declared those claims inadmissible. After fixing 31 August 2012 as the time-limit for payment of the compensation owed by the DRC to Guinea, with post-judgment interest accruing at an annual rate of 6 per cent in the event of late payment, the Court decided that each Party should bear its own procedural costs. The Court was informed that compensation was duly paid by the DRC within the time-limit fixed for that purpose.

*

I now come to the Judgment rendered by the Court in the case concerning *Questions relating to the Obligation to Prosecute or Extradite* between Belgium and Senegal. In this case, which it submitted to the Court by means of an Application dated 19 February 2009, Belgium complained that Senegal, where the former President of Chad, Hissène Habré, has been living in exile since 1990, had taken no action on its repeated requests to ensure that the latter be brought to trial in Senegal, failing his extradition to Belgium, for acts characterized as torture, crimes against humanity, war crimes and the crime of genocide, allegedly committed while he was President of Chad between 1982 and 1990. Belgium contended that Senegal was in breach of its obligations under Article 5, paragraph 2, Article 6, paragraph 2, and Article 7, paragraph 1, of the 1984 Convention against Torture and its obligations under customary international law. Senegal, for its part, submitted that there was no dispute between the Parties with regard to the interpretation or application of the Convention against Torture or any other relevant rule of international law; according to the Respondent, the Court therefore lacked jurisdiction in the case. Arguing, in particular, that none of the alleged victims of the acts attributed to Mr. Habré was of Belgian nationality at the time when the acts were committed, Senegal also objected to the admissibility of Belgium's claims because, in its view, the latter was not entitled to invoke the international responsibility of Senegal for the alleged breach of its obligation to submit the Hissène Habré case to its competent authorities for the purpose of prosecution, failing his extradition.

Given that the existence of a dispute was a condition of the jurisdiction of the Court under both bases of jurisdiction invoked by Belgium, namely Article 30, paragraph 1, of the Convention against Torture and the declarations made by the Parties under Article 36, paragraph 2, of the Statute of the Court, the Court began by considering that question: it found that, in view of the legislative and constitutional reforms carried out in Senegal in 2007 and 2008, any dispute that might have existed between the Parties with regard to the interpretation or application of Article 5, paragraph 2, of the Convention, which requires a State party to the Convention to 'take such measures as may be necessary to establish its jurisdiction' over acts of torture when the alleged offender is 'present in any territory under its jurisdiction', if it does not extradite him to one of the States referred to in paragraph 1 of the same Article, had ended by the time the Application was filed.

As regards Belgium's claims relating to Senegal's duty to comply with its obligations under Article 6, paragraph 2, and Article 7, paragraph 1, of the Convention against Torture, which respectively require a State party to the Convention, when a person who has allegedly committed an act of torture is found on its territory, to hold 'a preliminary inquiry into the facts' and, 'if it does not extradite him', to 'submit the case to its competent authorities for the purpose of prosecution', the Court, after analysing the diplomatic exchanges between the Parties, found that they had conflicting views concerning the interpretation and application of the above-mentioned provisions at the time of the filing of the Application. However, the

Court considered that the dispute which had thus arisen did not relate to breaches of obligations under customary international law.

After recalling that, in the words of its Preamble, the object and purpose of the Convention against Torture is to make more effective the struggle against torture throughout the world, the Court found that Belgium, as a State party to that Convention, had standing to invoke the responsibility of Senegal for the alleged breaches of its obligations *erga omnes partes* under Article 6, paragraph 2, and Article 7, paragraph 1; the claims of Belgium based on these provisions were thus declared admissible.

After assessing questions relating to the merits, the Court found that Senegal had violated its obligations under the two above-mentioned provisions of the Convention and that it had engaged its international responsibility. Noting the continuing nature of those violations, it declared that Senegal was required to cease them by 'tak[ing] without further delay the necessary measures to submit the case to its competent authorities for the purpose of prosecution, if it does not extradite Mr. Habré'.

*

I shall now turn to the Court's Advisory Opinion concerning *Judgment No. 2867 of the Administrative Tribunal of the International Labour Organization upon a Complaint Filed against the International Fund for Agricultural Development*. In that case, the Court was asked to examine the validity of a judgment rendered by the Administrative Tribunal of the International Labour Organization (hereinafter 'Tribunal' or 'ILOAT') concerning the contract of employment of Ms Saez García. It should be recalled that the latter had accepted from the International Fund for Agricultural Development (hereinafter 'IFAD' or 'Fund') an offer of a two-year fixed-term contract serving as a Programme Officer in the Global Mechanism, an institution housed at the Fund. That contract of employment had been renewed on two occasions. The Tribunal was seized of a dispute concerning the decision of the President of the Fund to reject the recommendations of the Fund's Joint Appeals Board following several internal procedures relating to the non-renewal of the contract of the individual concerned and the abolition of her post. In its judgment, the Tribunal set aside the President's decision and ordered the Fund to pay damages and expenses. In the course of the advisory proceedings before the Court, the Fund asserted, in particular, that Ms Saez García was a staff member of the Global Mechanism and not of IFAD and that her employment status had to be assessed in the context of the arrangement for the housing of the Global Mechanism made between the Fund and the Conference of the Parties to the UN Convention to Combat Desertification.

After examining the texts defining the respective powers of, and relationships between, IFAD and the Global Mechanism, the Court came to the conclusion that the Global Mechanism, which is devoid of any international legal personality, had no power and had not purported to exercise any power to enter into contracts, agreements or 'arrangements', internationally or nationally. With respect to Ms Saez García's employment status, the Court found that there was an employment relationship between her and the Fund, given that the staff regulations and rules of the Fund were applicable to her. Accordingly, the Court unanimously found that the Tribunal was competent, under Article II of its Statute, to hear the complaint introduced against IFAD on 8 July 2008 by Ms Saez García and that the decision given by the Tribunal in its Judgment No. 2867 was valid.

In the light of its concern 'about the inequality of access to the Court arising from the review process under Article XII of the Annex to the Statute of the ILOAT', the Court examined the principle of the equality before the Court of the Fund and Ms Saez García. It declared that the 'principle [of equality] must now be understood as including access on an equal basis to available appellate or similar remedies unless an exception can be justified on objective and reasonable grounds'. In this connection, the Court questioned whether the system established in 1946 allowed for the implementation of this modern-day concept of the principle of equality and access to justice, stating, however, that it did not fall to it to reform the current system.

In the case in question, the Court found that 'the unequal position before the Court of the employing institution and its official, arising from provisions of the Court's Statute, ha[d] been substantially alleviated' by its decision that

> 'the President of the Fund was to transmit to the Court any statement setting forth the views of Ms Saez García which she might wish to bring to the attention of the Court and [to fix] the same time-limits for her as for the Fund for the filing of written statements in the first round of written argument and comments in the second round'.

Moreover, the Court concluded that the situation of inequality was also alleviated by its decision not to hold hearings, pointing out that its "Statute does not allow individuals to appear in hearings in such cases, by contrast to international organizations concerned".

While the UN has reformed its system of administrative justice some time ago, it remains nonetheless still possible to request revision of a judgment of the ILOAT. In fact, the opportunity to challenge a judgment of the Tribunal is only available to international organizations duly authorized to do so under the Statute of the ILOAT, and not to any staff member affected by such a decision. In that regard, the question arises whether the time has not come for the International

Labour Organization to also consider initiating a reform of the current system, such as the one already carried out by the UN.

*

Turning to more practical matters, I am delighted to tell you that the Court is refurbishing the Great Hall of Justice in the Peace Palace. This project, which has received the support of the Carnegie Foundation, is the first major renovation of this Hall in 100 years. In the past, minor works were carried out in order to extend the bench in order to accommodate the enlarged composition of the Court's predecessor, namely the Permanent Court of International Justice. However, no renovation on the scale of the current project has previously been envisaged; furthermore, the newly-renovated Great Hall of Justice will also be equipped with improved modern technical facilities offering a wide range of possibilities.

I am therefore very pleased to assure Member States that, of course, we hear and shall continue to hear cases submitted to the Court faithfully and impartially, as required by the noble judicial mission entrusted to us, but that we are also modernizing the setting in which we exercise this function. We have thus been able to put the funds mobilized by the United Nations General Assembly to good use in this refurbishment and renovation project.

*

Mr. President,
Excellencies,
Ladies and Gentlemen,

I hope that I have conveyed to you the extent to which the Court seeks to meet the expectations of the international community as a whole, including, as in the last decision that I reviewed, in relation to particular aspects of the law of international organizations. This is why the Court has already discussed the schedule of its judicial work for 2013 and 2014 with a view to fixing several series of hearings. I have already mentioned that hearings will begin in the case concerning the *Maritime Dispute (Peru* v. *Chile)* in December. In addition, the Court envisages holding hearings in April in the case concerning the *Request for Interpretation of the Judgment of 15 June 1962 in the Case concerning the* Temple of Preah Vihear (Cambodia *v.* Thailand) *(Cambodia* v. *Thailand)*, and in early summer next year in the case concerning *Whaling in the Antarctic (Australia* v. *Japan)*.

Of course, the Court must do its utmost to serve the noble purposes and goals of the United Nations using limited resources, since the Member States award it less than 1 per cent, exactly 0.8 per cent, of the Organization's regular budget. Nevertheless, I hope that I have shown that the recent contributions of the Court are not to be measured in terms of the financial resources that sustain it, but against the great progress made by it in the advancement of international justice and the peaceful settlement of disputes between States.

I would like to thank you for giving me this opportunity to speak to you today. I wish you every success for this Sixty-Seventh Session of the Assembly."

———————

ANNEX 28

Owing to the adverse weather conditions in New York on this date (Hurricane Sandy), which disrupted work at the United Nations Headquarters, President Tomka was able to deliver only a shortened version of his speech (which is reproduced in full below) on the contribution of the Court to the development of the law of maritime delimitation. His speech was later recorded in full by the Codification Division of the United Nations Office of Legal Affairs: the video recording, which is 45 minutes long, is available in English on the website of the Audiovisual Library of International Law (www.un.org/law/avl). To view it, click on "Faculty Directory", and then select "T" (Peter Tomka). The video is entitled *The Contribution of the International Court of Justice to the Development of the Law of Maritime Delimitation.*

Herewith is the full text of the speech given by the President of the Court, Mr. Peter Tomka, before the Sixth Committee of the General Assembly on 2 November 2012:

"Mr. Chairman,
Distinguished Delegates of the Sixth Committee,

I am pleased to address your Committee today. The Court greatly appreciates this opportunity to further strengthen the bonds of harmony and co-operation which bind our respective institutions.

I congratulate His Excellency Ambassador Yuriy Sergeyev on his election as Chairman of the Sixth Committee for the Sixty-Seventh Session of the General Assembly.

*

Today, rather than going over the ground I already covered in the General Assembly in recounting the work carried out by the Court, I would like to take this opportunity to address you with a more narrow focus on what I consider to be a timely topic. In particular, I would like to discuss the contributions of the Court to the law governing maritime delimitation. It seems that there is an ever-increasing interest in the work of the Court on this front and, more specifically, with respect to maritime delimitation more broadly. One only has to glance at the burgeoning docket of international judicial and arbitral institutions to appreciate the timeliness of this topic and, correspondingly, the need to further bolster the principled legal approaches to maritime delimitation.

The International Court of Justice's delimitation-heavy docket is eloquent: in its history, some fourteen cases involving maritime delimitation issues have been submitted to the Court for adjudication with respect to maritime zones located in Western and Eastern Europe, North and South America, including the Caribbean, the Middle East and Africa[1]. There are currently two cases pending before the Court: the *Territorial and Maritime Dispute* opposing Nicaragua and Colombia, in which the Court began its deliberations last May, and the *Maritime Dispute* between Peru and Chile, in which the Court will hold public hearings next month.

Similarly, several other tribunals, including arbitral ones, have also considerably advanced the jurisprudential discourse in this field. For instance, ITLOS rendered a judgment last spring in its first ever maritime delimitation case in the *Dispute concerning delimitation of the maritime boundary between Bangladesh and Myanmar in the Bay of Bengal*. This case illustrated both the salience of maritime delimitation issues in contemporary international law and the influence of the Court's jurisprudence in further developing this legal field. Likewise, the docket of the Permanent Court of Arbitration has also been rich in recent years with cases involving maritime disputes, including the pending *Arbitration between the Republic of Croatia and the Republic of Slovenia*.

Thus, the Court's contribution to the advancement of the law governing maritime delimitation cannot be overemphasized, as evidenced by the wide reach and scope of the precedential value of its judgments and their influence in other decisional fora. When handling maritime delimitation cases, the Court not only interprets and applies relevant customary norms to reach equitable outcomes in maritime disputes in unique contexts, but it continuously contributes to the greater unification of the relevant rules applicable to different maritime areas while confirming its established methodology for achieving those equitable solutions. I propose sketching a broad picture of the major milestones in the evolution of the Court's jurisprudence, which has undoubtedly solidified the unity and coherence of the resulting normative scheme.

*

There is no doubt that a paramount contribution deriving from the Court's jurisprudence resides in its elaboration of the 'equidistance/ relevant circumstances' methodology when confronted with the delimitation of the continental shelf and the exclusive economic zone ('EEZ') with a view to achieving an equitable solution. I shall return to this aspect of the Court's jurisprudence in a moment but, for the time being, I would like to underscore a few important principles underpinning the most pertinent norms in the field.

---

[1] See, e.g., Shi Jiuyong, "The Wang Tieya Lecture in Public International Law: Maritime Delimitation in the Jurisprudence of the International Court of Justice", (2010) *9 Chinese Journal of International Law*, 271, 272.

1. General principles

Of particular relevance, and now firmly entrenched in the Court's jurisprudence, is the notion that maritime delimitation remains shaped and informed by international law, as opposed to leaving coastal States up to their own devices. Merely five years after the Court's inception in 1946, the *Anglo-Norwegian Fisheries (United Kingdom v. Norway)* Judgment had already consecrated this foundational principle, which I would equate with the primacy of international law in maritime delimitation matters, in the following terms:

> 'The delimitation of sea areas has always an international aspect; it cannot be dependent merely upon the will of the coastal State as expressed in its municipal law. Although it is true that the act of delimitation is necessarily a unilateral act, because only the coastal State is competent to undertake it, the validity of the delimitation with regard to other States depends upon international law.'[1]

Thus, the limits and outer boundaries of different maritime areas appertaining to a State in any given case are necessarily defined by international law[2]. As a corollary, such principle entails not only the conferral of rights and entitlements to States over their appurtenant maritime areas, but also the assumption, by those sovereign entities, of obligations owed towards other members of the international community. Such duties aim at protecting the maritime environment and, to a certain degree, also promote the protection of foreign persons and property against crimes perpetrated in States' areas of maritime entitlement, to list a few examples.

Equally important is the principle, commonly expressed as 'the land dominates the sea', according to which maritime entitlements flow from State sovereignty over land and are thus determined by reference to pre-existing territorial rights. The Court first referred to this principle in 1969 in its *Continental Shelf (Greece v. Turkey)* cases when addressing the delimitation of the sea-bed in the North Sea[3], only to reassert it several times in subsequent jurisprudence, including in the *Aegean Sea Continental Shelf (Greece v. Turkey)* case[4] and the *Territorial and Maritime Dispute between Nicaragua and Honduras in the Caribbean Sea (Nicaragua v. Honduras)*[5].

---

[1] *I.C.J. Reports 1951*, p. 132.
[2] See e.g., Sir Gerald G. Fitzmaurice, *The Law and Procedure of the International Court of Justice* (Cambridge, Grotius, 1986), p. 203.
[3] *I.C.J. Reports 1969*, p. 51, para. 96.
[4] *I.C.J. Reports 1978*, p. 36, para. 86.
[5] *I.C.J. Reports 2007 (II)*, p. 696, para. 113.

The Court had the opportunity to provide further contour to this principle in the *Qatar* v. *Bahrain* case, when it declared that '[i]t is thus the terrestrial territorial situation that must be taken as starting-point for the determination of the maritime rights of a coastal State'[1]. It is worth mentioning that, in that case, the Court attributed sovereignty to Qatar over a low-tide elevation, Fasht ad Dibal, given that such feature was situated on the 'right side' of the maritime boundary, once the delimitation line was constructed and adjusted[2]. The Court's reasoning may be best explained by the fact that since this maritime feature formed part of the sea, it would necessarily fall within the purview of entitlement of the State exercising jurisdiction over the territorial sea surrounding this low-tide elevation. Indeed, the opposite conclusion might have irreconcilably flown in the face of the 'land dominates the sea' principle.

2. Increasing requests for single maritime boundaries

In recent years, States have increasingly requested the Court to draw a single maritime boundary with a view to dividing, by a single line, all their respective maritime areas extending beyond the territorial sea, namely the continental shelf and EEZ. The single boundary approach, which closely followed the emergence of the legal framework governing the EEZ, was entertained by a Chamber of the Court for the first time in its 1984 *Gulf of Maine* Judgment. This was the first occasion on which the Court was called upon not only to delimit the respective continental shelf areas of the Parties, but also to determine the boundary pertaining to their respective superjacent water columns[3]. By contrast, the 1969 *Continental Shelf* cases and the 1982 *Tunisia/Libya* case remained confined to the delimitation of a single maritime area, that of the continental shelf.

Even in the absence of prior jurisprudence espousing such method, the Chamber in the *Gulf of Maine* case was receptive to the Parties' request that it draw a single boundary to apportion both maritime zones, 'in accordance with the principles and rules of international law applicable in the matter as between the Parties'. The Chamber went on to:

'observe that the Parties have simply taken it for granted that it would be possible, both legally and materially, to draw a single boundary for two different jurisdictions. They have not put forward any arguments in support of this assumption. The

---

[1] *Maritime Delimitation and Territorial Questions between Qatar and Bahrain (Qatar* v. *Bahrain), Merits, Judgment, I.C.J. Reports 2001*, p. 97, para. 185.

[2] *Ibid.*, p. 109, para. 220.

[3] *Delimitation of the Maritime Boundary in the Gulf of Maine Area (Canada/United States of America), Judgment, I.C.J. Reports 1984*, p. 267, para. 26.

Chamber, for its part, is of the opinion that there is certainly no rule of international law to the contrary, and, in the present case, there is no material impossibility in drawing a boundary of this kind. There can thus be no doubt that the Chamber can carry out the operation requested of it.'[1]

From that case onward, most parties to maritime delimitation disputes before the Court requested it to draw a single maritime line to divide their respective zones of entitlement, including in the 2009 case concerning *Maritime Delimitation in the Black Sea*, opposing Romania and Ukraine[2]. It is telling that the notion of a single maritime boundary appears nowhere in the United Nations Convention on the Law of the Sea ('UNCLOS'); rather, it originated in the practice of States and the Court has welcomed this development in its jurisprudence, while still upholding other relevant conventional and customary norms governing maritime delimitation.

3. Relevant coasts and baselines

It is of fundamental importance that the Court's determining of a delimitation line dividing the respective rights of the parties be carried out only when the baselines are known, while taking account of the relevant coastlines. In many ways, therefore, they amount to a preliminary consideration to be taken into account when the Court initiates the delimitation process. In the case concerning the *Land and Maritime Boundary between Cameroon and Nigeria (Cameroon v. Nigeria: Equatorial Guinea intervening)*, the Court spoke to this point:

'Before it can draw an equidistance line and consider whether there are relevant circumstances that might make it necessary to adjust that line, the Court must . . . define the relevant coastlines of the Parties by reference to which the location of the base points to be used in the construction of the equidistance line will be determined.'[3]

Unsurprisingly, the Court has often had to deal with cases in which the baselines to be used for the determination of the breadth of the territorial sea and, ultimately, for the delimitation of the final

---

[1] *I.C.J. Reports 2001*, p. 267, paras. 26-27.

[2] *I.C.J. Reports 2009*, p. 70, para. 17. In the pending case before the Court opposing Nicaragua and Colombia, a request for a single maritime boundary was also initially put forth by the Applicant to delimit the respective areas of continental shelf and EEZ. However, Nicaragua later rescinded its position in favour of claiming an extended continental shelf in the Caribbean Sea. See *Territorial and Maritime Dispute (Nicaragua v. Colombia)*, Reply of the Government of Nicaragua, Vol. 1, 18 September 2009, paras. 25-26.

[3] *I.C.J. Reports 2002*, p. 442, para. 290.

maritime boundary had not been specified by the parties. *Qatar* v. *Bahrain* is a case in point[1]. This happens because in many cases, before carrying out its delimitation, the Court first has to resolve sovereignty issues pertaining to certain maritime features that may have a bearing on the establishment of some baselines.

The 1951 *Fisheries* case, opposing the United Kingdom and Norway, contributed greatly to advancing the method of determining the relevant baselines from which the breadth of the territorial sea is measured seaward. Because of historical factors and the particular indented shape of its coast, Norway argued that it could use straight baselines to measure its territorial sea, as opposed to the habitual low-water mark along the coast. I should mention that the United Kingdom had conceded a breadth of four miles to Norway, so the actual breadth of that State's territorial sea was not in dispute[2]. Ultimately, the Court recognized Norway's entitlement to rely upon a general straight baselines system to measure the breadth of its territorial sea in light of the geographical peculiarity of its coast. In so doing, the Court significantly advanced the judicial appreciation of the relevant legal norms, many of which are now mirrored in UNCLOS.

That said, the *Fisheries* case likely consecrated the exceptional status of the straight baselines system, signifying that due deference is to be given to the habitual low-water mark standard in any given case. One need only read Article 5 of UNCLOS, which states: '[e]xcept where otherwise provided in this Convention, the normal baseline for measuring the breadth of the territorial sea is the low-water line along the coast as marked on large-scaled charts officially recognized by the coastal State'[3]. Similarly, Article 7 of the same instrument also reflects several of the elements offered by the Court in the *Fisheries* case when confirming the applicability of the straight baselines system, chief amongst them being the following: '[i]n localities where the coast line is deeply indented and cut into, or if there is a fringe of islands along the coast in its immediate vicinity'[4].

However, paragraph 3 of the same provision does impose some restrictions, indicating that straight baselines must not be drawn in a manner which 'depart[s] to any appreciable extent from the general direction of the coast', and that 'the sea areas lying within the lines must be sufficiently closely linked to the land domain to be subject to the regime of internal waters', thereby reflecting the views expressed by the Court in the *Fisheries* case[5]. Interestingly, while not forming a

---

[1] *Maritime Delimitation and Territorial Questions between Qatar and Bahrain (Qatar* v. *Bahrain), Merits, Judgment, I.C.J. Reports 2001*, p. 94, para. 177.

[2] *Fisheries (United Kingdom* v. *Norway), Judgment, I.C.J. Reports 1951*, pp. 119-120.

[3] United Nations Convention on the Law of the Sea (Montego Bay, 10 December 1982, United Nations, *Treaty Series*, 1833).

[4] *Ibid.*

[5] *Fisheries (United Kingdom* v. *Norway), Judgment, I.C.J. Reports 1951*, p. 97, para. 183.

full-fledge independent element driving the reasoning of the Court, economic factors, such as reliance by local communities on fishing activities in a given maritime area, did nonetheless inform its decision to ascertain whether the straight baselines system was applicable to the Norwegian coastline. Article 7, paragraph 5, of UNCLOS ultimately incorporated a similar approach, that is only where the method of straight baselines applies may account be taken of 'economic interests peculiar to the region concerned' when determining particular baselines.

Some 60 years later, in the *Qatar* v. *Bahrain* case, the Court revisited the question whether a State may draw straight baselines in order to effect delimitation of its maritime areas, this time in a decidedly different scenario. Drawing inspiration from the method prescribed by UNCLOS by reference to its status as a *de facto* archipelagic State, Bahrain felt it was entitled to draw archipelagic baselines. Indeed, Article 47 of that Convention provides that such States may draw 'straight archipelagic baselines joining the outermost points of the outermost islands and drying reefs of the archipelago'. However, given that Bahrain had not subsumed this request under its formal submissions to the Court, the International Court of Justice declined to rule on this question; rather, it construed its role as confined to drawing a single maritime boundary in accordance with international law, as requested by the Parties[1].

Recalling the binding force of its judgments pursuant to Article 59 of its Statute, the Court insisted that its delimitation would remain unchanged by Bahrain's eventual decision to declare itself an archipelagic State, or by any other such unilateral action undertaken by either Party. In short, the Court affirmed the paramount importance of the stability of maritime boundaries[2].

Equally interesting was the Court's consideration of the relevance and impact of maritime features, other than the main coast, on the determination of the baselines. Relying on UNCLOS, the Court underscored that

> '[i]n accordance with Article 121, paragraph 2, of the 1982 [Convention], which reflects customary international law, islands, regardless of their size, in this respect enjoy the same status, and therefore generate the same maritime rights, as other land territory'[3].

Article 121, paragraph 1, of UNCLOS excludes low-tide elevations from the ambit of the definition of 'island', and provides that such feature is 'a naturally formed area of land, surrounded by water, which is above water at high tide'.

---

[1] *Maritime Delimitation and Territorial Questions between Qatar and Bahrain (Qatar v. Bahrain), Merits, Judgment, I.C.J. Reports 2001*, p. 97, para. 183.

[2] *Ibid.*

[3] *Ibid.*, para. 185.

However, when a boundary is to be drawn between two opposite or adjacent States with overlapping maritime areas, complications ensue and it may well be that some islands might be disregarded when establishing baselines, should they bring about a disproportionate effect on the resulting boundary. Of course, it remains a matter for interpretation whether this operation should occur before the Court even posits a provisional line, or whether it should rather be addressed at the adjustment stage of the delimitation, when the Court considers relevant factors warranting correction of its provisional line, or during both stages of the delimitation. What Article 13 of UNCLOS tells us is that when a low-tide elevation is 'situated wholly or partly at a distance not exceeding the breadth of the territorial sea from the mainland or an island', 'the low-water line on that elevation may be used as the baseline for measuring the breadth of the territorial sea'[1].

4. Equitable outcomes when delimiting the territorial sea, the continental shelf and EEZ

Another monumental contribution in the Court's jurisprudence lies in the introduction of the concept of 'equity' in maritime delimitation contexts. This development is explained, in large part, by the fact that the applicable legal rules cannot exhaustively cover all situations of overlapping maritime claims. The 1969 *North Sea Continental Shelf* cases were instrumental in introducing the notion of equity, in which the Court was called upon to ascertain the legal rules applicable as between Germany and the Netherlands and Germany and Denmark with respect to the delimitation of their respective continental shelf areas in the North Sea. In the Court's view, such delimitation had to be carried out 'in accordance with equitable principles, and taking account of all the relevant circumstances'[2].

UNCLOS ultimately mirrored the Court's pronouncements in its provisions pertaining to delimitation of the continental shelf and the EEZ between States with opposite or adjacent coasts. Indeed, the attainment of an 'equitable solution' remains the central objective in both Articles 74 and 83 of UNCLOS. The ensuing delimitation must, therefore, be effected in conformity with customary principles and rules regulating the continental shelf and EEZ, as UNCLOS provides no further guidance on how the equitable aspects of a given solution are to be envisaged. By contrast, Article 15 of the same instrument, which reflects customary international law as confirmed by the Court

---

[1] United Nations Convention on the Law of the Sea (Montego Bay, 10 December 1982, United Nations, *Treaty Series*, 1833), Art. 13.
[2] *I.C.J. Reports 1969*, p. 53, para. 101.

in the *Qatar* v. *Bahrain* case[1], expressly mentions the equidistance/
special circumstances method with respect to delimitation of the
territorial sea as between adjacent or opposite States.

In the *North Sea Continental Shelf* cases, the Court had to ascertain
whether the equidistance principle, enshrined in Article 6 of the
1958 Geneva Convention on the Continental Shelf, formed part of
customary international law, Germany not being a party to that
instrument. Ultimately, the Court held that neither the equidistance
method, nor any other delimitation methodology, had to mandatorily
be applied between the Parties to determine their respective continental
shelf entitlements in the North Sea[2]. Several years later, this time in the
Continental Shelf case opposing Libya and Malta, the Court similarly
declined to 'accept that, even as a preliminary and provisional step
towards the drawing of a delimitation line, the equidistance method
is one which *must* be used'[3].

Despite this initial resistance exhibited by the Court, the method
by which it posits a provisional equidistance line in the area to be
delimited before adjusting that line, if necessary, by taking account
of special circumstances for the purposes of achieving an equitable
solution ultimately became its preferred delimitation approach.
In fact, virtually all cases brought before the Court since the *Gulf
of Maine* Judgment in 1984 were disposed of by reference to this
methodology, which was applied by the Court to all maritime areas
in dispute, with the notable exception of the 2007 case between
Nicaragua and Honduras. Because of the particular geographical
situation in that case, the Court ultimately resorted to a bisector line
as it was unfeasible to construct an equidistance line. However, it
underscored that '[a]t the same time equidistance remains the general
rule'[4].

Thus, the Court's jurisprudence has been instrumental in ensuring
greater unity in the field of maritime delimitation. In its view,

---

[1] *Maritime Delimitation and Territorial Questions between Qatar and Bahrain (Qatar* v.
Bahrain), Merits, Judgment, I.C.J. Reports 2001, p. 94, para. 176.

[2] *North Sea Continental Shelf* cases (*I.C.J. Reports 1969*, p. 53, para. 101).

[3] *Continental Shelf (Libyan Arab Jamahiriya/Malta), Judgment, I.C.J. Reports 1985*,
p. 37, para. 43 (emphasis in original).

[4] Given the instability of the mouth of the River Coco near the Nicaragua-Honduras
land boundary, coupled with the uncertain nature of some maritime features located
offshore, thereby affecting the position of the appropriate base points to construct an
equidistance line, the Court discarded the equidistance approach on the basis that it would
not produce an equitable solution. In order to depart from the traditional rule, the Court
found support in the wording of Article 15 of UNCLOS, which it did not interpret as
precluding geomorphological problems from amounting to "special circumstances" and,
therefore, from falling within the purview of the exception laid down in that provision. The
Court took note of the fact that the Parties had raised, in their pleadings, the possibility of
using a different delimitation methodology. See *Territorial and Maritime Dispute between
Nicaragua and Honduras in the Caribbean Sea (Nicaragua* v. *Honduras), Judgment,
I.C.J. Reports 2007 (II)*, pp. 742-745, paras. 275, 277-282.

there exists a solid connection between the legal regime governing delimitation of the territorial sea, which it termed the 'equidistance/ special circumstances rule', on one hand, and the principles regulating delimitation of the continental shelf and EEZ, which it expressed as the 'equidistance/relevant circumstances rules', on the other hand. As it confirmed in the *Qatar* v. *Bahrain* case, both régimes warrant the application of a similar delimitation approach, rooted in principles of equity and taking into account particular circumstances relevant to each case[1].

Moreover, the concept of 'median line', which was appreciated interchangeably with 'equidistance line' in the recent *Maritime Delimitation in the Black Sea* case with respect to delimitation methodology[2], and was defined in both UNCLOS and the earlier Geneva Convention, was described by the Court as follows in *Qatar* v. *Bahrain*: 'the line every point of which is equidistant from the nearest points on the baselines from which the breadth of the territorial seas [or the continental shelf and EEZ] of each of the two States is measured'[3]. Conversely, identifying particular circumstances susceptible of affecting the direction of a provisional equidistance line is more challenging, as no exhaustive list of such relevant/ special circumstances exists[4]. In any event, State practice and the arguments submitted by parties to the Court have largely shaped the development of those relevant factors, which also progressively appeared in the Court's jurisprudence. I now turn to a few of these special circumstances.

5. Special/relevant circumstances

The coastlines of the parties has undoubtedly proven to be one of the most important factors taken into account by the Court as a relevant circumstance justifying a correction to a provisional delimitation line so as to achieve an equitable solution. However, it is not of recent vintage, as the Court had alluded to it for the first time in the *North Sea Continental Shelf* cases when it determined the rules and principles applicable to the delimitation of the Parties' respective continental

---

[1] *Maritime Delimitation and Territorial Questions between Qatar and Bahrain (Qatar* v. *Bahrain), Merits, Judgment, I.C.J. Reports 2001*, p. 111, para. 231.

[2] Indeed, the Court opined that no legal consequences flow from the use of both terminologies since "the method of delimitation is the same for both". See *I.C.J. Reports 2009*, p. 101, para. 116.

[3] *Maritime Delimitation and Territorial Questions between Qatar and Bahrain (Qatar* v. *Bahrain), Merits, Judgment, I.C.J. Reports 2001*, p. 94, para. 177.

[4] As the Tribunal observed in the *Guyana/Suriname* Arbitration, "special circumstances that may affect a delimitation are to be assessed on a case-by-case basis, with reference to international jurisprudence and State practice". See Award of 17 September 2007, pp. 95-96, para. 303. See also *ibid.*, para. 304 (equating "[n]avigational interests" with "special circumstances").

shelf areas. When laying down the portion of the *dispositif* regarding factors to consider during the negotiations of an equitable boundary, the Court referred to the notion of having 'a reasonable degree of proportionality . . . between the extent of the continental shelf areas appertaining to the coastal State and the length of its coast measured in the general direction of the coastline'[1]. It is unsurprising that the 'proportionality' factor has been invoked frequently by parties before the Court so as to substantiate an adjustment to an equidistance line provisionally drawn.

In the 1982 *Tunisia/Libya* case, concerned with preserving the rights that other States could claim in the future, the Court determined that it was reasonable to initiate a proportionality analysis. The Court grounded this conclusion on a hypothesis that the entire maritime area between the two States had been divided, even if, in actuality, the delimitation line could not completely be drawn in the relevant area. A contrary conclusion would have made the prospect of an equitable delimitation challenging until all other delimitations in the relevant area — including those concerning the rights of third States — had been effected[2]. In this connection, the Court insisted upon the fact that it was 'not dealing here with absolute areas, but with proportions'[3].

The Court then proceeded to ascertain the ratio between the length of the Libyan coast, measured alongside its coastline, and the length of the Tunisian coast, measured in a similar manner, leading it to identify a proportion of approximately 31:69 in favour of the Tunisian coast. The Court arrived at a similar proportion when it conducted the same operation, this time with the use of straight lines drawn along the two coasts. Again, a very similar ratio was generated by the Court's assessment of the ratio representing the two States' respective sea-bed areas. Ultimately, the Court concluded that '[t]his result, taking into account all the relevant circumstances, seems to the Court to meet the requirements of the test of proportionality as an aspect of equity'[4].

In the *Qatar/Bahrain* case, the Court was again confronted with arguments concerning a considerable disparity in coastal lengths. The Court did not carry out a precise assessment of the coastal ratios as it had done in the *Tunisia/Libya* case; rather, it observed that the Qatari contention as to disparity hinged solely on the assumption that the disputed Hawar Islands fell under its sovereignty. Having rejected this line of argument, the Court then proceeded to swiftly dismiss

---

[1] *North Sea Continental Shelf* cases, (*I.C.J. Reports 1969*, p. 54, para. 101).

[2] *Continental Shelf (Tunisia/Libyan Arab Jamahiriya), Judgment, I.C.J. Reports 1982*, p. 91, para. 130.

[3] *Ibid.*

[4] *Ibid.*, p. 91, para. 131.

Qatar's claim for an appropriate correction of the boundary it had provisionally posited[1].

Parties to maritime disputes before the Court have also invoked another relevant circumstance, rather unsuccessfully so far, namely that of the existence of economic activities undertaken by the parties in the maritime areas subject to delimitation. In the *Qatar* v. *Bahrain* case, for example, Bahrain insisted that the presence of pearling banks on the northern coast of the Qatar peninsula, home to a long-standing culture of Bahraini fishing, should affect the delimitation in its favour. In responding to this argument, the Court highlighted that pearl fishing in that area was always considered 'as a right which was common to the coastal population', not exclusively reserved for Bahraini fishermen; furthermore, the Court took note of the cessation of the pearling industry along those banks, which occurred some time before. Dismissing Bahrain's claim, the Court held that it did 'not consider the existence of pearling banks, though predominantly exploited in the past by Bahrain fishermen, as forming a circumstance which would justify an eastward shifting of the equidistance line as requested by Bahrain'[2].

Several other claims grounded in economic concerns were similarly put forth by the Parties in the *Tunisia/Libya* case. For instance, Tunisia lamented its lack of access to the same natural resources that Libya could secure, primarily mineral and agricultural, and argued that it was in a state of relative poverty compared to the wealth of resources enjoyed by Libya. Tunisia further contended that the fishing resources situated in the waters claimed on the basis of 'historic rights' was a way for Tunisia to supplement its national economy in order to ensure its survival[3]. For its part, Libya argued that the presence or absence of oil or gas resources in the continental shelf of either Party should be a significant factor to be considered in the delimitation process[4].

The Court rejected the Tunisian contentions, equating them with 'extraneous factors' that may vary over time. It went on to say that '[a] country might be poor today and become rich tomorrow as a result of an event such as the discovery of a valuable economic resource'[5]. Conversely, the Court did not categorically pronounce on the argument concerning oil and gas resources located in the

---

[1] *Maritime Delimitation and Territorial Questions between Qatar and Bahrain (Qatar v. Bahrain), Merits, Judgment, I.C.J. Reports 2001*, p. 114, paras. 241-243.

[2] *Ibid.*, p. 113, para. 236.

[3] *Continental Shelf (Tunisia/Libyan Arab Jamahiriya), Judgment, I.C.J. Reports 1982*, p. 77, para. 106.

[4] *Ibid.*

[5] *Ibid.*, p. 77, para. 107. Similarly, in the *Libya/Malta* case, the Court dismissed the contention that the wealth of States constitutes a relevant circumstance that should affect maritime delimitation. See *Continental Shelf (Libyan Arab Jamahiriya/Malta), Judgment, I.C.J. Reports 1985*, p. 41, para. 50.

continental shelf to be delimited, opining that it could have its place in a series of relevant factors to be considered on the road to an equitable solution[1].

In the *Qatar* v. *Bahrain* case, Qatar also raised the existence of a division of a sea-bed between the Parties that had been decided by the British authorities in 1947, when both Parties were under their protection. This contention did not sway the Court, as neither Party had argued that the British decision was binding upon it, rather both invoking parts of the decision to support their own claims. What is more, the Court was mandated by the Parties with delimiting, by a single boundary, both the continental shelf and the EEZ areas of the Parties, whereas the British decision of 1947 was solely confined to dividing the sea-bed of the two States[2].

A grant of concessions for offshore exploitation of oil and gas constitutes another special circumstance considered by the Court as a potential justification for adjusting a delimitation line. In the *Tunisia/Libya* case, concerning the delimitation of the respective continental shelf areas, the Court opined that the granting of oil concessions in certain spaces revealed the existence of a *de facto* line. Short of instituting an implicit agreement between the Parties on a particular line of demarcation, the Court nonetheless concluded that the location of the concessions amounted to a relevant factor, if only as a starting-point, in effecting the delimitation of the continental shelf[3].

A similar contention was advanced by Nigeria in the *Cameroon* v. *Nigeria* case, namely whether 'the oil practice of the Parties provide[d] helpful indications for purposes of the delimitation of their respective maritime areas'[4]. Upon canvassing its own jurisprudence and other arbitral awards on the subject, the Court concluded that

> 'although the existence of an express or tacit agreement between the parties on the siting of their respective oil concessions may indicate a consensus on the maritime areas to which they are entitled, oil concessions and oil wells are not in themselves to be considered as relevant circumstances justifying the adjustment or shifting of the provisional delimitation line'[5].

Thus, the Court declined to take account of this circumstance given the absence of any agreement between the Parties concerning their oil

---

[1] *Continental Shelf (Tunisia/Libyan Arab Jamahiriya), Judgment, I.C.J. Reports 1982,* pp. 77-78, para. 107.

[2] *Maritime Delimitation and Territorial Questions between Qatar and Bahrain (Qatar v. Bahrain), Merits, Judgment, I.C.J. Reports 2001,* pp. 113-14, paras. 239-240.

[3] *Continental Shelf (Tunisia/Libyan Arab Jamahiriya), Judgment, I.C.J. Reports 1982,* p. 84, para. 118.

[4] *I.C.J. Reports 2002,* p. 447, para. 302.

[5] *Ibid.,* pp. 447-48, para. 304.

concessions. This approach was also followed more recently in the *Maritime Delimitation in the Black Sea* case[1].

Lastly, the presence of islands and other maritime features in the relevant area also warranted consideration in the Court's jurisprudence as a circumstance justifying a correction to a provisional line. In cases where competing claims exist in a given maritime area, islands and other features have sometimes been disregarded in the delimitation process so as to do away with their disproportionate effect, especially when dealing with insignificant maritime features. It is with this in mind that the Court in the *Qatar* v. *Bahrain* case excluded Qit'at Jaradah from the base points used to construct the equidistance line between the two States, a tiny uninhabited island situated halfway between the main island of Bahrain and the Qatar peninsula[2].

Similarly, in *Libya/Malta* the provisional equidistance line posited by the Court remained unaffected by the uninhabited islet of Filfla for equitable purposes[3]. In the *Cameroon* v. *Nigeria* case, Cameroon argued that the presence of Bioko Island off its coast could serve as a ground for shifting the median line. However, Bioko Island was subject to the sovereignty of a third State, Equatorial Guinea, prompting the Court to declare that 'the effect of Bioko Island on the seaward projection of the Cameroonian coastal front is an issue between Cameroon and Equatorial Guinea and not between Cameroon and Nigeria, and is not relevant to the issue of delimitation before the Court'[4].

6. Concluding thoughts: towards greater unity and coherence in maritime delimitation

The Court's jurisprudence has thus played a central role in further developing the law governing maritime delimitation. Its influence has been pervasive in the works of arbitral tribunals and other relevant international decision-making bodies. By way of example, the equidistance/special circumstances methodology, whose genesis was first mapped out in the 1985 *Libya/Malta* case[5], was referred to and confirmed by the tribunals in the *Guyana/Suriname* and *Barbados/*

---

[1] *I.C.J. Reports 2009*, pp. 124-126, paras. 193-98.

[2] *Maritime Delimitation and Territorial Questions between Qatar and Bahrain (Qatar* v. *Bahrain), Merits, Judgment, I.C.J. Reports 2001*, pp. 104, 109, para. 219.

[3] *Continental Shelf (Libyan Arab Jamahiriya/Malta), Judgment, I.C.J. Reports 1985*, p. 48, para. 64.

[4] *I.C.J. Reports 2002*, p. 446, para. 299.

[5] *Continental Shelf (Libyan Arab Jamahiriya/Malta), Judgment, I.C.J. Reports 1985*, p. 46, para. 60.

Trinidad and Tobago arbitrations as the leading delimitation approach in public international law[1].

There is no doubt that one of the Court's most recent contributions might become one of its most enduring pronouncements in the field. The unanimous decision in the *Maritime Delimitation in the Black Sea* case brought the coherence and unity of maritime delimitation law into sharp relief, first by confirming the validity of the delimitation methodology, and second, by further advancing the extant legal scheme. In short, the Court indicated that three defined steps must be contemplated when it is called upon to delimit the continental shelf or EEZ, or when it must determine a single maritime boundary.

To summarize, the Court first posits a provisional delimitation line by reference to geometrically objective criteria that accord with the geography of the area to be delimited. When faced with delimitation between adjacent coasts, the Court specified that 'an equidistance line will be drawn unless there are compelling reasons that make this unfeasible in the particular case'[2]. Moreover, the 'provisional delimitation line will consist of a median line between the two coasts' when delimitation is to be effected between two opposite coasts[3]. In the *Maritime Delimitation in the Black Sea*, the Court first posited a provisional equidistance line between the adjacent coasts of Romania and Ukraine, which then transformed into a median line between their opposite coasts, in light of the particular geography of the relevant area.

Keeping in line with Articles 74 and 83 of UNCLOS, the Court stressed that the 'course of the line should result in an equitable solution'[4]. Consequently, the second stage of the inquiry requires the Court to consider relevant factors or circumstances in determining whether an adjustment or shift of the provisional equidistance line is warranted to achieve an equitable outcome[5]. Finally, the Court went on to describe the third and last stage of its delimitation approach, which is supported by State and jurisprudential practice. It is commonly referred to as the 'disproportionality test'. In short,

'[T]he Court will verify that the line (a provisional equidistance line which may or may not have been adjusted by taking into

---

[1] Indeed, the Tribunal stated that "[t]he case law of the International Court of Justice and arbitral jurisprudence as well as State practice are at one in holding that the delimitation process should, in appropriate cases, begin by positing a provisional equidistance line which may be adjusted in the light of relevant circumstances in order to achieve an equitable solution". See *Barbados/Trinidad and Tobago*, Jurisdiction and Merits (UN Law of the Sea, Ann. VII, Arb. Trib., 11 Apr. 2006), para. 242.

[2] *Maritime Delimitation in the Black Sea (Romania v. Ukraine) (I.C.J. Reports 2009*, p. 101, para. 116).

[3] *Ibid.*, p. 101, para. 116.

[4] *Ibid.*, p. 101, para. 120.

[5] *Ibid.*, pp. 101, 103, paras. 120-121.

account the relevant circumstances) does not, as it stands, lead
to an inequitable result by reason of any marked disproportion
between the ratio of the respective coastal lengths and the ratio
between the relevant maritime area of each State by reference to
the delimitation line . . . A final check for an equitable outcome
entails a confirmation that no great disproportionality of
maritime areas is evident by comparison to the ratio of coastal
lengths.'[1]

By way of final comment on this third step, the Court offered the
following clarification: '[t]his is not to suggest that these respective
areas should be proportionate to coastal lengths'[2].

There is every indication that this three-step methodology now
constitutes the usual approach to be espoused in appropriate cases
of maritime delimitation. Its validity as a tried and true reflection
of the current state of international law has recently been affirmed
by ITLOS in its first ever maritime delimitation case. Thus, ITLOS
endorsed the Court's three-step methodology in a case where it was
called upon to determine a maritime boundary between Bangladesh
and Myanmar in the Bay of Bengal[3].

*

Mr. Chairman,
Distinguished Delegates,

Maritime delimitation jurisprudence has evolved harmoniously
and coherently over the last two decades, with the International
Court of Justice playing a central role in the progressive development
of the relevant legal scheme. Indeed, a rich horizontal dialogue and
cross-fertilization actuate various judicial and arbitral processes
confirming the validity of the relevant rules applicable to delimitation
exercises. Such unity in decision-making appears to have assuaged
initial fears and concerns, voiced in some circles most notably in the
1980s, that the law of maritime delimitation was headed towards a
fragmented future. What is more, it vindicated the assertion of the
then International Court of Justice President, Dame Rosalyn Higgins,
that 'so-called 'fragmentation of international law' is best avoided by
regular dialogue between courts and exchange of information'[4].

---

[1] *I.C.J. Reports 2009*, p. 103, para. 122.
[2] *Ibid.*
[3] Dispute concerning *Delimitation of the Maritime Boundary between Bangladesh and Myanmar in the Bay of Bengal (Bangladesh/Myanmar)*, judgment of 14 March 2012, paras. 233-40.
[4] Statement by H.E. Judge Rosalyn Higgins, President of the International Court of Justice, at the Meeting of Legal Advisers of the Ministries of Foreign Affairs, 29 October 2007, available at www.icj-cij.org/presscom/files/7/14097.pdf.

Relevant guiding principles and consecration by the Court of the provisional equidistance line/relevant circumstances methodology — or the three-step approach I have just described if the final verification of the boundary line is envisaged as a separate stage of the inquiry — is now firmly entrenched in maritime delimitation decision-making. In this light, there is every indication that the lockstep march and practice of States and international judicial and arbitral bodies will continue onward, and toward greater unity and coherence in the application and interpretation of the relevant legal principles."

ANNEX 29

History (1996-2012) of the United Nations General Assembly
Resolutions on *Legality of the Threat or Use of Nuclear Weapons*

By a note dated 15 October 1996 the Secretary-General of the United
Nations transmitted the text of the Advisory Opinion given by the Court
on 8 July 1996 to the General Assembly (United Nations doc. A/51/218).
At the 79th plenary meeting of its fifty-first session, held on
10 December 1996, the General Assembly adopted resolution 51/45M, at
the 67th plenary meeting of its fifty-second session, held on 9 December
1997, resolution 52/38 O, at the 79th plenary meeting of its fifty-third
session, held on 4 December 1998, resolution 53/77 W, at the 69th plenary
meeting of its fifty-fourth session, held on 1 December 1999,
resolution 54/54 Q, at the 69th plenary meeting of its fifty-fifth session,
held on 20 November 2000, resolution 55/33 X, at the 68th plenary
meeting of its fifty-sixth session, held on 29 November 2001,
resolution 56/24 S, at the 57th plenary meeting of its fifty-seventh session,
held on 22 November 2002, resolution 57/85, at the 71st plenary meeting
of its fifty-eighth session, held on 8 December 2003, resolution 58/46, at
the 66th plenary meeting of its fifty-ninth session, held on 3 December
2004, resolution 59/83, at the 61st plenary meeting of its sixtieth session,
held on 8 December 2005, resolution 60/76, at the 67th plenary meeting
of its sixty-first session, held on 6 December 2006, resolution 61/83, at
the 61st plenary meeting of its sixty-second session, held on 5 December
2007, resolution 63/49, at the 61st plenary meeting of its sixty-third
session, held on 2 December 2008, resolution 64/55, at the 55th plenary
meeting of its sixty-fourth session, held on 2 December 2009, at the 60th
plenary meeting of its sixty-fifth session, held on 8 December 2010 and
at the 71st plenary meeting of its sixty-sixth session held on 2 December
2011, the General Assembly adopted resolution 66/46, the full texts of
which are reproduced in *I.C.J. Yearbook 1996-1997*, pp. 205-206,
I.C.J. Yearbook 1997-1998, pp. 286-288, *I.C.J. Yearbook 1998-1999*,
pp. 313-315, *I.C.J. Yearbook 1999-2000*, pp. 278-280, *I.C.J. Yearbook
2000-2001*, pp. 317-319, *I.C.J. Yearbook 2001-2002*, pp. 306-307,
I.C.J. Yearbook 2002-2003, pp. 325-327, *I.C.J. Yearbook 2003-2004*,
pp. 343-345, *I.C.J. Yearbook 2004-2005*, pp. 278-280, *I.C.J. Yearbook
2005-2006*, pp. 278-279, *I.C.J. Yearbook 2006-2007*, pp. 297-299,
I.C.J. Yearbook 2007-2008, pp. 346-347, *I.C.J. Yearbook 2008-2009*,
pp. 368-371, *I.C.J. Yearbook 2009-2010*, pp. 413-415, *I.C.J. Yearbook
2010-2011*, pp. 310-312 and *I.C.J. Yearbook 2011-2012*, pp. 340-342,
respectively. At the 48th plenary session of its sixty-seventh session, held
on 3 December 2012, the General Assembly adopted resolution 67/33,
the text of which appears in Annex 30.

ANNEX 30

Full Text of General Assembly Resolution A/RES/67/33 of
3 December 2012 on the Advisory Opinion of the International
Court of Justice on the *Legality of the Threat or Use of Nuclear
Weapons*

"The General Assembly,

Recalling its resolutions 49/75 K of 15 December 1994, 51/45 M of 10 December 1996, 52/38 O of 9 December 1997, 53/77 W of 4 December 1998, 54/54 Q of 1 December 1999, 55/33 X of 20 November 2000, 56/24 S of 29 November 2001, 57/85 of 22 November 2002, 58/46 of 8 December 2003, 59/83 of 3 December 2004, 60/76 of 8 December 2005, 61/83 of 6 December 2006, 62/39 of 5 December 2007, 63/49 of 2 December 2008, 64/55 of 2 December 2009, 67/76 of 8 December 2010 and 66/46 of 2 December 2011.

Convinced that the continuing existence of nuclear weapons poses a threat to humanity and all life on Earth, and recognizing that the only defence against a nuclear catastrophe is the total elimination of nuclear weapons and the certainty that they will never be produced again,

Reaffirming the commitment of the international community to the realization of the goal of a nuclear-weapon-free world through the total elimination of nuclear weapons,

Mindful of the solemn obligations of States parties, undertaken in Article VI of the Treaty on the Non-Proliferation of Nuclear Weapons, particularly to pursue negotiations in good faith on effective measures relating to cessation of the nuclear arms race at an early date and to nuclear disarmament,

Recalling the principles and objectives for nuclear non-proliferation and disarmament adopted at the 1995 Review and Extension Conference of the Parties to the Treaty on the Non-Proliferation of Nuclear Weapons, the unequivocal commitment of nuclear-weapon States to accomplish the total elimination of their nuclear arsenals leading to nuclear disarmament, agreed at the 2000 Review Conference of the Parties to the Treaty on the Non-Proliferation of Nuclear Weapons, and the action points agreed at the 2010 Review Conference of the Parties to the Treaty on the Non-Proliferation on Nuclear Weapons as part of the conclusions and recommendations for follow-on actions on nuclear disarmament,

Sharing the deep concern at the catastrophic humanitarian consequences of any use of nuclear weapons, and in this context reaffirming the need for all States at all times to comply with applicable international law, including international humanitarian law,

Calling upon all nuclear-weapon States to undertake concrete disarmament efforts, and stressing that all States need to make special efforts to achieve and maintain a world without nuclear weapons,

Noting the five-point proposal for nuclear disarmament of the Secretary-General, in which he proposes, *inter alia*, the consideration of negotiations on a nuclear weapons convention or agreement on a framework of separate mutually reinforcing instruments, backed by a strong system of verification,

Recalling the adoption of the Comprehensive Nuclear-Test-Ban Treaty in its resolution 50/245 of 10 September 1996, and expressing its satisfaction at the increasing number of States that have signed and ratified the Treaty,

Recognizing with satisfaction that the Antarctic Treaty, the treaties of Tlatelolco, Rarotonga, Bangkok and Pelindaba and the Treaty on a Nuclear-Weapon-Free Zone in Central Asia, as well as Mongolia's nuclear-weapon-free status, are gradually freeing the entire southern hemisphere and adjacent areas covered by those treaties from nuclear weapons,

Recognizing the need for a multilaterally negotiated and legally binding instrument to assure non-nuclear-weapon States against the threat or use of nuclear weapons pending the total elimination of nuclear weapons,

Reaffirming the central role of the Conference on Disarmament as the sole multilateral disarmament negotiating forum,

Emphasizing the need for the Conference on Disarmament to commence negotiations on a phased programme for the complete elimination of nuclear weapons with a specified framework of time,

Stressing the urgent need for the nuclear-weapon States to accelerate concrete progress on the thirteen practical steps to implement Article VI of the Treaty on the Non-Proliferation of Nuclear Weapons leading to nuclear disarmament, contained in the Final Document of the 2000 Review Conference,

Taking note of the Model Nuclear Weapons Convention that was submitted to the Secretary-General by Costa Rica and Malaysia in 2007 and circulated by the Secretary-General,

Desiring to achieve the objective of a legally binding prohibition of the development, production, testing, deployment, stockpiling, threat or use of nuclear weapons and their destruction under effective international control,

Recalling the Advisory Opinion of the International Court of Justice on the *Legality of the Threat or Use of Nuclear Weapons*, issued on 8 July 1996,

1. *Underlines once again* the conclusion of the International Court of Justice that there exists an obligation to pursue in good faith and bring to a conclusion negotiations leading to nuclear disarmament in all its aspects under strict and effective international control;

2. *Calls once again upon* all States immediately to fulfil that obligation by commencing multilateral negotiations leading to an early conclusion of a nuclear weapons convention prohibiting the development, production, testing, deployment, stockpiling, transfer, threat or use of nuclear weapons and providing for their elimination;

3. *Requests* all States to inform the Secretary-General of the efforts and measures they have taken with respect to the implementation of the present resolution and nuclear disarmament, and requests the Secretary-General to apprise the General Assembly of that information at its sixty-eighth session;

4. *Decides* to include in the provisional agenda of its sixty-eighth session the item entitled 'Follow-up to the Advisory Opinion of the International Court of Justice on the *Legality of the Threat or Use of Nuclear Weapons*'." [Footnotes not reproduced but are available on the website of the General Assembly under "A/RES/67/33".]